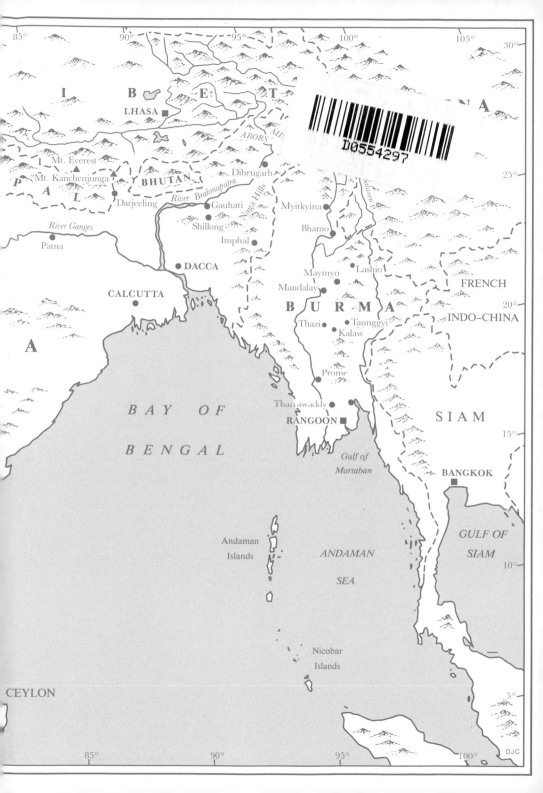

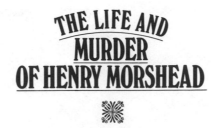

THE LIFE AND
MURDER
OF HENRY MORSHEAD

Henry Morshead self portrait, aged 22, 1904

THE LIFE AND
MURDER
OF HENRY MORSHEAD

Ian Morshead

A TRUE STORY FROM THE DAYS OF THE RAJ

with an introduction by
Mark Tully
British Broadcasting Corporation, New Delhi

THE OLEANDER PRESS LTD

The Oleander Press Ltd
17 Stansgate Avenue
Cambridge CB2 2QZ
England

British Library Cataloguing in Publication Data

Morshead, Ian
    The life and murder of Henry Morshead.
    1. Morshead, Henry   2. Mountaineers—
    Great Britain—Biography
    I. Title
    796.5'22'0924   GV199.92.M/

    ISBN 0-900891-76-9

Text design and layout by Ron Jones
Jacket design by Leigh Taylor
Maps drawn by David J. Charles

Printed and bound in Great Britain

Contents

List of Illustrations

To Evie

'So soon it Passeth'

Introduction by Mark Tully

I can well understand how filial piety inspired a member of the Morshead family, long connected with India, to investigate the death of his father. Filial piety is very much an Indian quality. The Indian family and all that goes with it has not suffered the ravages of Western family life.

The ultimate in filial piety is the Hindu cremation. The eldest son must be present to perform the last rites, otherwise there is no hope of his parent's escaping this world and achieving salvation. A Christian friend of mine was once summoned to the cremation of an aunt to perform that function, as she had no son. The Pandit, or Priest, brushed aside the fact that he came from a branch of the family which had been converted to Christianity in the previous generation. That makes sense because an orthodox Hindu recognises neither apostasy nor conversion: you can become a Hindu only by birth, and once a Hindu you cannot opt out of the religion. So my friend was ordered to take off his bush shirt and trousers and put on a *dhoti*. I have never known the best way to describe that Indian garment. The *Shorter Oxford English Dictionary* says simply 'the loin-cloth worn by Hindus'. But that does not convey the dexterity needed to tie a *dhoti*, or the fine flowing effect achieved by an expert. My friend had to have his *dhoti* tied for him. The Pandit next produced a barber to shave his head, but he baulked at that. The Pandit reluctantly accepted his fine head of curly black hair and the rites went ahead. My friend did not believe one jot or tittle or the ritual but the Pandit and the family did, and the road to salvation was considered open.

Hinduism is certainly one of the world's oldest religions, if not the oldest. It is also the most complicated. Hinduism is so far removed from the later religions of the book like Christianity and Islam that we Westerners find it very hard to sympathise with it. I have always believed that one reason why the British in India found it easier to sympathise with Muslims or even Sikhs is because of the Hindu pantheon and the gaudy images of the gods. After all, two of the main tenets of the Protestant Englishman of those days were 'there is one God' and 'thou shalt not bow down thyself to graven images, nor serve them'. In fact it can be argued that Hinduism is monotheistic and it is certainly true that idol-worship is not obligatory. Nevertheless, there is no doubt that Hinduism was distasteful to many of our forefathers who served in India. But I am sure it was not distasteful to Henry Morshead. Hence his son's filial piety!

Henry Morshead was an explorer too. He not only climbed Kamet, but also led the team of surveyors on the first expedition to Everest, the highest of the Himalayas, which are holy to Hindus. Those Englishmen who went on the first expeditions to Everest were known as Everesters. James Morris in his colourful trilogy of empire *Pax Britannica* describes those Everesters as 'Englishmen...who went to Everest in a spirit of uncomplicated bravado'. Although such a spirit is no longer fashionable in our sceptical scientific age, something of it must live on in Henry Morshead's son Ian to have taken him from suburban Surrey back to the scene of his father's mysterious death.

Perhaps because those Everesters and the other stalwarts of British India were so unlike the Englishmen of today there has recently been something of a boom in Anglo-Indiana. The boom has been one-sided, for it has not presented the Englishman in India complete with all his warts, nor has it presented him as seen by contemporary Indians, except for loyal sepoys or faithful family retainers. Indians did have views of the English and they were by no means always entirely favourable.

One of the great scholars and wits of Delhi in the nineteenth century was Nazir Ahmad (1836–1912). He was a man of wide interests. On the one hand he translated Macaulay's Penal Code into Urdu, on the other, the Qur'an. He was also one of the first Urdu novelists. His novel *Ibn ul Vaqt* (1888) is the story of a Muslim so impressed by the seeming invincibility of the Raj that he determines to become more English than the English. In this book, Nazir Ahmad describes the experience of a friend of his who went to meet an Englishman in his club—but of course the friend, like Aziz in Forster's *A Passage to India*, was not actually allowed inside the club.

'A friend told me that once he needed to see a particular Englishman. When he got to his house he found that it was the time of the day he spent in his club. So he was forced to go there. The *chaprassi* (footman) was looking for a chance to tell the Englishman that he'd come, when my friend heard that there was a crowd of Englishmen inside. They were mimicking Indian English and roaring with laughter. My friend did say that the English which they found so funny *was* worth laughing at and native speakers had the right to laugh at foreigners but Indian English..., if that is laughable, then

Englishmen's *Hindustani* is fit to make you weep. Indians only learn English through books. In contrast, besides books, the English live out their entire lives in Indian society and still speak the same "Well, *tum kya mangta?*".' ["Well, what you asking for?", an example of the incorrect, badly-pronounced Hindustani many Sahibs habitually used.] The English were and still are great condescenders. But there were some Englishmen who did not spend their time in clubs mocking the 'natives'. They loved India as they saw it and they did look very deeply into it. They were not the great and the famous: generals, successful bureaucrats in the Indian Civil Service, the wealthy Calcutta merchants or box-wallahs were too busy pursuing their careers to have much time for Indians and India.

John Beames was a member of the Indian Civil Service who preferred to spend his life in remote districts rather than wielding great power in the Secretariat. His habit of pointing out the idiocy of the instructions he received from the great Nabobs of the Bengal Secretariat debarred him from promotion anyhow. Beames described himself in his autobiography as an 'obscure' person. But his memory still lives on because of the original work he did on Indian languages, quite apart from his delightful autobiography, *Memoirs of a Bengal Civilian*.

In that autobiography Beames quotes some lines of verse written by one of his colleagues about a particularly pompous pronouncement by a Lieutenant Governor on the imperative need for all Indian Civil Service officers to devote their entire energies and time to their jobs.

> 'The model magistrate our rulers say,
> Decides all night, investigates all day.
> The crack collector, man of equal might,
> Reports all day and corresponds all night.'

Beames would certainly have approved of Henry Morshead, who preferred exploring in Tibet to climbing up the ranks of the Indian Army. The curious circumstances surrounding his murder in a remote corner of Burma were in some ways characteristic of his adventurous life, though hitherto inexplicable in others, for he had no obvious enemies. Far from the bright lights of Calcutta, the decadence of Simla, or the new 'Babu Bureaucracy' of Delhi, he died a seemingly pointless death, the mystery of which has at last been solved.

Yet it was men like him, dedicated to discovering rather than ruling India, whose memories deserve to live on. It was the obscure officers in the districts, not the Viceroys, Governors and Generals, who founded and nurtured the Englishman's reputation for honest administration; it was they who opened up the remoter corners of the empire, and it was they who catalogued the munificence of India's flora and fauna, and who wrote grammars of India's many languages.

I don't think Nazir Ahmad, if he had known him, would have been scornful of Henry Morshead.

Author's Foreword

The unsolved mystery surrounding my father's assassination in the Burmese jungle in 1931 hung over my mother for the remaining 47 years of her life. After her death in 1978 I had access to her letters and newspaper cuttings. The cuttings I had long been familiar with, but the letters were new to me. They named names, expressed opinions freely and, as they continued up to the day of his death, I felt they might provide a clue.

The wording of the official enquiry had always seemed ineffectual. A labyrinth of rumour existed, and it had been finally declared, somewhat arbitrarily I thought, that the case must remain a mystery. Now, all these years later, as I read and re-read the last few letters, in conjunction with the official documents, I found myself turning the spotlight of suspicion on to each name in turn. I decided to delve deeper, and this book is the result. My quest became an Odyssey when, with every known fact at my fingertips, I paid a return visit to the scene of my father's death nearly fifty years after the event. As a result, the first and last chapters are autobiographical.

I would stress that, as regards the murder, any solutions offered, or hypotheses put forward, are mine and mine alone, and cannot be taken as fact. Where I have interposed words of my own in a quoted passage I have used square brackets, and, where necessary I have used fictitious names.

I acknowledge with gratitude the gracious permission of Her Majesty the Queen to quote from letters in the Royal Archives.

I am indebted to the Surveyor General of India, Major-General Kishori Lal Khosla, for his personal interest and for permission to draw on Survey of India Records.

I am most grateful to Miss Helen Mason for giving me access to the memoirs of her father, the late Prof. Lt.Col. Kenneth Mason, M.C.; and to Lady Morshead for making available to me the papers of my uncle, the late Sir Owen Morshead, G.C.V.O., K.C.B., D.S.O., M.C.

I am grateful to Authors and their Publishers or Representatives for permission to quote from the following: *No Passport to Tibet* by F.M. Bailey, Granada Publishing; the Bailey collection (MSS EUR F.157) at the India Office Library and Records; *Mount Everest—The Reconnaissance, 1921* by C.K. Howard-Bury, Arnold; *The Assault on Mount Everest, 1922* by C.G. Bruce, Arnold; *The Last Secrets* by John Buchan, Nelson; *The Kelly Book* by Margaret and Mary Kelly, Mrs. Margery Kelly; letters of Henry Morshead in the archives of the Royal Geographical Society; *The Military Engineer in India* by E.W.C. Sandes, R.E. Institute, Chatham; *Gino Watkins* by J.M. Scott, A.P.Watt; *After Everest* by T. Howard Somervell, Hodder & Stoughton; *Himalayan Frontiers* by Dorothy Woodman, Barrie & Jenkins. The Author and Publisher would like to thank the following for permission to reproduce photographs: *The Sphere* on pages 18—19; *The Graphic* for photos on pages 88 and 104; India Office Library & Records for photo on page 24; Edward Arnold (Publishers) for photo on page 79; P. & O. Group Library for photo on page 131; and the Royal Geographical Society Library for photos on pages 25, 29, 39 and 41, which are from an album of Henry Morshead's donated to them by his widow.

I acknowledge the help given by: Leonard Aspinal; Mrs. Ann Barclay; Mrs. Margaret Bennett; Colonel Jamshed Dalal; Mrs. Emma Dalzell; Major-General R.C.A. Edge, C.B., M.B.E.; Major J.T. Hancock, Corps Librarian, Royal Engineers Institute; Lt.Col. B.S. Hartland; Professor J.N. Hazard; J.W. Hunt, Central Library, Royal Military Academy, Sandhurst; Mrs. Gwen de Graaff Hunter; R. Lawford, Hon.Librarian, Alpine Club; Sir Robin Mackworth-Young, K.C.V.O., F.S.A.; V.K. Nagar; Michael O'Keefe, The India Office Library; H.F. Oxbury, C.M.G.; H. David Phillimore; Stephen Rabson; Mrs. Mary Rowlatt; W.R. Trevelyan; W.S.C. Tully, C.B.E.; Philip Ward; Mrs. Theo Wilkinson; C.E. Willoughby; Lt.Col. H. Westland Wright, O.B.E.; The Foreign Office; The National Army Museum; The National Motor Museum at Beaulieu; and the Officers' Pension Society.

I thank all those who assisted me during my return visit to India and Burma. Mark and Margaret Tully and the Staff of the B.B.C. Bureau in New Delhi were my sheet-anchor. To Mr. John Fenton, aged 91, to Dr. Game and to the Bernard family, in Maymyo, I owe an especial debt of gratitude.

1 | L'Avant-propos

A schoolmaster's voice interrupted my daydream during break that afternoon early in the summer term. 'Run and find your brother', it was saying, 'and then both of you report to the Headmaster's Study.'

The words offered a menacing range of possibilities. Horris Hill, Newbury was a Spartan establishment in 1931, with discipline strictly enforced. There were cold baths every morning, lessons before breakfast, and long school walks on Sundays. One could get pushed over backwards into a hollybush, or clipped about the face by an older boy, or even dragged into a classroom and beaten when no master was looking. Having an elder brother helped, but one learned to look after oneself.

'We can't both have done something wrong, so I think it's alright' said my brother. 'And I've only been here a fortnight' I added, encouragingly.

Looming large and imposing, the Headmaster, J.L. Stow, ushered us in—and was kindness and consideration personified. Had we by any chance seen today's paper, or yesterday's *Evening News*?

Few, if any, newspapers circulated in the school so the answer was no. 'Good', he said, and without beating about the bush went on to tell us that my father had been shot dead while out riding in the Burmese jungle near Maymyo. He treated us as if we were his own children. Would we please spend the afternoon in his garden if we liked, and not go back into class that day. His wife, a kindly Scots lady, would bring us tea later. We filed out in awed silence.

Some memories flashed by as time stood still for an afternoon.

Sleeping on the roof and watching the stars come out one by one... Jackals barking... Bandicoots... Being chased from the kitchen outhouse by Cook brandishing a red coal... Terrifying. Could he have discovered that those round holes in every cabbage leaf had been made by the cork from my popgun? Was he really after me?... What was that single point of light in the pitch dark room? Approach it cautiously. 'Yes, dear, that's only a joss-stick burning to keep away the mosquitoes.' Thirst... The tell-tale trail of ants leading all the way from the window to the carefully-hidden sweet. (You were supposed to take one, not take two and hide one. . .) You will never die, Daddy, will you?

'There's a White Star liner berthing alongside. You can get dressed again and stay up late to watch it as a treat.'

I had already, at the age of nine, made that passage to or from India five times. When we had first arrived in London, we children had found it quite inexplicable that we were not allowed to sleep outdoors. If that meant on the pavement in winter, well why not?. . . The visit to the ship's engine-rooms, and a mechanically-minded Royal Engineers officer exasperated that his five-year-old son could not follow his explanation of how the engines worked. . .

'Did you say that was Egypt on the left, Nanny, and Arabia on the right, or was it the other way round?' How interesting; although through the heat haze they both looked much alike. Another treat; we were to be allowed up on to the bridge and permitted by the captain to sound the ship's siren. 'Where are you bound for, sonny?' said a P. & O. crewman as the ship hove to in Suez roads. 'Back to England to go to school.' 'What does your father do then?' 'He's in the Army. . . The Survey of India, actually.' The larger-than-life memories of an Indian childhood already formed an indispensable part of one's education.

'You'll never die, Daddy, will you?' Every child says it at some stage. We said it many times and really meant it. It was something near to being an obsession with both of us, and now it had happened. Mr. Stow spared us the details of the jungle outrage, and we accepted the finality of the event in the realistic manner of young children that invariably surprises adults. When had we last seen him? The elder boy not for eighteen months when he had been sent home to school in England. The rest of us had waved goodbye three months before, on the banks of the Irrawaddy at Prome, en route for Rangoon, the S.S. 'Chindwin' and home.

Later, one would hear about, and read, Kipling's poem, and it would mean more to a schoolboy who had seen it. Good Gracious! The Road to Mandalay was in reality a river; and there really were flying fishes playing on it. Part of the journey had been on an armoured train. A strange foreboding was felt at this parting. Why was an armoured train necessary? What were we English doing in the country anyway? Why, why, why had it happened?

Tomorrow was a normal school day, a half-holiday what was more, and life would go on again.

2 | Family Background

The earliest records of our family are to be found in the Lay Subsidies for the 'parochia de Seynt Ive' in the East Hundred of Cornwall in 1544 in the reign of Henry VIII. A Ricus, a Waltus and two Johes Morsheads appear. No others appear until 1610 when Eduardus, of Penherget, comes in a list of nineteen names.

The subsidy rolls were compiled in connection with financial support granted by Parliament to the King and each name is followed by the Latin words *vidua valet in bonis*, which means widow validated in possession. So the family were Cornish yeomen. Edward's son William, of Penherget, died in 1645 and his Inventory was appraised at £1,252.6.8d, a surprising sum for that day for a small-estate farmer in a far-away Cornish parish.

Four generations later, in 1745, William Morshead, of Cartuther, cut quite a dash as he rode forth, at the age of twenty-two and just down from Oxford, to claim his bride Olympia Treise, eventually sole heiress of her brother Sir Christopher Treise, Kt. of Lavethan. Only the previous month young William had suitably equipped himself with a Coat of Arms; a few years later, at thirty-one, he was High Sheriff of Cornwall.

These two old homesteads of Cartuther and Lavethan, both still privately occupied, lie about fifteen miles apart on different sides of Bodmin Moor, near Liskeard and Blisland respectively. Cartuther is mentioned in the Domesday Book as Croutedor. The Cornish language had, by the time a 1576 map was drawn, converted this to Cortyther, and later still to Correther on a map by Robert Morden.

When, in 1778, their eldest son John married Elizabeth Frederick, the heiress of Sir Thomas Frederick, Bart. (the same family that founded the former Frederick Hotels Ltd.), she brought with her half the borough of Paddington and more at Richmond. It was said that they owned land in thirty-two different parishes. A baronetcy (now extinct) followed, and Sir John, who was Callington's M.P. for four years and Bodmin's for eighteen, became Lord Warden of the Stannaries and Surveyor General to the Prince

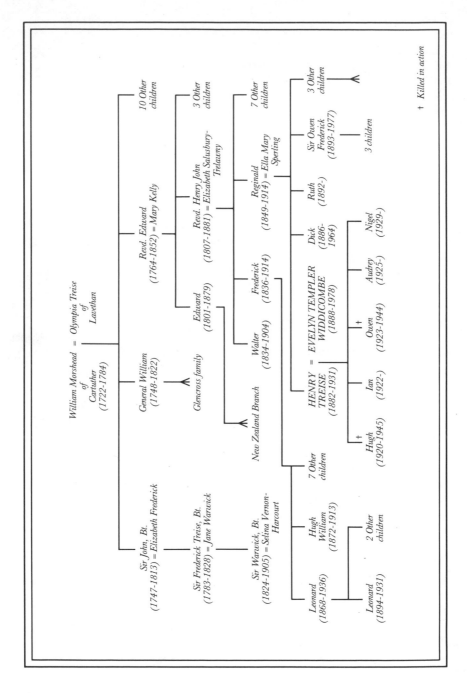

William Morshead = Olympia Treise
of
Cartuther
(1722-1784)
of
Lavethan

Sir John, Bt.
(1747-1813) = Elizabeth Frederick

General William
(1748-1822)

Revd. Edward
(1764-1852) = Mary Kelly

10 Other
children

Glencross family

3 Other
children

Sir Frederick Treise, Bt.
(1783-1828) = Jane Warwick

Edward
(1801-1879)

Revd. Henry John
(1807-1881) = Elizabeth Salusbury-
Trelawny

Walter
(1834-1904)

Frederick
(1836-1914)

Reginald
(1849-1914) = Ella Mary
Sperling

7 Other
children

Sir Warwick, Bt.
(1824-1905) = Selina Vernon-
Harcourt

New Zealand Branch

Dick
(1886-
1964)

Ruth
(1892-)

Sir Owen
Frederick
(1893-1977)

3 Other
children

7 Other
children

HENRY = EVELYN TEMPLER
TREISE   WIDDICOMBE
(1882-1931)   (1888-1978)

3 children

Hugh
William
(1872-1913)

Hugh
(1920-1945) +

Ian
(1922-)

Owen
(1923-1944) +

Audrey
(1925-)

Nigel
(1929-)

Leonard
(1868-1936)

Leonard
(1894-1931)

2 Other
children

+ Killed in action

of Wales. Family fortunes seemed to be reaching an apogee, and in those days the fortune all went to the eldest son.

There is an old proverb, no doubt Chinese, which says that the moon starts to wane when at its fullest. In this case the eldest son had a weakness for the gaming tables where he would run up accounts and borrow from other gamblers. A fool and his money are soon parted. A bigger fool merely parts with bigger amounts. John was already in trouble as early as 1777 when he suffered a Common Recovery, the contemporary legal device for disentailing land.

In 1780 *The English Chronicle* contained the following: 'John Morshead, Esq. the other Member for Callington is a young gentleman of family in the neighbourhood of this borough. He is distinguished for a most amiable disposition and the strictest honour in all his engagements. He has lived in the politest circles of life, and has been involved in several of those fashionable difficulties which result from an imprudent attachment to gaming and gamesters; he has been reduced to the last extremity of pecuniary difficulty, and has been compelled to borrow money on the worst terms to discharge the worst engagements, yet in all this unfortunate complication he never forgot his promise given to a creditor, nor disappointed the just demands of his honest tradesmen. His conduct under such circumstances much more than compensates for the original indiscretion that reduced him to it, and has sufficiently established his character as a man of inviolable integrity, honour and honesty. Mr. Morshead married Miss Frederick, one of the daughters of Sir Thomas Frederick, by whom he got a fortune of upwards of an hundred thousand pounds, which for various causes no man perhaps ever better deserved.'

By 1796 he had mortgaged his future by selling annuities on his own life to the tune of £47,000 and one estate had to be sold by order of the Chancery. It was probably to elude his creditors for a period that he slipped across to France in 1802 after the Peace of Amiens. But the Peace of Amiens, a Peace which "everybody was glad of but nobody was proud of", did not last, and he found himself benighted and held captive for some years among Napoleon's *détenus* at Verdun: as motley a collection of fugitives, sharpers, aristocrats, black sheep and genuine prisoners-of-war as you are ever likely to find living in a closed community. Here he added further to his financial problems by being fined twenty thousand francs for calumny, before eventually being released in 1809.

Between 1809 and 1811 he was forced to sell off all his estates. A Rowlandson caricature exists in the Victoria and Albert Museum depicting him felling his trees to settle his play debts. Drawing from memory three years after Sir John's death, Rowlandson has misnamed him Sir Henry in his handwritten inscription.

The moon was by now giving off only a niggard and fitful light, and it finally went behind the clouds as Sir John died in the Isle of Man worth £4,000. This he left to his dearly-loved wife Elizabeth. Her comments do not survive, but she seems to have stood by him. If thrift is a virtue, it is more so in an ancestor. Small wonder that his descendant Sir Warwick sold off the Romney portraits of his grandparents and one suspects that, when he built the seventeen-bedroom mansion of Tregaddick (also at Blisland and still privately occupied) in 1888, it was built with money from his well-connected bride from the Vernon-Harcourt family.

While this was going on, John's younger brother William was living an altogether different life. Colonel and A.D.C. to the King in 1780 he earned his further promotion in the field, in the Wars with the French Republic that followed the French Revolution and the subsequent Reign of Terror. He embarked in 1793 with the troops for Holland, which was protected from invasion by a treaty with England. Austria and Prussia were our allies. Halfway through the campaign the Dutch joined sides with the French and it was difficult to tell friend from foe. The terrible scenes of the retreat from Amersfoort in 1795 are described in letters to his brother, then living comfortably in his Hampton Court property, but no comment is ever made therein on their contrasting life-styles, or any criticism of his brother's conduct.

William's promotion came from none other than the Duke of York (the Grand Old one): Royal Archives, Windsor Castle: Georgian Papers No.8571. Letter from Frederick Duke of York to H.M. King George III:

Broadstairs, August 5th 1797

'Sir, I have the honour to report to your Majesty the death of Lord Amherst which happened on Thursday morning, and the Government of Guernsey are become vacant.

As Your Majesty has already been pleased to express Your intention of appointing Lord Cathcart to the command of the 2d Regiment of Life Guards whenever the vacancy should happen, the 29th Regiment of Infantry will thereby become vacant.

As this is an old Regiment I should suppose that Your Majesty would approve of a Colonel of a junior Regiment being promoted to the command of it and the one who appears to have the fairest pretensions to Your Majesty's favor, is Major General Forbes.

Should this arrangement meet with Your Majesty's approbation I beg leave to lay before Your Majesty the names of three officers, who seem to have the most claims from their rank and services to the Command of the 81st Regiment for Your Majesty's decision, they are Major Generals Sir Hew Dalrymple of the 66th Regiment, Major General Morshead of the Coldstream Regiment of Guards, and Major General Ross of the 78th Regiment. Sir Hew Dalrymple is the Senior Officer and commands at present in Guernsey; Major General Morshead is now in the West Indies, has been upon actual Service from the very first day of the war, and has now for the second time volunteered remaining in the West Indies after having received Your Majesty's permission to return to England; Major General Ross's situation and merits are too well known to Your Majesty for it to be necessary for me to enter upon them. He is the junior of these three officers.

As for the Government of Guernsey ... etc
I have the Honour to be Sir
Your Majesty's most dutiful son
and subject
Frederick.'

Born in 1748, the General married late in life and his great-grandson Julian Glencross, as I write these lines, is still alive in his mid-90s.

With a squire and a general there had to be a parson: the Revd. Edward, my father's great-grandfather, was the youngest son of this family of thirteen children. Chaplain to the Prince of Wales and the Duke of York, he was presented to the Crown living of Calstock by the King in 1796 and remained Vicar of the little village on the west bank of the Tamar estuary for the next 57 years. The Revd. Edward married Mary Kelly, daughter of squire Arthur Kelly of nearby Kelly, Colonel of the South Devon Militia. The *Kelly Book* tells how, when the Colonel died in 1823, an epitaph was written by a carpenter, but it was not thought suitable to be placed in the church:

Here lies my old Tom Cat I tell 'y
He died, same day as Squire Kelly
One hunted hares, t'other rats;
Squires must die as well as cats!

When in due course the squire's son-in-law Henry John Morshead also took Holy Orders he became, predictably, Rector of Kelly, remaining so until his death 48 years later. An elder brother had meanwhile emigrated to New Zealand and it is probably no coincidence that the Australian G.O.C. troops at Tobruk in 1943, General Leslie Morshead, bore a striking resemblance to some members of the family. 'There'll be no Dunkirk here' he said; and there wasn't. Earlier still a branch had emigrated to Prince Edward Island and thence to the United States.

The next village to Kelly was Dunterton, where the Revd. Parramore had freshly arrived as Rector in 1867. The Morshead ladies called. Parramore became a great character, and two stories have been handed down in our family by Sir Owen Morshead:

Voice from back of church: 'You'm playzed to spake up—us caant yurr'ee down yurr.' Parramore, cupping his hands, from the pulpit: 'YEW AWE ME TEW YURR'S TITHES—Can'ee yurr *thaat*?'

'Ah reckon old Parramore's the man to prayche,' said a farmer years later to a member of the family ... 'stand up in the pulpit, give out 'is text like a man—and tear'n all to *rags* in ten minutes.'

Just over the fence from Calstock churchyard, where the Revd. Henry John's father was still Rector, lived a family perhaps more ancient than even the Kellys. Sir William Salusbury-Trelawny, the eighth baronet and father of twelve children, presided at his estate of Harewood. The building no longer exists. Sir William's ancestor, the third baronet, had been one of the seven bishops who defied King James II in 1688 and were sent for trial and subsequently acquitted.

> A good sword and a trusty hand,
>   A merry heart and true:
> King James's men shall understand
>   What Cornish lads can do.
>
> And have they fixed the where and when?
>   And shall Trelawny die?
> Here's twenty thousand Cornish men
>   Will know the reason why!
>
> Trelawny he's in keep and hold,
>   Trelawny he may die;
> Here's twenty thousand Cornish bold
>   Will know the reason why!

Contrary to popular belief, the 'Song of the Western Men' was not contemporary with the incident. It is usually attributed to the Revd. Robert Stephen Hawker (1803–1875) but is equally applicable to the first baronet, whose life was endangered in 1628 by the House of Commons. Another Trelawny had been Governor of Jamaica, which is perhaps the reason for finding Jamaica Inn in the middle of Dartmoor.

Sir William himself had no time for clergymen: so much so that when he died in 1856 he would not allow himself to be buried in the churchyard. Only his head lay in the churchyard with his legs sticking out on to his own property. Both his father and his maternal grandfather were clergymen; and when the former used to swear he would claim that he swore, not as a clergyman, but as a baronet and a country gentleman.* Nevertheless, out of his five daughters who lived, four married clergymen and one became a nun, all within his lifetime. The Revd. Henry John Morshead married the eldest, and Evelyn's grandfather, the Revd. F.T. Batchelor, married the youngest; by which time one assumes he must have forgiven them all. So, notwithstanding the old Trelawny prophecy:

'Trelawny's course through cousins run
Shall weep for many a first-born son'

the wedding of Henry and Evie, my parents, was another wedding of second cousins.

Marlborough College had been founded in 1843 for the sons of West Country clergy, just in time for the Revd. Henry John to send three of his children there. Walter, the eldest, was the school's first Senior Prefect. His brother Frederick went as a scholar to Winchester. Great was the friendly rivalry between them, and great was the joy at Kelly Rectory as seldom a term went by without a prize being brought home. Walter went on to become a scholar of Trinity, a barrister of the Middle Temple and Examiner at the High Court of Justice; while Frederick went on to become a Fellow of New College and founder and housemaster of the eponymously-named house, known affectionately to generations of Wykehamists as 'Freddie's.'

By far the youngest was Reginald, my grandfather. His brother Freddie was already Headmaster of Beaumaris School, Anglesey, when Reginald left Marlborough a term or two early to cram under him for his Maths Degree at St. John's, then the great mathematics college, at Cambridge. The modern pressures of 'O' and 'A' levels are as nothing compared to the constant barrage of religious and moral exhortation kept up by the Revd. Henry John to his son Reginald. "Remember, *festina lente*, hasten slowly, and make yourself a perfect master of each step and not move on till you have. This is the sure and only way to knowledge." About every tenth letter bears a small message to "mind he does not overdo it". Reginald eventually became twentieth wrangler, high enough to be congratulated by some but commiserated with by his vicariously-ambitious father.

Armed with a handful of academic references, Reginald too started his career as a teacher but was soon offered a partnership in the Tavistock bank Gill & Sons (Registered in 1791), which changed its style in 1878 to Gill, Morshead & Co. The partnership was offered partly as a result of a death-bed reconciliation between father and son effected by the Revd. Henry John.

So it happened that, in June 1880, when Ella Sperling aged 27 came down from Edgeworth Manor, Glos., on a brief visit to her Aunt Janet, Squire Kelly's wife, it was at Kelly Rectory that she met the Rector's son, the young banker Reginald, aged 31, still living with his parents. My grandparents fell in love at once.

Speed was essential. Reginald's note must have been written in the middle of the night. The envelope is marked:

Mrs. Kelly   Immediate

Inside, it reads: Wednesday morning (actually 16 June 1880)

> 'Dear Janet,
> Can you give me a few minutes in private
> immediately after breakfast this morning
> or at any rate before your visitors leave?
> I will come down any time you fix.
>   Yours aff^y, Regd Morshead'

The Rector's meticulously-kept diary for the same day reads

'Plans upset. R.M. to dinner'

The visitors leave and a series of daily letters follows. Reginald's sister 'Tish' accompanies Ella on a visit to the latter's grandparents at Stowlangtoft Hall, near Bury St. Edmunds and playfully describes him to his future in-laws as having red hair and a squint... Reginald declines to comment on the weather. 'It is bad enough talking on this unfailing topic, one ought to be restrained from writing about it by Act of Parliament.' 'Do you still want me in Devonshire?' asks Ella a month after they have parted. 'My darling, if you do not come soon my pent up feelings will get the better of me and I shall come straight up to Suffolk and carry you off regardless of Mrs. Grundy or anyone else' — by return of post.

Exactly three months later, on 16 September, they were wed. A year later the old clergyman was dead. The letters continue after the wedding but there are few of them. The first starts 'My more than Better Half', the second 'Dearest and Oldest of Wives' and the third 'Dear Old Wife'. Married life was to remain rose-coloured for them till death intervened about the time of World War I.

The eldest by four years of a family of seven, Henry had to create his own entertainment, inventing for himself games and stories about imaginary people with imaginary names. An early delight was being taken round the house to frighten all the stuffed birds. 'Exercise round table' he exclaimed on his second birthday, and immediately got up and began trudging round the

Ella, with Henry aged 5, and Dick aged 1

hall table with long steps. This was the earliest reference I found to a pre-disposition to walk anywhere and everywhere which would remain with him for life. 'Take care of the damp passages of the house for him,' advised his grandmother, 'I have such a pretty bed for him during your absence.'

A working model of a steam engine and a box of carpenter's tools were his favourite toys, but formal schooling did not begin until he was nine-and-a-half. Before this he did English and French with his mother: Arithmetic, Euclid, Algebra and Latin with his father. The latter had time to spare as the family banking firm, with its four branches, was taken over by Fox, Fowler & Co. with fifty-five branches. They in turn were later merged into Lloyds Bank.

After a few terms at Waynflete, Clifton, where a cousin was Second Master, Henry was sent at the age of eleven to Kelly College, Tavistock, which had been founded in 1875 by a cousin, Admiral B.M. Kelly. In the Napoleonic Wars the Admiral had made a fortune in Prize Money of a size quite unexpected by his family. This he left in trust for the foundation of a Public School, Kelly College, at Tavistock.

Henry regularly won good reports and form prizes at both schools, and in 1896 sat for the Winchester scholarship examination but failed. He came fifth in the Maths paper, however, and secured a good place in the school, entering the House of his Uncle Freddie, who was then nearing the end of his term as a founder Housemaster. Freddie, an early Alpinist and a member of the Alpine Club since five years after its foundation in 1861, had stood on the top of the Matterhorn at least five times, and had made a solitary ascent of Mont Blanc as far back as 1864. He also thought nothing of cycling from Winchester to Tavistock at the end of term.

Six years earlier the Housemaster's son, Hugh William, had won or captained just about every event or team in the school's calendar. A search of the annals reveals that Henry might hardly have been in the school at all; his uncle certainly never made him a prefect. His time appears to have been spent quietly getting on with his work, as testified by his row of prize books. He moved quickly up the school to the 'Army Class', and came second in the Duncan (Maths) prize and the chief Science prize in his last year.

It was therefore a disappointment when he came only 88th out of 200 in the Woolwich exam in September, 1900. The position was improved upon during the ensuing year and he passed out 20th, high enough to be able to choose Royal Engineers. He also developed physically during the course, coming eighth in Aquatic Sports and representing the Academy in the Gymnastics Team. A well-knit 5 foot 9 inches, he was developing into something of a pocket Hercules.

Reginald and Ella with their children, 1903, at Hurlditch Court, Tavistock

The legendary figure of the British Army's last Commander-in-Chief, Field Marshal Earl Roberts of Kandahar, 'Bobs' Bahadur, who had won the V.C. in the Sepoy Revolt, and relieved Kimberley the previous year, took the salute at the passing-out parade and addressed the newly commissioned officers:

> '... If you will set yourselves a high standard, and not be satisfied with mediocrity, you will do credit to the Corps to which you belong, and to the Royal Academy in which you have been trained. Make yourselves acquainted with the duties of the non-commissioned officers, the gunners, the sappers; help them, take an interest in their games and make them comfortable in barracks. Do not let your men hear you utter an oath or a filthy word. Soldiers very soon discover which officers take an interest in them, the officers they can trust and respect, and when the hour of danger comes the soldiers will follow them. I wish you all good-bye and every possible success in your career.'

A salute of 19 guns was fired on the departure of the diminutive but bemedalled septuagenarian.

Leaving the R.M.A. Woolwich as a 2nd Lieut. R.E., Henry's leave, like his school holidays before, was spent with horse or shot-gun at the family home, Hurlditch Court, near Tavistock. A further two years' training followed at the School of Military Engineering at Chatham, where he was awarded the Fowke Memorial Medal given, typically, for a young officer who has distinguished himself in the school of Fortification Construction. He passed his course of instruction in Military Topography, the parchment certificate, headed unambiguously 'No duplicate of this certificate can be issued', giving his standard as Very Good. On the river he rowed stroke for his year of intake.

The top twenty had all applied for service in India, and as there were only seven vacancies Henry thought he had no chance, but he was wrong. Duly presented at the King's Levee, he came home for six weeks embarkation leave over Christmas 1903. On 4 February 1904 Reginald and Ella went to Southampton to see him off in the troopship 'Plassey' 'for five years if all goes well'.

His first posting was to the Military Works Department of the United Provinces of Agra and Oudh, now the State of Uttar Pradesh, where he performed the mundane duties of a Garrison Engineer. These were interspersed with bouts of fever and with local leave, the fever being occasioned rather by his habit of living rough than any inherent weakness in health. 'Henry is just off on a month's leave and hopes to get some hunting and shooting in the jungle. His Colonel is lending him tents and rifles' writes his mother. This is followed by 'Henry is going to send us the heads of a deer and an antelope he has shot, to be put up in the hall.' The Urdu language came easily to him.

An opportunity to join the Survey of India came in 1906; the majority of its gazetted officers were drawn from the Royal Engineers. The Survey, besides having an international reputation, offered an open-air life with the possibility of adventure and exploration, an irresistible combination. Dehra Dun was its headquarters, and the duties ranged from latitude to magnetic operations, the Forest Map Office, the Computing Office and the Triangulation Party.

Surveyors traditionally took little with them on their expeditions; their instruments came before their personal belongings, their profession before their comfort. This suited Henry, whom a contemporary described as being 'small and dark, and hard as nails'. His idea of a good weekend was an eighty-mile tramp in the hills, carrying his shirt in his hand (and sometimes his trousers too) and only the lightest of equipment. 'Blest with the digestion of an ostrich, he could do with impunity things that would put most men on the sick list.'

After one spell under canvas, soon after joining the Survey, Henry too succumbed to a bout of typhoid, then known as enteric. It lasted ten weeks, and he nearly ended in the 'padre's godown'. 'We have such good accounts of Henry;' wrote his mother eventually in May 1907, 'one from Mr. Eccles, one from Captain Lewis and best of all a letter from himself written in pencil from his bed at Grey Castle Nursing Home in Mussoorie. He had just been allowed an egg for the first time after nothing but milk and Benger's Food for many weeks. Nothing is said in any of the letters as to his coming home... He is learning to walk again.'

Two months later he arrived home on sick leave, still somewhat thin and pale. His brother Dick, a medical student at Bart's, went out from Plymouth in the tug at 6 a.m. to meet him on board the P. & O. 'Peninsula'. Typically, he tried to walk too far too soon and his left leg swelled up with phlebitis like a balloon. For most of six solid months he was tied to a sofa, vegetating, in scarcely endurable inactivity.

'Henry is back in camp near Rurki trying to calculate whether certain hills have risen about 7 inches in consequence of earthquakes', wrote Ella to her youngest son, Owen. 'It involves 40 miles of levelling with the theodolite and does not seem worth the trouble!... H. is still on the move and has just completed 5,000 miles of railway travel in three months... H. has not been able to write while on leave in the wilds of the Himalayas. He got a big he-bear and some mountain sheep.' Some weeks later two boxes of his heads and skins arrived in England with the suggestion that his youngest brother employ his carpentry skill in mounting some of the heads during his holidays.

'Henry has been carrying on his work on magnetic observation in some of the wildest and least known parts of India... H. is just starting on the 20,000-mile tour he has to do in the next six months. He may be ordered to do the Survey of Ceylon... H. has gone on a six-week shooting expedition on the borders of Tibet with a gunner friend, Lieut. Gerald Burrard, of the Royal Field Artillery.'

Recalling this expedition in a letter to Evelyn, after Henry's death, Sir Sidney Burrard wrote: 'My son went on a trip with Henry to the sources of the Ganges about 1910. My wife was anxious because Gerald took so little baggage, but Gerald always replied that he had much more than your husband had. He wrote us angry letters, when his mother in her anxiety sent a hill-coolie after him with jam and tins and biscuits and tea, saying they did not want such nuisances.'

Then, in 1911: 'Our great news is that Henry is off at four days notice to accompany the Abor expedition under General Bower up on to the Chinese frontier. The Abors murdered Mr. Noel Williamson and Dr. Gregorson in the spring and this is the expedition which could not be sent up earlier because of the rains. No part of Asia is so little known as the district between the head of the Irrawaddy and the Brahmaputra, and there does not exist the vestige of a map on which to base the boundary with China; so eight survey officers are going up with the expedition, of which Henry is one. He is elated, but it will be dangerous work. The Abors are a treacherous lot and are, I fancy, backed up by their Chinese neighbours.'

3 | Abors & Mishmis

'I see that the Abor Expedition started yesterday from Dibrugarh', wrote Ella in October 1911. 'Henry's last letter was written on the steamer going up the Brahmaputra. The two Gurkhas were on board and they were having a jovial time... The survey were separating into two parties following the two branches of the Brahmaputra, into quite unknown and almost impenetrable jungle... We had an unexpected but welcome letter from Henry last mail, written from a camp in the jungle. All going well; any amount of game, large and small, but no time to hunt it.

Henry says he cannot get leave till this time next year, which is disappointing... I have not seen his name in the list of promotions as yet; he expected to get his Captaincy this month... H. has started for the wilds again and we shall only get letters at rare intervals... Did I tell you that his Pamirs job is off, which means that he may get home next summer?'

The Captaincy came in December 1912, the leave would have to wait.

Lord Hardinge, the Viceroy, was aged fifty-three and had served in the Foreign Office in eight different capitals; he wished to see the clarification of this 600-mile eastern frontier during his Viceroyalty if possible. The area stretched from the state of Bhutan across the district now known as Arunachal Pradesh and into North Burma. It was in order to get back with maps that survey detachments accompanied the Abor Expedition, and the Mission to the adjacent Mishmi tribe. These could then be used by the Foreign Secretary Sir Henry McMahon, at the next Conference with the Chinese, to help in drawing frontiers which corresponded with geographical and ethnic facts.

Noel Williamson, political officer at Sadiya in Assam, had visited the village of Kebong in response to an invitation. On emerging from his tent to talk to the villagers he had been cut down from behind with a dao, the broad, pointless knife used for all purposes from digging and peeling vegetables to house-building and hacking at the jungle. Gregorson too had been killed, and their fifty porters, trying to escape, had found every

Embarking on the river steamer in Calcutta for the Abor Expedition

avenue held. Rope bridges were guarded, their raft sank, and they were chased by Abors with dogs. Only five had returned to tell the tale.

Reporting the Abor expedition for the *Daily Telegraph* was their well-known special correspondent Perceval Landon. It was as much the geographical as the political aspect of the expedition that was attracting attention, and Landon, who was also a dramatist and author, described for his readers on 4 November 1911 the demoniac vegetation of the Assam terai, as Nature responded to the humid glasshouse climate:

'The alluvial flats are choked with a matted and intertwined growth that one might almost saw down in sections. Overhead, there is the dense pall of leaf and branch, of creeper, liana and epiphyte, looped and knotted, strangling for sheer want of room; underneath there is a straining and jostling tangle of 30 ft. high undergrowth, in which the same struggle for life is carried on, only ten times more strenuously. It is a fight for every cubic inch of sunlit air in which a shoot can be thrust or a leaf gasp for nutriment. Through all this cats-cradle of living cables and dense, compact foliage stand up the trunk pillars that uphold it; but they are as invisible as the sodden and plaited masses of blind, whitened ground

creepers, jointed grasses and brown clogged pools below, which never see the sun.'

We need not concern ourselves here with the nature of the fighting except to notice that it formed the background to the surveying work that Henry was employed upon. Suffice it to say that it was of the pointed-wooden-stockade variety, with the Abors relying on their tactical skill in the dense cover, home-made guns, daos and arrowheads dipped in aconite paste. From Kohima in Manipur State, scene of a famous battle in World War II, came 1,500 Naga coolies to assist General Bower, each one carrying a spear and a dao, glad of the employment at twelve *annas* a day, and many yelling their own war cries.

Militarily, the only result was to break up the local domination of the Kebong-Rotung group of villages and to enable the tribes in the interior to trade with India, which they expressed a desire to do.

The Surveyor General of India at the time was Colonel S.G. Burrard, who divided his surveyors into four teams. Each team had either two or three British officers, assisted by either two or three Indian surveyors, and some thirty to forty *khalasis*. The teams were based on the four respective

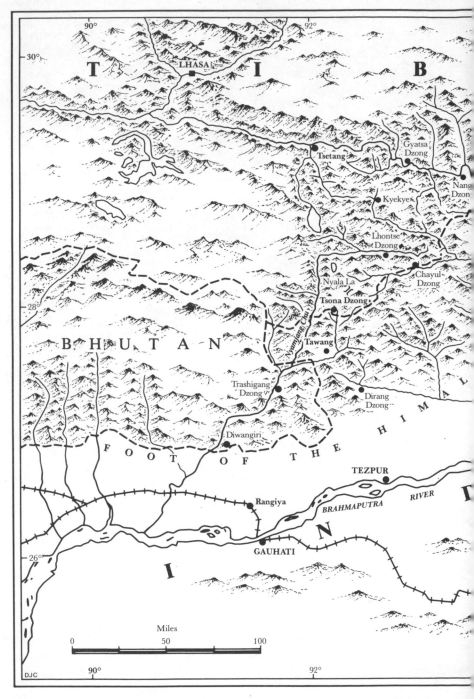

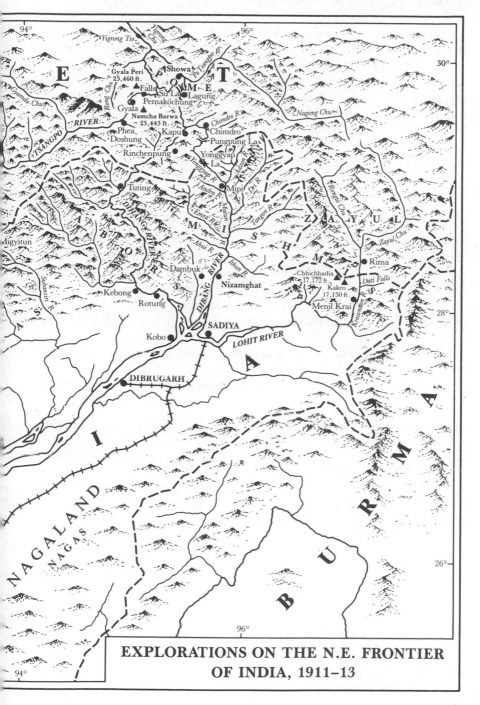

**EXPLORATIONS ON THE N.E. FRONTIER
OF INDIA, 1911–13**

drainage systems of this huge area of 28,000 square miles that was about to be mapped for the first time; that is to say the basin of the upper Irrawaddy and the four principal feeders of the Brahmaputra itself.

With the teams on the extreme east and extreme west this book is not concerned. Of the other two teams, one led by Capt. O.H.B. Trenchard, with Lieutenants Oakes and Field, was attached to the main Abor column and their instructions were to explore and map the basin of the Dihang river, as the Tsangpo is known is this part of its course. The other, led by Capt. C.P. Gunter with Lieutenant Morshead, was attached to the Mishmi Mission and was to explore the other two large eastern tributaries of the Brahmaputra, namely the Dibang and the Lohit.

Trenchard's team was thus nearer the scene of the Abor fighting, while Gunter's was nearer that of the recent Chinese penetration. The Political Officer, never far from the scene, was Capt. G.A. Nevill and the Intelligence Officer ('the man from Simla') was Capt. F.M. (Eric) Bailey, who had been with Younghusband to Lhasa and who had, that very year, completed an adventurous journey alone from China into Assam. 'Everyone thinks Eric is fortunate to be on this expedition,' wrote Bailey's mother to his father, 'but I think the expedition is fortunate in having him.' She was right.

That the Dihang was in fact the same river as the Tsangpo, which flowed behind the Himalayas, had not as yet been proved by actual physical exploration. John Buchan, writing in 1923, had stated in his book *The Last Secrets*:

> 'Fifty years ago one of the questions most debated among geographers was the origin of the Brahmaputra. The great river, navigable for 800 miles from its mouth, was familiar enough in its course through the plains of India; but it flowed from the wild Abor country, and no part of the Indian borders was less known than those north-eastern foothills. Meantime in Tibet, north of the main chain of the Himalayas, there was a large river, the Tsangpo, flowing from west to east. Did the Tsangpo ultimately become the Brahmaputra, or did it flow into the Irrawaddy or even into the Yangtse Kiang?'

By 1911 the actual identity of the Tsangpo and the Brahmaputra was already known. What was arousing public interest now was the supposed existence of high falls on the Dihang section of the Tsangpo. Artists' impressions in the illustrated weeklies were already visualising them for the readers of their despatches from Aborland. There *had* to be a high fall. How else did the river drop from 9,000 ft. to 1,000 ft. in what appeared to be about 100 miles? Burrard himself had an open mind on the subject; the

Ganges and the Sutlej had even bigger drops without falls, although these were over much greater distances; the Kali river in Eastern Kumaon had the steepest gradient so far discovered and that had no falls.

Surveyors Abdul Haq and Allah Ditta joined Gunter and Morshead with 32 *khalasi*s and we find them at Kobo base camp, in October 1911, opposite Sadiya, near where three great rivers meet: the Dihang, Dibang and Lohit. Here they spent ten days in torrential rain which turned Kobo into a swamp. It was not until 25 November that actual plane-tabling was started, and each surveyor was given a small escort.

The country to be surveyed was of an inhospitable and mountainous character, the main ranges varying from 15,000 ft. to 17,000 ft. in height and dropping in a distance of four or five miles to the level of the main valley at about 4,000 ft. The slopes of the Lohit gorge were often nearly 40° making it difficult to climb out of the valley except up the larger side streams; while the general fall of the river was over 40 ft. a mile, causing it to be a torrent until it debouched into the plains.

The rainy climate caused continual difficulty, and mist and cloud were prevalent even on the finest days; during the four months only 38 days were without rain. In January the snowline came as low as 7,000 ft. for a few days, but 10,000 ft. was usually the limit of snow; above this height the mountain tops were bare of trees, rocky and precipitous.

Mishmi villages consisted of one or two long *basha*s built on piles with several families living in each house. At first sight it appeared surprising that human beings could find a living at all in such surroundings, but at the bottoms of the valleys where there was soil it was very fertile; crops of millet were also grown on hill-side clearings. Occasionally a more prosperous village might have 20 to 30 houses and possess some cattle and pigs. The expedition's transport was entirely by Naga coolies who were excellent in the low hills, but who were not properly clothed for work above the snowline.

Gunter started by exploring the Lohit, following the right bank as far as the Yepak river at Menil Krai, a place where the murdered Williamson, probing the loyalty of the border Mishmis, had earlier that year reported seeing a Chinese flag, red with a blue four-clawed dragon. The expedition found a wooden Chinese 'boundary' post, and themselves carved a rival inscription on a granite boulder. The survey was carried on a further 20 miles to within three miles of the recently Chinese-occupied Tibetan border village of Rima, which Bailey had passed through in 1911. Henry took a traverse ten miles up the Rongtö Chu, mapping in its approximate source, and Captain Dundas, of the Political Department, suggested this stream as the best Tibetan boundary.

The detachment completed 3,370 square miles of detail survey and 1,010 square miles of reconnaissance survey, both on the ¼ in. scale. They put on the map the twin peaks of Kakro, 17,150 ft., and Chhichhadia, 17,172 ft., overlooking Rima, and the Dati falls where a sidestream plunges 3,000 ft. to the Lohit; but it was becoming clear that three of the four survey teams were going to have to return the following cold weather, preferably starting earlier in the season, as the work was far from complete.

Their orders for the next season, 1912–13, were to discover the source of the Dibang river and to find out whether the Nagong Chu was one of its tributaries. Gunter proposed to take charge of the plane-tabling himself, and Captain Morshead was to undertake the triangulation of as much of the area 'as it was possible for one man to do'. An early start was important to Henry because the plane-tablers would soon be waiting for the results of his observations from three stations on the first high range; so every effort was made to engage local labour to enable them to start work at once. To clear a jungle hilltop for use as a survey station was in itself sometimes a week's work.

Unfortunately, the Political Officer was called away at the critical

F.M. Bailey in 1907. He wears the Tibet Medal of 1904

Captain W.C.M. Dundas stands beside the wooden 'boundary' post. The inscription reads 'The Glorious Manchu Empire—Zayul Province Southern Limit'

moment and the promised labour force was late arriving. The weather broke after a week, and by 19 November snowstorms caused their retirement from the bivouac at 10,250 ft., and the death of one Mishmi by being frozen. This was an ominous start for the triangulation. On the man's death every other Mishmi bolted, leaving Morshead and Surveyor Muhammad Salik to get back to Nizamghat as best they could with all the kit. The latter included a heliograph, which could hardly have been of much use in these conditions. The points fixed from the first two stations were, however, of value and gave them a good idea of how far north their work was going to take them.

Meanwhile Surveyor Abdul Haq had been finding that the Abors in his area were friendly and did not interfere with his work although they did not put themselves out to help. The combination of an escort of 25 military police and the offer of very high wages actually persuaded some of them to offer their services. The Mishmis were friendly and anxious to help but appeared to be overawed by the Abors of Dambuk, a large and prosperous village of 400 houses, and could do nothing without their permission.

By the beginning of December there were assembled at Nizamghat 1,100 coolies, 350 military police and four British officers, and by the end of the month the survey parties had got to the furthest point reached the previous year in the Dibang valley, and even the Mishmis were speculating on the reception that lay ahead. Certainly it was *terra incognita* to any European. The supply of rations broke down, and they paused while a system of convoys was evolved. Gunter and Morshead were together on 10 January on the top of Achi Hill, where stations were established at 10,433 ft. and at 9,560 ft., commanding views of the Matun, Dri and Tangon valleys ahead.

The days spent at Achi were full of interest as they were fixing on the map of the world rivers, peaks and valleys which had not been seen or even heard of by Europeans: the views too were very fine and impressed on them all the utter wilderness of the country. At Etalin village, on the junction of the Tangon and the Matun (Dihang), Henry was seedy and required a rest, and also had a week's computation to do. So Gunter pressed on up the Tangon valley for three marches and back, in the heavy rain which had started again. There were very few days on which his plane-table could be set up without its having to be protected by means of a water-proof sheet stretched tent-wise on poles. All the Mishmis up that valley appeared very friendly, though the curiosity of some of the ladies trying to get their first view of a European was rather trying, especially when that European was struggling to wash and get dressed inside a 30 lb. tent.

Etalin village became an advanced base and Major Bliss, the Escort Commander, came up and a conference was held to settle the future programme. Gunter was to lead the main column up the Dri valley, a singularly inappropriate name in view of the weather. Morshead would leave for the Iliyi Hills, 9,928 ft., and the Tondondi Hills, 9,627 ft.

As no information about the country up the Dri could be obtained except that there were Tibetan villages there, peopled by Pohs, who were very fierce and went for one on sight with a drawn sword, the officer commanding the force did not consider it safe to proceed without a large escort. Halting at the junction of the Dri and Matun rivers, Gunter moved about with his escort and managed to 'cut in' many useful points ahead. The jungle had thinned out and plane-tabling was simplified along the main spurs at about 7,000 ft.

On Tondondi Hill it snowed almost continuously, but a single fine day enabled Henry to complete a large part of his observations. As the main advance had commenced he did not delay on this hill but joined the main column at Mipi, a small Tibetan hamlet where a base had been established a few days before, near the junction of the Matun and Andra rivers. The village had first been reconnoitred and found to contain only harmless Kambars and not the fierce Pohs that the Mishmis had led them to expect.

Nevertheless, a stockade was built round the camp for protection at night.

A week's halt was necessary at Mipi to enable rations to be collected for a further advance; and a few fine days enabled the surveyors to do a lot of plane-tabling from several high fixings, while Henry cleared and observed from the highest point in the vicinity. Captain Bailey, who was a good Tibetan scholar, managed to extract useful information from the Tibetans about the Tsangpo and the country north of the Andra and Adzon watershed, and the plan began to take shape of his crossing over into the Chimdro valley, with Henry, to unravel the mystery of the 'falls' and the unmapped section of the Tsangpo.

In 1906 some thousands of Tibetans had come south, over the Andra and Yonggyap passes, and ejected the few Mishmis whom they had found in the Matun valley. It did not take them long to discover that it was not a land flowing with milk and honey and that the country could not maintain them. Those who were able soon quit and returned to Tibet leaving many hundred dead along the route. A small party of 80 souls, mainly those too old or feeble to travel, remained; and it was these who formed the community of about 60 still living in Mipi.

As the Tibetans were so few, and friendly withal, the escort was reduced and parties were sent simultaneously up the Tangon river to the east and up the Andra and Adzon rivers to the north. Using Mipi as a base the three captains, Gunter, Bailey and Morshead, moved slowly up the Andra valley, able to make only three or four miles a day owing to the incessant snow and rain, and continually coming across the depressing remnants, cooking pots, clothes and dried bones, of the Tibetans who had died there from exhaustion and starvation six years before.

On 10 March 1913 the Naga coolies could go no further and they were snowed up for five days in their camp at 7,000 ft. The last fixing up the Andra valley was made at an elevation of 9,000 ft. at a distance (up the Andra valley) of 130 miles from Nizamghat. Bailey and Morshead were unable to make their dash for the pass, and fix it by a time and compass traverse, owing to the depth of snow, and the return journey was commenced; but not before Bailey had found shelter in a cave for a few days and travelled a few miles further on his own. On the 29th the bridge at Ta-aron carried away and 'Captain Morshead left at once to repair it' records Bailey's diary. The Mishmi bridging technique was new to Henry, however, and he could only supervise the work.

Gunter and Morshead then moved up the narrow gorge of the Adzon, hoping to run a theodolite traverse; the dense jungle precluded this, so they had recourse to a range-finder traverse instead. Fixings were not to be expected as it was impracticable to climb the hills on either side.

Mr. Abdul Haq explored the Emra river valley until, with the snowline down to 5,000 ft., further advance had to be abandoned. The Mishmis in this valley appeared to be the only ones to have established trading relations with the Mipi Tibetans; they had no communications with the Dihang Abors over the pass at the head of their valley, the last attempt made by them in this direction resulting in the annihilation of the whole party except one man; a tactic presumably thought more effective than destroying them all.

Haq, with Surveyor Sheo Lal, explored the Tangon river for six weeks, spending four nights on Tangon Hill at a 12,500 ft. camp where the only water was melted snow. On the summit of a 15,000 ft. peak Sheo Lal had a bad fall and Haq took over his plane-table as well. Finally snow-blindness and frostbite among the *khalasi*s together with shortage of rations drove them back to base.

Gunter made his last fixings up the (exceedingly wet) Dri valley, compensated somewhat for the atrocious conditions by the sight and sound of several sidestreams in full flood leaping the 3,000 ft. fall of rock in two or three magnificent cascades and thundering on to the river flats below. One of his *khalasi*s fell down a precipice, but was fortunately caught up in a tree some 80 ft. down and on being rescued informed everyone that he was 'dead'. The gorge for the last 40 miles was so restricted and shut-in by precipices on both sides that it was impossible to climb out of the valley anywhere until the river bed had attained an altitude of 10,000 ft. At 142 miles (up the Dri valley) from Nizamghat he turned back and decided to leave the forsaken place free for 'the *Takin* to wander about in at their leisure'.

All the tributaries of the Dibang had been found to have grades of well over 100 ft. per mile, many for distances of 20 or 30 miles; but the steepest stretch of 'milk water' of them all was the rise from 7,500 ft. to 9,500 ft. in only 1½ miles on the Dri, a gradient of 1 in 4. It was not surprising, concluded Gunter, that the Dibang river rushed through the gorge at Nizamghat with such terrific force.

Morshead meanwhile made prolonged stays on three hills called Agidzu, 10,426 ft., Karundi 11,267 ft., and Deshindi 12,027 ft. The first took five days to clear, while the two latter were already clear hilltops of pure snow some 12 ft. deep lashed by the wind and necessitating the erection of a pole. He found it necessary to bivouac 3,000 ft. lower down and climb to his hilltop each day. It was not until 7 May that the weather permitted him to take a round of angles from Karundi. Gunter visited him there, and heavy snow and rain kept them imprisoned in their tents for six days.

On 28 April Gunter had received urgent appeals from Major Bliss to close down and return to Sadiya; and on 5 May came a letter reporting that the Ithun bridge had been carried away by floods and that all persons were to be put on short rations. Nothing could be sent up the line until the Mishmis had constructed one of their suspension bridges of twisted bamboo across the Ithun river; these could be anything up to 350 ft. long. The party had sufficient rations to last only until 16 May and it was evident that they would have to start retiring on 10 or 11 May at the latest, leaving Henry to continue his exploration as planned with Captain Bailey.

As the survey establishment repaired to Shillong to undertake the mapping of their field work, Gunter could reflect that the whole programme laid down by the Government of India had been accomplished. To have got only 21 days of fine weather in four months, even fewer than in the previous season, had been a trying experience for a triangulator. The patience, endurance and professional ingenuity of every member of the party had been taxed to their utmost, but the course of the Dibang had been traced to the source of each of its five large constituents. The Nagong Chu was not a tributary but, according to Tibetan information, flowed into the PoTsangpo and thence into the Dihang. The watersheds connecting the

Computations at Nizamghat. Captains Nevill and Nicolay assist Henry (on left) with the logarithm book

exterior boundaries of his survey had been satisfactorily connected with those of the surveys to his east and west.

In the Lohit valley the previous year they thought they had found the wildest and most precipitous country in India; but they had yet to visit the Dibang gorges, which made the Lohit pale into insignificance. The 'road' up the Dibang had been one succession of dips down into deep gorges and ascents up over high spurs. One march (from Angolin to Imbolin) had entailed ascents totalling 7,100 ft. and descents totalling 4,200 ft.; another (over the watershed between the Ahui and Emra rivers) involved a continuous climb of 5,000 ft. The only piece of country approaching flatness was the 'Downs' at the junction of the Dri and the Matun, 3 miles long by 1½ miles wide.

Gunter had praise for his staff. Captain Morshead 'completed the computations of every triangulated point within a few hours of the observations having been made and sent the results to the plane-tablers before the latter required them. As this was mostly carried out in snow and under difficult conditions it can be realised what a fine record he has to show for his season's work'. The season's work, however, was not yet over.

4 | The Tsangpo Gorges

The Abor Exploration Survey under Captain Trenchard was working in the main Dihang valley to the westward. There must have been an element of professional rivalry between the two teams, although this is not obtrusive. All knew they were breaking new territory and all wanted to be in on the act.

Lieutenants G.F.T. Oakes and J.A. Field of Trenchard's 1912 survey were the first to measure the height of the great peak of Namcha Barwa, previously seen by explorer Nem Singh in 1879, by Kinthup in 1881, and by Capt. C.L. Robertson, R.E. in 1900. Henry confirmed its height from the other side[1] and, in his journey with Bailey the following year, discovered the peak to be right in the great knee-bend of the Tsangpo. He translated the meaning of its Tibetan name as 'Lightning burning in the sky'.

At 25,445 ft. its height took geographers by surprise. It was the highest peak east of Kanchenjunga and the 35th highest in the world. The two lieutenants, Oakes and Field, by then captains, were to be tragically killed within two days of each other in the Battle of the Somme in 1916.

Conditions in Trenchard's valley, as the season advanced, were not dissimilar to those described by Landon; owing to the excessive humidity 16,000 ft. was found to be the limit to which plane-table or theodolite could be carried. Leeches abounded, the obnoxious *damdim* fly put in its appearance, and 'malaria-carrying sandflies' made life a plague. Limbs were bathed in permanganate of potash, and quinine was consumed in prophylactic quantities; unattended bites, sores and cuts usually put far more men on the sick list than did fever and other diseases.

Trenchard's column finished up with a brave little dash, which would have been pushed to further conclusion if it had not been known that Bailey and Morshead had better chances of success. Captains Trenchard and Pemberton succeeded in crossing the main ridge to the north-west and reached the Tsangpo above Gyala, about six days march above the spot where the falls were supposed to be. A barometer height for the river confirmed that an enormous drop occurred in the river bed, and from such enquiries as could be made it was evident that the local people thought there was something worth being evasive about.

Supplies and coolies were short, however, and the two officers had to return to the main column as quickly as they could. The return of the latter down the Dihang was much hampered by sickness. The medical officer had a rule-of-thumb fitness test; a man whose temperature was 101° had to carry a full load, 102° a half load; 103° was left to stumble along by himself, and 104° formed part of the baggage. There was not a man who did not rejoice to see the plains of Assam once more after eight months struggling through the hills.

Captain F.M. Bailey, Indian Army, told the story of his exploration with Captain Morshead in his book *No Passport to Tibet*. The title was well chosen because the two officers had been told, by telegram from Simla before starting, not to enter Tibet; but Captain Nevill, head of the mission, agreed to maintain the fiction on their behalf that they had already left. I have drawn on the book, together with the reports and papers of both officers. Very few photographs exist, because it was decided to leave Henry's camera behind to save weight, and Bailey's was soon lost.

'As soon as I met Henry Morshead he impressed me with his keenness, efficiency and his extra-ordinary powers of physical endurance. He was my first, and as it proved my only, choice for a colleague, for as soon as I put the idea to him he leapt at the opportunity.'

Bailey had been educated at Wellington and Sandhurst and was the older by a year. The two men were well matched, for both could work long hours in almost impossible conditions and both seemed oblivious to the normal requirements for sleep and food. Comfort meant nothing to either of them. Henry left Mipi on 15 May 1913, Bailey joining him the next day at a place called Basam (a Tibetan word meaning 'cane footbridge'), where he found Henry down with fever. This was a worry right at the beginning of the journey; but next morning Henry said he was better, and left before dawn to take a compass bearing up the valley from a 7,000 ft. hill. He was expected back in the evening, but night fell and there was no sign of Morshead.

'All his kit is here. He was alone', records Bailey's diary starkly.

'Morshead was quite fearless and thought so little about danger that he didn't realise that there was such a thing as risk. I sent men down the road with torches, in case he might have missed the way in the dark, but they returned without having met him.

I hardly slept that night for worrying over his disappearance. Had he had an accident or another more violent attack of fever? It might be impossible to find him in this dense uninhabited country, and even supposing we did find him and he was in some way incapacitated, what then? This heaven-sent opportunity of exploring the gorges was unlikely ever to come our way again.'

Bailey returned to Basam, where there was still no sign of Morshead; but he appeared soon afterwards in a high fever. The two men had misunderstood each other as to which bank of the river they were going to follow. Then, after leaving his survey station, Henry had been led astray by a fresh blaze, which he thought Bailey had made for his guidance. It turned out to be one of the nomadic cultivation blazes; the whole hillside was alight, the noise from the bursting stemjoints of the bamboo clumps sounding like salvos from an artillery bombardment.

'Not finding any further traces and being overtaken by darkness, he had spent the night without food, trying ineffectually to shelter from the pouring rain under a rock. This not being one of the cures for fever, Morshead began to run a high temperature and so, instead of trying to catch us up, he made for Basam to which he reckoned I would return... It was plain that he could do no more that day, so I gave him some tea, laced with whisky, of which we had one bottle for such emergencies as these. Then, seeing that he was comfortable, I left him and went ahead to my camp of the night before. By the next morning he had recovered completely and he joined us very early and we moved on in heavy rain.

20 May. Camp, 8,150 ft. We had now climbed high enough to be free at last of those pests of the damp forests, leeches and ticks. While we were still below that altitude I had noted another characteristic of Morshead's which rather alarmed me. No one can avoid picking up leeches and one cannot stop to remove them while one is on the march. On one occasion described by me[2] I found at a halt that I had 150 leeches on me and my clothes. Morshead appeared indifferent to them. I thought at the beginning that this indifference might be a residue of his fever; but later I found that this was not the case. When his temperature was indubitably normal, he would stand there covered with leeches and with blood oozing out of his boots, as oblivious as a small child whose face is smeared with jam. It worried me, because I felt that I had to be responsible for Morshead's tropical hygiene as well as my own.'

On 24 May they reached the *latsa* or hut at the foot of the Yonggyap La.

The next day snow fell heavily all day, and their guides, who confessed they were already lost, declared that it would be madness to attempt the pass. On the 26th, the weather having slightly improved, they started early, doing much of their own carrying so as to have every possible coolie available for carrying rations. In the thick mist the guides had difficulty in finding the pass, which was reached by an ascent of 1,500 ft. through waist-deep snow, and it was dusk when they reached the *latsa* on the north side of the pass. There they halted for a day as four of the coolies were incapacitated by snow-blindness. There had been no apparent glare on the snow, owing to the dense mist all day, and the possibility of snow-blindness had not occurred to either. They received a lesson thus early from which they were not slow to profit.

Since leaving Mipi not a single triangulated peak had been visible through the cloud and mist, and Henry began to realise the impossibility of carrying on a system of connected triangulation, or of executing anything more rigorous than a traverse by 'time and compass'.

They measured the altitude of the pass by hypsometer, at 12,020 ft., but could not find a stick long enough to measure the depth of the snow. On a rock nearby it was twelve feet, and on the ground was probably twenty. While waiting for the coolies to recover their eyesight Bailey took his gun and supplemented their rations, shooting a blood pheasant, two Brahminy duck and a mallard. A puppy which they had picked up locally, and named 'Roarer', enjoyed chasing the pheasants but could not catch them. Henry's report does not mention that at this point he discovered that his sight-rule was missing. It must have been dropped as they were crossing the pass. 'This is a disaster.' he said. 'Without a sight-rule I can't make a plane-table survey. My work will be practically useless.' He spent the day trying to make a new sight-rule out of a ration tin.

As they dropped down into the Chimdro valley they were getting decidedly short of food. Morshead needed to travel more slowly than Bailey in order to do his survey work as he went. So it made good sense for Bailey to press on over the Pungpung La, itself another pass under 20 feet of snow, and down into the Chimdro valley to exercise his best Tibetan on the *Dzongpön* in the vital matter of inducing him to grant them supplies and transport, at a fair price, for the next stage. Theoretically, once granted, the privilege would not be disputed at the next village, and so on. They would find later that the closer together the villages were, the more off-loading and re-loading was necessitated, as each village was jealous of not exceeding its allotted stage.

Henry followed along, 'swearing gently each time he remembered the loss of his sight-rule', and traversing up the side valleys to their furthermost villages and back, caught up Bailey at a village called Bulung:

'He looked bad. We were back in leech country again and he was still doing nothing about them... While I was at the monk's house, one of our coolies, a Monba called Anay, came and drew me on one side. Morshead was "very ill", he said. "How was he ill?" I asked. "Very ill" he repeated, and then said that Morshead had fainted.

It seemed callous to leave him at such a time, and yet our position with the Tibetans of Chimdro was such that I did not want to leave the monk, or let him know that Morshead was ill. Any betrayal of weakness might tip the balance against us. I remembered how whisky had pulled him round before. The bottle would probably do him far more good than I. Unpacking it, I gave it to Anay and with difficulty managed to borrow a pony.

Morshead rode in on the pony soon after this. The whisky had revived him and he was already looking much better. He was a man with marvellous powers of recuperation, but I remembered what had happened in the Yonggyap valley and was frightened that he might have a recurrence of his fever.'

Arthur Swinson, in his biography of Bailey, makes the fair comment at this moment[3] that already Morshead's neglect of elementary health precautions was beginning to annoy Bailey. However, the fever did not recur (what, never? well, hardly ever) and we can safely leave Bailey's own comments on Henry until the end of the chapter.

On 5 June they reached Kapu, where the Chimdro joins the Tsangpo, and took a hypsometer reading of the height, 2,606 ft. Henry decided to send a runner to Captain Trenchard, asking for the co-ordinates of any triangulated points he might have fixed, and at the same time borrow another sight-rule from him. Trenchard was thought to be at Tuting, about fifty miles further down the Dihang, and the people of Kapu said that it would take ten days to get an answer. (The runner did not have to go all the way back to Mipi, as stated by Swinson.)

While waiting for a reply they traversed unhurriedly down the Dihang valley to meet the returning runner, taking latitudes by the stars when the weather permitted, as far as Rinchenpung. The moist damp heat of June was most tedious, and combined with the perfect plague of mosquitoes, *damdims*, leeches and gadflies would have been unbearable were it not for the excellent quality of the *marwa* beer which was brewed there in large quantities. Bailey shot a 90-inch snake with his pistol; both men were good shots.

The *damdim* is black and yellow and about the size of a housefly.

According to R.H. Phillimore it would make for the tenderest part of your anatomy when you went behind the bush, and each bite made you scratch for three days. The local beer was quite simply made by boiling up barley in a large pot and, before it was cool, tossing in a piece of yeast. After a few days the resultant milky-looking fluid would have a considerable alcoholic content, and could be distilled to produce a crystal-clear *arak*. Fermenting millet seeds could also be used to similar effect.

After vainly waiting three days in Rinchenpung for a reply, they retraced their steps to Kapu and continued up the Tsangpo valley to Lagung, where they found trouble in the form of the Nyerpa or Minister of Pome, Namgye by name, waiting for them. Namgye was returning from a cold weather tour in Pemakö. He viewed Bailey and Morshead with suspicion, regarding their arrival as a breach of faith. It was agreed that the latter would have to abandon their intention of following the valley of the Tsangpo, and would accompany him over the Su La to Showa, capital of Pome, on the PoTsangpo, where a council would be held as to their disposal.

Tibet at the time was at a momentous period in its complicated history. Nearly 200 years of Manchu suzerainty had come to an end in 1912, only a year previously. During this long time the Chinese had protected the Tibetans from Dzungar (Mongol) and Nepalese (Gurkha) invasions, but, latterly, the Chinese had had to struggle hard to assert their authority by force. A 100-strong Chinese garrison had arrived in Showa in August 1911 and left in January 1912. During this time they beheaded the Pöba (Tibetan) King and four of the five chiefs under his authority, together with eight ministers, thus at a stroke removing anyone of any authority in the country. They also burned the Palace and the Gompa (monastery) and many houses and villages.

Ironically, His Holiness the XIIIth Dalai Lama (Thubten Gyatso, 1876–1933), who had fled to China from the Younghusband expedition in 1904, found himself fleeing from the Chinese in 1910, and taking refuge in India, from where he declared the independence of Tibet.

With the outbreak of the Chinese Revolution in 1911 the Chinese troops had murdered their own officers and retreated back to the Mekong river; but the recent outrages were fresh in Tibetan memory.

The unfortunate Bailey was soon to be subjected to another shock, which showed the nervous tension under which they were operating in the early stages of the journey. As they approached Showa, with Bailey leading the way through fields high with wheat, barley and peas, suddenly a shot rang out. My God!, he thought, they have ambushed Morshead. If they had, Bailey would be next; but it turned out to have been a shot fired by someone scaring parrots from the crops.

Reaching Showa, 8,250 ft., on 25 June they were kept prisoners in the travellers' house for several days, while Bailey spent many hours pressing their case before the council, who affected to believe that they represented a flank attack on the part of the returning Chinese. Matters were eventually settled satisfactorily, and they were given a mounted guide and promises of supplies and transport to take them to the Tibetan border when, at the last moment, suspicions were again aroused and the negotiations imperilled at the sight of some Chinese writing on Henry's tablet of Indian ink.

Mistrust flared up anew and their voices grew harsh and accusing. Had not two letters arrived recently from W.C.M. Dundas of the Political Department, both of them inside Chinese envelopes? It was not until later that they learned that Dundas had gone to enormous trouble to procure them, under the impression that the sight of an English envelope would alarm the Tibetans with its strangeness. In the event the familiarity of the Chinese envelopes had alarmed them even more, and the Nyerpa asked them why Dundas used such envelopes if he was not Chinese; a question to which it was difficult to give a convincing answer.

'The incident seemed amusing enough in retrospect, but actually our lives were at stake', Henry told Lt.Col. E.W.C. Sandes, who goes on to describe Henry's interview with the *Dzongpön*: 'After the customary enquiries about the visitors' health and hardships of the journey, the next question was regarding their ages. In Tibet the calendar is reckoned by a 12-year cycle, each year being given the name of one of 12 animals. Thus a "horse-year man" must have been born in such a year as 1882, 1894 or 1906, and the enquirer is left to guess from his visitor's appearance, the particular cycle of his birth. When Morshead replied that he was a horse-year man, the *Dzongpön* raised his eyebrows in feigned polite astonishment and murmured: "Really your dignity is such that I should have thought you were at least twice that age". As the inhabitants were then reputed to kill all travellers who were worth looting, Morshead and Bailey were very fortunate to escape harm.'[4]

Henry's runner arrived back about this time with a reply dated 12 June from Trenchard. I found this, torn from the latter's field-service notebook, folded inside Henry's copy of his own report. Trenchard enclosed a list of recently triangulated points, together with a replacement sight-rule:

'What chance any of us have of persuading Dundas to allow us to lose ourselves in Tibet as you are doing remains to be seen. It would be great if we could meet somewhere on the Tsangpo north of the main range.

Whatever happens go everywhere and survey everything you can: we have not staked out any area as a preserve & even if we duplicate bits of work it will make it a better map. Above all get to Gyala and the Falls somehow. I hope you will have a successful trip and a safe return. No time to send you a trace of our work or the points mentioned in this letter. I hope you will be able to follow it clearly when you get our trig points plotted on your plane-table.'

Showa was a straggling village of about 40 houses with the remains of a large palace and a monastery which, together with the bridge over the Tsangpo, had been destroyed by the Chinese in 1911. A new cantilever log bridge, of 50 yards span and ten feet wide, had recently been completed.

Up to this point Henry had concealed the fact that he was making a map. Having now made friends with Namgye, he discussed the matter with him and showed him his survey instruments. No objection was made and thereafter he was able to work openly; although Namgye remarked that once many years previously a Chinaman who had come from the west, counting his paces and writing down the numbers in a book, had been quickly bundled out of the country.

The arrival of the replacement sight-rule had a dynamic effect on Henry. He climbed every hill in sight to take his observations, yet in the evening Bailey was perplexed to see him running round a field. 'What's the matter?' Bailey shouted. 'Nothing,' he shouted back, 'just taking a little exercise.'

On the fourth day out from Showa they came to an undamaged stone house, the palace of the king, who had been beheaded at the order of the Chinese. A little further on, the PoTsangpo, which they were following in a north-westerly direction, turned suddenly south-west; but a broken rope-bridge necessitated a two-day excursion northwards up the Yigrong Chu (river) to where there was a ferry across the Yigrong Tso (lake). Morshead went up the lake and mapped it.

Villagers told them how, thirteen years previously, the lake had been formed. A tributary of the Yigrong Chu ceased to flow for three days while rumblings were heard up the valley. Suddenly an immense mass of mud and stones, too hot to walk on, came down the valley fanning out and engulfing two villages on each bank and forming a dam across the river 350 ft. high and 1¼ miles wide. For over a month the Yigrong remained dammed, while a huge lake formed, submerging many villages; when the dam was topped a flood was released which was noticed in Assam as carrying the corpses of strange men and pine trees of an unfamiliar variety. Dejectedly the villagers asked B & M if they could take away the lake, and get them back their land for cultivation.

Fourteen miles downstream from the lake they were shown the site of an old village, 170 feet above the river, which had been washed away in this

Ferryboat on the Yigrong Lake

flood. It was the displaced Tibetans, wandering southwards in search of new homes, who had founded the colony of Mipi in the Mishmi hills.

'The snow-clad peak which Morshead and I had discovered from Mipi half hidden by its rival Namcha Barwa was now revealed in its true magnificence. Its name was Gyala Peri, and it towered to 23,460 ft. In itself it was one of the great mountains of the world; but what made it so astonishing was that only thirteen miles away was the peak of Namcha Barwa, 25,445 ft., and between them flowed the Tsangpo 14,000 ft. below the one and 16,000 ft. below the other. The two peaks are supposed to be the breasts of Dorje Pagmo, the Diamond Sow, whose incarnation lives at Samding Monastery on the Yamdrok Tso. It was an example of the power of water as startling as that of the Colorado River in the Grand Canyon.

One night Morshead was ill and I took the bearings for him. Another night we camped in a cave under a high precipice with a stream coming down in a cataract, a couple of hundred yards away, and wild strawberries, raspberries and gooseberries growing in the clearing. There were also redcurrants, which we were told were uneatable; but Morshead ate them all the same. His digestion seemed to be as insensitive to food as his body was to leeches. He ate any fruit he found.'

Finding his compass affected by the iron in the earth, Henry located an iron mine nearby. He went in some way, but did not reach the workface. The tortured landscape also yielded glaciers, hot springs and a sulphur mine with gas bubbling out among the rocks. They had marched right round the back of Gyala Peri by the time they arrived back on the Tsangpo opposite Phea Doshung, to which they crossed, missing Trenchard and Pemberton by about a week.

They followed the right bank of the Tsangpo downstream to Gyala, and there, across the river *on a small side stream*, were the falls of Shingche Chogye. The limestone rocks which formed the bed of the stream had been hollowed out into curious caverns by the water, which fell in three successive cascades of some fifty feet each into the Tsangpo below. A demon, carved on the rock and giving his name to the falls, was popularly supposed to be chained behind the waterfall, by a chain with bells hanging from it, but visible only at times of low water.

Below Gyala the valley narrowed and the Tsangpo changed from placid river into a roaring torrent fifty yards wide. Pemaköchung, ten miles further downstream, which they reached on 21 July, was the last Tibetan habitation. It consisted merely of a humble monastery and one other occupied house. Bailey found it a dead-and-alive sort of place—one of the world's dead ends. Certainly it was a dramatic and austere site for a place of pilgrimage. A Tibetan shepherd boy told him, more or less, that he should see it when the pilgrims came; this was once a year and they got a crowd of 30 to 50 people then. He had not the heart to tell the boy that Pemaköchung was not at the head of his list of desirable summer resorts.

A mile or so above the monastery the Tsangpo itself went over a cliff some 30 ft. high, sending spray up 50 ft. in the air, and from there onwards was a seething, boiling mass of water; but there were no high falls. Nor was there any track down the valley. Henry took a boiling point at the top of the fall, 8,381 ft., and an azimuth observation to Namcha Barwa, eight miles away to the south.

Determined to cut a road for themselves as long as their rations lasted, they succeeded in reaching a prominent spur from which they could trace the general course of the Tsangpo downstream for the next 30 or 40 miles and fix the position of the high snowy range round which it bends. Bailey, with a single coolie, followed a party of Monbas for a few miles further before they gave him the slip at an almost impossible precipice, and he had to return, after taking a hypsometer reading at the lowest point reached. Everyone questioned agreed that there were no more actual falls.

A table of gradients in Henry's report shows that from Pemaköchung, at the top of the 30-foot falls, the gradient for the next 35 miles averages 76 feet

Tsangpo falls from below

per mile, or 1 in 69. The steepest short stretch is the first three miles below the falls, where it averages 97 feet per mile, or 1 in 54. This is about the same as the steepest grade on the West Highland Railway, Scotland, where the train, leaving Rannoch station for Fort William, is confronted by a gradient of 1 in 53; where two West Highland 4-4-0s, pulling ten coaches, used to fill the glen with the stentorian bark and hiss of their exhausts.

So imagine the maddened Tsangpo, careering down the same gradient, ever faster as it narrows into a gorge, all white water now except for an occasional flash of jade. Compare it also with the more leisurely pace of the Ganges, which Eric Newby found to drop only 22½ feet per mile on the steepest 25 mile stretch of his voyage between Hardwar and Balawali bridge; and which was still only 50 feet per mile at the point where Sir Edmund Hillary's jet boats were forced to give up. Yet fifty miles upstream Bailey and Morshead would find the same river wide enough and slow enough to give the appearance of a lake.

It was in the shadow of Gyala Peri that Bailey, a lifelong collector and naturalist, discovered the Himalayan blue poppy, Meconopsis Baileyi, and 'won immortality through a seedsman's catalogue'. When Captain Kingdon Ward, the famous plant hunter, revisited the area in 1924 with Lord Cawdor, he brought back its seeds. The two explorers each had a new species of Primrose named in their honour by Ward.

Tracks were seen of bear, takin, serow and musk deer, with occasional herds of gooral and bharal, one of the latter containing 43 head of those slate-blue Himalayan sheep. Bailey's specimen collections of mammals, birds and butterflies were to become famous. The last alone, as catalogued by Brigadier W.H. Evans in the *Journal of the Bombay Natural History Society* eventually numbered 2,000. Henry himself discovered a couple on this expedition, and I am indebted to Miss Mary Rowlatt for the following:

'I was passing the Natural History Museum in London yesterday and went in to ask about the Morsheadi butterfly; the idea of finding out about it appealed to me greatly. I was politely ushered into the offices and research departments of the butterfly section and was met by a Mr. Howeth with enthusiasm. He was able to look it up in a minute. There are two, actually, both small and somewhat dingy, but apparently of the greatest interest to experts.

Mr. Howeth gave me their names: one is Celestrina Morsheadi and the other Agriades Morsheadi. They had been catalogued and named in 1913 by a Brigadier Evans. Mr. Howeth had actually known Brigadier Evans, who had worked for three years in the Natural History Museum, cataloguing all Indian butterflies.'

By the standards of the outward journey the return was less political though not less arduous. The reverberations of the Abor expedition were still manifest as they made their way westwards. Once they were taken to be the advanced scouts of a force of two or three thousand. Another time they found an official with a rather threadbare parrot which had been trained to recite *Om Mani Padmi Hum* (Oh, thou (Sakya) of the lotus and the jewel), a veritable feathered prayer-wheel in the form of a bird which has given the word of repetition to our language.

'I've been thinking of us as going up the Tsangpo making a map,' says Henry, 'but really we are going back to India via Tsona, in a way.' 'Yes,' agrees Bailey, 'but rather a long way.'

Local rope bridges were made of twisted bamboo bark two or three inches in diameter. Over this would be laid a wooden saddle, a few inches long, which slid over the rope with its load slung beneath on leather thongs. Any contact with the rope while descending could inflict a spiteful wound. The better rope bridges had two ropes, a separate one for each direction, enabling a good high take-off point from each side. Single-rope bridges had a big sag in the middle and were very tiring as they reached the opposite bank. It was good going to get three people across in an hour.

At the end of August they reached Tsetang, some 70 miles south-east of Lhasa, where they found a Kashmiri colony, 800 strong, who gave them news of the outside world. This seemed to be mostly about Bulgaria, Serbia, Montenegro, Austria and Russia. Amazingly, one of them greeted Bailey as an old friend, and they talked of Lhasa in 1904. Within a week he was to prove a friend in deed as well.

Tsetang was an important place in Henry's survey. Pandit Nain Singh, C.I.E. had positioned it accurately in 1875 and, having linked it on to the new map, the explorers were able to turn south again. There was still three months travelling ahead of them, with plenty of jungle hacking, food shortages and coolies throwing down their loads; but why was it that Anay had been volunteering to carry the heaviest load? That happened to be the one with the money box in it, containing Rs.600/-, and the fact had already aroused a faint suspicion in Bailey:

'September 4th. Kyekye, 14,600 ft. We both slept soundly, but towards sunrise I was awakened by a noise. It was the voice of a woman, the kitchen servant who was supplied under the system; and she kept calling, "Anay, la! Anay, la!" She wanted to make tea for the men and there was nothing strange in her calling Anay. But there was something very odd in his not answering.

I sat up immediately, wide awake. The sun had not risen, but it was light enough to see that the things stacked under the outer fly had been tampered with. The money box was missing.

I woke Morshead and shouted for the Coolies to come. The Lepcha cook was the first to arrive and as he reached the tent, he picked up something from the ground. It was a dao, one of those cutlasses with which each coolie was provided, for cutting the jungle. The thief or thieves had obviously brought it in case either of us woke up. I thanked God we were both heavy sleepers. Two Pöba swords which we had bought had been taken by the thieves. The muster of our coolies showed that three of them were missing. Anay and the two Dawas; Anay, of whom I had been suspicious when I was alone with him in the gorges below Pemaköchung, the Dawa who had lost his temper and the Dawa who had hidden.'

This left them with only seventy rupees, and the five English sovereigns that Henry had in his belt. The sovereigns would have been worth about Rs.27/- each, or about twice their face value. Bailey wrote a letter in Urdu, and sent it by messenger to the head of the Kashmiri community back in Tsetang, Qazi 'Ata Ulla, informing him of their plight and asking if he would cash them a cheque on Calcutta, at Tsona. Their spare warm clothing, cartridges, tea and soap had also been in the box, which was later found ransacked.

It was seven weeks before they reached Tsona, but 'Ata Ulla did not let them down. He provided 250 rupees which was more than they had asked, and himself travelled as far as Lhontse Dzong with the money. Meanwhile ten days later, after leaving Migyitun[5] they separated, with Henry keeping to the south and mapping the limits of Tibetan authority. He was by now beginning to master the language himself. One site he chose for taking fixings of his snow peaks happened to be the funeral ground above a monastery, where the bodies of the dead were cut up and fed to the vultures in the usual Tibetan way. Seeing Henry and his attendant coolies, all the vultures in the neighbourhood converged on the spot, expecting a funeral banquet. They filled the air with their indignation when the survey party descended, leaving nothing succulent behind.

Two marches out of Chayul Dzong they were interrogated again by a petty official. Where were their passports? Why were they coming this way? It appeared they were not going to be offered the usual facilities. Then Bailey produced his photographs of the Dalai Lama, taken by himself on the Younghusband expedition, and the official started to mellow. The official produced his own photographs: Bailey showed the official his guns. Then they all went up on the roof, from which Bailey spotted a herd of bharal on the mountain above. They were about two miles away, and everyone took turns at looking at them through Bailey's telescope. This delighted the children, who seeing them suddenly so large, asked Bailey to shoot the bharal from the roof. 'They are too far away', he said. 'No,' said the children, 'not if you shoot them through the telescope.'

The whole incident pleased their host so much that he became quite friendly and not only asked them what transport they wanted but offered to buy two of the sovereigns to make into earrings. This was fortunate as they were still some weeks from Tsona and were down to 15 rupees. On another occasion, when they had been told the local *Dzongpön* was away, they found out that he was in fact hiding from them, reluctant to take the responsibility of giving assistance. The journey could be hilarious at one moment and terrifying the next. It was pointed out to them what their fate would be if they were unable to convince the Tibetans they were not Chinese. They would be sewn up in sacks and floated down to India. Were they looking for gold? They were British? But, surely, the British were going to help the Chinese take over Tibet?

Near Tsona, 14,500 ft., on 24 October Henry took the rifle and went after some *Ovis Ammon* he had seen, but wolves had also seen them and drove the *Ovis Ammon* away. 'They were more afraid of the wolves than they were of me' said Henry. *Ammon*, which stand 4 ft. high at the shoulder, with thick, curved horns, are the largest species of mountain sheep, and are seldom found below 15,000 ft. Two days later Henry did manage to bag two, and the supplies of meat were welcome, as by this time they were very hungry. On 12 November, long after the meat had passed its prime, they were still living on it, assuring one another that they were probably the first people ever to eat *Ovis Ammon* on the plains of India. 'Judging from its taste by then' said Bailey 'I think it is likely we shall be the last.'

Henry closed his survey at Trashigang Dzong, 3,250 ft., on 9 November. The 70 miles from there to the railhead at Rangiya had already been mapped (a motor road exists today), and he was now free from the care of seeing that no feature they passed was omitted from the map. Only a few days ago they had nearly lost two porters in a blizzard at 15,000 ft. Ahead of them now lay only descent; through forests to the perspiring plains of India.

It was six months since they had left Mipi, and over a year since they had been in any sizeable city. Once, they had seen in the distance the smoke of a train on the plains of Assam and had felt a seductive nostalgia; but now that they were returning they found their reluctance to leave Tibet growing stronger with each step. There was so much left to explore; they were conscious less of what they had achieved than of what they had failed to achieve, the missing section of the Tsangpo River, and the uncharted valleys they would like to have visited. This had been the chance of a lifetime and would probably never recur. For a time the snowline descended with them, reluctant to release them; neither was enamoured of the thought of returning to regular duties.

Crossing the east Bhutan frontier into Assam at Diwangiri they found the path washed away and followed the rocky bed of a river. It was necessary to ford it 32 times in one day. At Tamulpur, where they were able to hire three buffalo carts, they met a police inspector and tried to get him to cash a cheque. He gave them a strange look and asked a number of disbelieving questions. He had no money but agreed to give them a letter to the sub-inspector at the prosperous tea-town of Rangiya.

'I began to look at Morshead more closely. I had not paid any attention to how he was dressed while we were in Tibet. The values there were spiritual, not sartorial. But face to face with the police inspector, I was forced to admit that sartorially Morshead did not look impressive. He looked a tramp, and a rather unsuccessful tramp at that.

Morshead told me later that he began to look critically at me about the same time. He said that if he had just met me at Tamulpur, he would not have spoken to me. Even after having marched over 1,600 miles with me, he felt pretty ashamed.'

Arriving at the station (at 2.30 a.m.) they woke up one of the staff and asked about trains. There was a train next day as far as Lalmanir Hat. From there they could get a train to Calcutta, if they could buy the tickets. The police inspector's letter was of no avail, and the sub-inspector never turned up. 'How many tickets do you want and what class?' asked the man in the office. They did not know how many they wanted until he told them the cost. It was possible for them all to get to Lalmanir Hat, and Morshead to go on to Calcutta second class and wire back the money for Bailey to pay off the coolies and follow. 'We can't travel first class, dammit,' Morshead said 'Not with you looking the way you do, Bailey.'

Bailey had shaved every day while in Tibet, but Henry had grown a fine beard. Annoyed with themselves at rushing to conform again, they visited the barber and put on respectable clothes. The Tibetan part of their journey was still considered secret. 'We are living here in terror of reporters', wrote Bailey from Calcutta to his parents. 'I see some sort of garbled telegram has been sent home about us, and that old ass Holdich[6] says he does not believe we have enough evidence to prove the falls are not there.' Bailey concludes his book with some words about Henry:

'We became companions almost by chance, but if I had been given the widest choice, I could not have found better. Few men can be in one another's company uninterruptedly for six months without a certain fraying of tempers. But I can say with truth that there was never a word of difference between us. He was fond of singing, but he had only two songs, one of which Gerty Miller had sung better. I remember wishing sometimes that his repertory was a little wider—but if there had been friction between us two, those songs would have been enfuriating. What my habits were which might have enfuriated him I cannot tell, and unfortunately Morshead is not alive to tell his side of the story.

He had to travel slowly with delicate survey instruments, which had to be manhandled. My stuff could be carried on yaks and I could ride ahead, camp early and make enquiries about the country and the routes ahead. He came on behind, having climbed every significant eminence on the way... It was a terrific feat. When we separated he did my work as well, gathering the information I required and helping to supplement my report.

He was an imperturbably adventurous man. He distinguished himself in the First World War, in exploration in Spitzbergen and on Mount Everest, where he lost several fingers from frostbite. I suppose he took no more notice of the cold than of the jungle leeches. I was always afraid that that sort of carelessness would kill him one day. But I was wrong. He was taking a peaceful ride one morning in Burma when he was murdered.'

There was no mention of revolution or dacoity here; here was a life-long friend who called Morshead's death 'murder'.

How had the legend of the 'Falls' come about? The explanation was soon forthcoming, and remarkably simple and straightforward it proved. Bailey managed to locate the venerable old explorer of 1880, Kinthup, living in Darjeeling and working as a tailor. Sir Sidney Burrard authorised funds for Kinthup to visit Simla. Kinthup had *never said* that the 150 ft. falls were on the Tsangpo. Kinthup was illiterate and his dictated report had been taken down; when the English translation appeared there was no way for him to check it. Vindicated in a remarkable way, he went back to Darjeeling with a thousand rupees from Burrard, but not long to live, probably the greatest Himalayan explorer of them all.

Henry filed his report within a few weeks, and Burrard wrote back on a personal basis: 'It might be interesting to give a list of all new peaks discovered above 20,000 ft. You hardly make enough mention of the great Pemakö peak. The discovery of this peak was most remarkable. A description of it will be valuable; also a list of new glaciers, lakes and rivers.'

One such river, never previously shown on any map, was the important Nyamjang Chu, in Eastern Bhutan; another was the Chimdro tributary; the great bend of the Tsangpo itself had been shifted some sixty miles eastwards of its previously estimated position; and the Himalayan range had been extended some 300 miles to the East. A modest account of the journey in the *Royal Engineers Journal* won Henry the Montgomerie Prize from the R.E. Institute Council, and, for their contribution to the knowledge of this frontier, both were awarded the Macgregor Medal by the United Service Institution of India. It would not have surprised them to find instead that they had incurred the displeasure of the Governor General in Council, as Bailey had done only two years previously. 'It is impossible you should have been unaware of the stringent rules about exploration in tribal territory beyond the outer line of the Assam border' ran the letter, as he was fined 20 days' pay for departing from his authorised route and overstaying his leave.

Arthur Swinson, in his biography[7] of Bailey, ranks him as an explorer with Younghusband and Sven Hedin, Livingstone and Speke. Sir Olaf Caroe considered him the 'greatest explorer of the Indian Political Service in the last half century of its existence'. Yet in a long career as soldier, explorer, linguist, secret agent and diplomatist, he was never to be decorated beyond a C.I.E. in 1915. Presumably, in the official view it was not policy to heap honour on to an acknowledged individualist like Bailey; such a thing could conceivably backfire and make a fool of somebody; better to save the honours for the predictable middle-of-the-road man. Bailey was never offered what was regarded as a First Class Residency. His collection of avifauna, 2,306 in number, was presented to the British Museum; his butterfly collection to the United States.

When one recalls the difficulties that had previously attended Tibetan exploration, the contrast with that of Bailey and Morshead is remarkable. The 1904 Younghusband expedition was called a peaceful mission; but it had available a mountain battery, a Maxim gun detachment and 1,000 rifles. The orders were never to fire unless fired upon; but inevitably the guns were fired. The Chinese were believed to have departed from Tibet in 1911. They were not to reassert their claims until 1949, after the British had left.

The general area of the Mishmi Survey is an interesting one geologically. The worst earthquake ever experienced there took place in 1950 and lasted intermittently for several weeks. Mountains up to 18,000 ft. were rent apart and areas up to twelve square miles sagged into new positions. Mercifully the population was sparse. A description of the scene as he found it six years later is given by Henry Gibbs in his book *The Hills of India. The Standard Encyclopaedia of the World's Rivers and Lakes*[8] makes the astonishing claim that after the 1935 earthquake 'the river (Brahmaputra) is recorded to have flowed backwards for some seconds, causing widespread chaos and disaster'. I take my last words on the subject from John Buchan's book *The Last Secrets:*

'Their (Bailey and Morshead's) evidence may be finally considered to have solved the riddle of how the great river breaks through the highest range on the globe. It does it by means of marvellous gorges, where the stream foams in rapids, but there is no fall more considerable than can be found in many a Scottish salmon river. The mightly current is not tossed in spray over a great cliff, but during the aeons it has bitten a deep trough through that formidable rock wall... I am not sure that the reality is not more impressive than the romantic expectation.'

Notes

1   Records of the Survey of India, Vol.IV p.3 footnote, 1914; also *Sketch of the geography and geology of the Himalaya Mountains and Tibet*, S.G. Burrard & H.H. Hayden, 2nd ed., pp.45–46.
2   *China—Tibet—Assam*, p.166.
3   *Beyond the Frontiers*, Hutchinson, 1971, p.94.
4   *The Military Engineer in India*, Vol.II, p.250.
5   Scene of a border dispute in the Chinese offensive of 1962.
6   Sir Thomas Holdich, an ex-President of the R.G.S.
7   *Ibid.* p.233.
8   Weidenfeld & Nicolson, 1965, p.51. On the same page the Dihang is confusingly referred to as the Dibang.

5 | He may be home for Christmas

In ten years of service Henry had returned home once (on sick leave) and that was in 1907. Now if ever, with World War I only six months away, would be the time to enjoy some holiday. His idea was to come home for six months in the winter, and join the Italian exploring expedition into Central Asia in April, an expedition intended to embrace two seasons and bring him back to Europe in the autumn of 1915.

Back home, his mother Ella was combing through the papers for intelligence. A cable from the India Office on 7 November contained encouraging, if out of date, news. A fortnight later she had Henry's own cable from Calcutta, so 'he may be home for Christmas'.

'We have had no further news of Henry since Monday's wire, but I am daily hoping for one to say he is coming home. Many cuttings reach us from various papers; in a long one from the Morning Post he is called Captain Moorsom all through!... We think he must be in London as the Delta reached Marseilles on Saturday morning.'

By 5 February he had still not arrived, but by the 10th 'Henry and Jack have gone off to Plymouth to buy Henry some clothes'... One of the earliest d-i-y-ers, he was soon busy levelling a tennis court, putting a new fence round the garden and fitting a new bath and a large boiler in the house, with his younger brothers and sisters harnessed in to fetch and carry.

Captain Trenchard, already in England on leave, had been trying to get in touch. His letter went all the way to India and back, for the price of a single penny stamp, before catching up with Henry in Devon six weeks later:

'Many congratulations on your safe return to India, and for what you both achieved at the back of beyond. You must have had a very hard time—even for your amazing constitution. I am looking forward to reading your report when a copy reaches me, and have asked MacLeod to let me have one of his 8-inch provisional maps as soon as he has got all your new work on to his. Gunter wrote the other day from Switzerland to say he had heard from you; it was a great disappointment to hear that you had not managed to reach the Falls.

Is there any chance of your coming to stay for a while when you do reach England? I am living with my people and they will gladly put you up. I shall have a car of sorts in work at the beginning of March and can give you some golf. I hope too I shall be a bit fitter by then.'

Trenchard himself, at this stage, still seems to have thought there were high Falls. Certainly the 'Captain Moorsom' article in the *Morning Post* had refused to accept that there were none. Bailey's words on reading it were 'Well, Captain Moorsom, it looks as if we've just been wasting our time for six months'. Trenchard's health was not badly impaired; he died in California in December 1976, aged 94.

Major Gunter arrived for a visit, a pleasant man with white hair and a youngish face. They rode to the Lamerton Fox Hounds; and drove to Tintagel and Boscastle. The new fence down the drive was finished and pronounced an immense improvement; and Gunter painted a water-colour of Hurlditch Court which still hangs on my wall today. A holiday in Switzerland for some practice in ice-and-snow work was followed in quick succession by tours in North Wales, Scotland and Ireland, interspersed with the occasional Livery Company dinner and the reading of a paper before the Royal Geographical Society, of which Bailey was already a distinguished member. 'Please don't trouble to mention my name in your announcement in the June Journal', was Henry's response to the Secretary's wish to associate Morshead's name with Bailey's paper. His own election to the R.G.S. was proposed and seconded later the same year.

Mount Everest was now occupying Henry's thoughts. Since its discovery in about 1850, no climber had come within 75 miles of the mountain, access through Nepal and Tibet being closed to European travellers. Access through the latter had now become a possibility and, in May 1914, Henry wrote to Bailey inviting him for a visit:

'. . . I wanted to consult you about our proposed N. to S. trip through Mongolia and Tibet. You may have heard that Major C.G. Rawling is running an expedn to survey & climb Mt. Everest during the summers of 1915—16. The party will comprise besides himself—a doctor & botanist, a survey officer, 2 Swiss guides & a Tibetan interpreter from the Darjeeling *cutcherry*.

Burrard has offered to give me the job of surveyor if I cancel the last 10 months of my leave & return to India in April 1915, & the offer seemed too good to refuse. I am spending next weekend with Rawling at the

Somerset's Depot at Taunton, when I shall learn more details. The thing would be for you to get taken on as Tibetan interpreter instead of the Darjeeling *munshi*; I will square Rawling at this end.

During the winter of 1915—16 while the rest of Rawling's party return to vegetate in Darjeeling before the final attack, you and I could go off & explore the N. border of Bhutan, & possibly revisit those *Ammon* on the Nyala La. You & I would then have to postpone our big Tibet journey till our next furlough is due—viz April, 1918, when we'd take it on the way home.

I rather contemplate raising the wind a bit by going out to British Columbia in July—a man in the Canadian land business offered me a job marking out his prairie into 10-acre orchard plots. Fact is it's impossible, even for a man of my simple tastes to live on £500 a year, doing nothing. More than half my screw has gone already, & I've been doing nothing except hunting on a boarded-out troop horse of the 4th D.G.'s, followed by a short bust in town.

Send me a line, & above all for heaven's sake don't go and leave me to do the lecture, as I won't be back from Switzerland till the day before.'

When World War I broke out, Henry, who had just returned from Ireland, was promptly shipped out to India on the trooper 'Dongola', only to be promptly shipped home again to train the sappers of the new armies. 'I am sorry for Henry having to go off to India instead of to the front,' wrote his mother, Ella. 'It will be tantalising being cut off from all war news for the three weeks voyage. One does not know what may have happened by that time.'

On the morning of 11 August 1914, three special trains left Waterloo station carrying 1,000 officers of the Indian Army to Southampton. The ticket-collector said that in his 25 years' experience he had never seen so much luggage go by any train as went on the special luggage train that followed.

When it arrived at Southampton there was utter chaos as everyone, from subaltern to general, rushed about trying to locate their own boxes in the 15 luggage vans. To add to the confusion, a list was posted in the shed of some 200 'lucky' officers who were ordered not to embark, but to report back to the War Office. The few available cabins were soon allocated to the 10 generals and 105 colonels on board. Captains and most of the field officers were slinging their hammocks on the troop deck as the ship sailed slowly down Channel at 10 p.m., a sitting duck for the 'Goeben' and the 'Breslau', or indeed any enemy vessel mounting a gun.

On returning to England, Henry found himself posted to the 75th Field

Company, R.E. of the 16th (South Irish) Division, stationed at Kilworth, Co.Cork. For political reasons they were slow in recruiting, and leave was possible. The death had occurred of his father while he was away. This, combined with the War, detracted somewhat from the celebration of his first Christmas at home for eleven years.

6 | War & Wedding

Plans for climbing Everest were far from people's thoughts in June 1915. Ypres, poison gas and Gallipoli had taken their place; Rawling himself would be killed as a Brigadier-General in France in October 1917. The 75th Field Company, R.E. were at Ardnacrusha Camp outside Limerick. Things were on the move and the unit was to be incorporated in the Guards Division, then near St. Omer. They crossed the Channel on 21 August and after a few weeks at G.H.Q., which Henry described as very dull, took part in the battle of Loos.

His brother Dick was already out there, a captain in the R.A.M.C., and in the front line. A letter to his sister, datelined 'Everybody knows where, 25th Aug /15', goes on to say 'your other brother (the Indian one who does so well) has not turned up yet.' He did not do so badly himself, getting the M.C. at Beaumont Hamel, a most unhealthy spot and the very symbol of discomfort.

Ella: 'We had such a pleasant surprise on Sunday, H. meeting us on our way to morning church, having arrived before his letter. The weather has been wet, but he got horses for himself and Jack and they hunted from Sourton Cross; fair sport but no kill; very few out. On Tuesday he hired the Bedford motor and took us all for a joy-ride to Plymouth and Launceston, a most successful round. Today they are hunting from Ivy House and must be back in time for Henry to catch the night train back to London before crossing again on Sunday.' On the way back to the front, in French cattle-trucks labelled Hommes 40 Chevaux 8, he became separated from his kit. 'Slept on floor of hut no food or kit' as his diary puts it.

Early in 1916 he was made company commander but remained still a captain; this seemed unfair to Ella, unversed in the ways of the army. The following month he was posted to command the 212th Field Company, R.E. in the 33rd (Domino) Division still as a captain, and joined them in the Vermeilles sector during the combat for possession of the Hohenzollern redoubt.

'We had much looked forward to seeing Henry, whose leave had been due, but he sees no chance of getting away just now. He has had a second sharp attack of 'flu and needs a change badly, but his senior subaltern had just been shot on his way up to the trenches when he last wrote.' He was able to look in for a couple of days on his way back to Limerick, and she described him as looking well but thin. Returning to the front, he commanded his company in the battle of the Somme (High Wood-Les Boeufs). With half a million casualties in the muddy trenches of the Somme (more on the first day alone than in the whole eleven days of El Alamein) a sense of humour was essential for survival. Who but the Paymaster himself would have thought of Separation Allowance as a funny subject?

Dear Sir,
    We received your letter, I am his Grandfather and Grandmother, he was born and brought up in this house in answer to your letter.

Dear Sir,
    Mrs ... has been put to bed with a little lad, wife of Peter...

Dear Sir,
    You have changed my little boy into a little girl. Will it make any difference?

Sir,
    I write these lines for Mrs... who cannot write herself. She is expecting to be confined and can do with it.

Dear Sir,
    I have received no payment since my husband has gone from nowhere.

Dear Sir,
    My husband has now gone to the Mind Sweepers ...

Dear Sir,
    I am expecting to be confined next month, will you please let me know what to do about it?

Dear Sir,
    My husband Bill has been put in charge of a Spitoon. Shall I get more pay?

Sir,
    Will you please send my money as soon as possible as I am walking about BOLTON like a damned pauper and oblige.

Dear Sir,
  My husband has joined the Army, and shall be glad if you will send me his elopement money.

Dear Sir,
  In accordance with instructions on the ring paper I have given birth to a daughter on October 21st.

It was never long before something would bring them sharply back to sullen reality; the piper's quick-stepping reel would change suddenly to a lament. The buff envelope is marked 'If away Acting Adjutant to open'. Inside is a note addressed to Henry, written in indelible pencil, from No.2 Stationary Hospital:

'The wound has turned out to be more serious than expected, gas gangrene having set in. I shall probably be dead by tomorrow morning. Give my love to Tommy and whoever are left and remember me to my section. I must thank you for the kind manner with which you entered into all my peculiarities. Take care of my batman . . .'

Henry's letters home tended to be long ones, written over several days, with postcards in between; the postal service was remarkably good. From the Somme he replied to a letter from Eric Bailey who, after service in France and Gallipoli, was now back in the Political Department in India, and on the threshold of even more dramatic adventures in Kashgar and Tashkent, such as securing his recruitment by Bolshevik counter-espionage to *search for himself*:

'. . . What I feel is that your scheme covers too much of our old ground over again. For instance, I regard the Tsangpo valley as a dead dog now—the two dotted bits we left are hardly worth revisiting. For purely personal reasons I'm keen on visiting Lhasa for a day or two—the Foreign Office oughtn't to make any bones this time. Thence I'd prefer to go eastward, filling in the country between A.K.'s route and the Tsangpo, including, of course, the whole of the Gyamda chu basin.

I'm keen on allowing ourselves plenty of time for exploring Po Tö & the rest of Pome. . . These are only ideas—one can't do much without a map to refer to, which I can't get till I next go on leave. . . Another idea is that once we've cut the painter, we'll take sufficient money & clothes to last us 2 or 3 years if necessary so as not to have to come home hurriedly like last time (this of course needn't be mentioned to the F.O.).

I see I have another of yours unanswered. I quite agree with you about

Shackleton[1]—he ought never to have gone off like that with a war on. Indeed I'm not engaged, nor anywhere near it! Don't know what I could have said to make you think that—they won't look at me. If such a thing *should* ever happen I know it's jolly well not going to interfere for a moment with our work in Tibet.

Don't go and get strafed on the old N.W. Frontier; you've stopped enough bullets already in France & Gallipoli [three to be exact]. If there was any chance of your getting back to Europe after the war I'd vastly prefer going out by Trans-Siberian & striking S. from Urga [now Ulan Bator, Capital of Outer Mongolia]. I have 18 months unexpired leave after the war & a further 6 months to my credit if necessary.'

On return from a week's leave in October 1916, his Colonel failed to recognise him. He had cut off his moustache, and had met Evelyn Widdicombe, whom he was to wed within six months. Evie's father had failed to make his fortune in Alberta, Canada. Judging by the skyline of Calgary today he was just a hundred years too soon. Evie's mother decided to cut and run. Leaving her husband out there, she brought her three children home again on the Royal Mail (twin screw!) liner 'Lake Champlain' in May 1901; she never saw him again. Evie the eldest was twelve years old.

With bank assistance her mother acquired leaseholds in Pimlico and founded a ladies' residential club, the Warwick Club Ltd, which flourished strongly until long after her death. It was before the bedsit revolution and the days of flat sharing, and fulfilled an undoubted need in its day. Various members of the family made use of the club while passing through or staying in London. For a brief period it put her mother into the chauffeur and limousine bracket.

Evie, under the circumstances, had always earned her own living, a fact which appealed to Henry. Leaving a career position as Secretary and Librarian to the Froebel Society, she had been helping to run the club for three years. A cake was packed up and despatched to the front line for Henry's 33rd birthday, and he was mentioned in despatches the same month. Ella again:

'December 5th, 1916. A letter from Henry mentions possible leave at Christmas, but quite uncertain. He is in rest again after a hard time at the front. His name is sent for promotion and employment on the Staff, but he doubts if anything will come of it. He has just had a belated communication from the Secretary of State for India and Governor General in Council conveying their thanks for his 'adventurous journey in Tibet the results of which are of permanent geographical value'. What has reminded them of this expedition after the lapse of three years!?...[2] I can't tell you where he is, but they were expecting to move again soon. He has been doing Staff Captain work as well as his own.

January 2nd, 1917. We are so excited at seeing Henry's name for D.S.O., I feel a very proud mother with two sons in the Honours List! [His brother Owen had just beaten him to it] We are all so pleased and are being inundated with congratulations on all sides.'

Promotion to Major came through on 21 December 1916, with orders to form and train a Pioneer Battalion for the 46th (North Midland) Division. A week's leave in January enabled him to become engaged. It took him four tedious days to rejoin his unit. The weather was so cold that winter that he wished he had taken his skates back with him. All the food froze, even bread. Henry's brothers approved of his choice of a wife; but the choosing of a date was going to be difficult. He returned to the command of his 212th Field Company, then in the Quéant-Drocourt sector, in time for the battle of Arras. 'Evelyn says they hope to be married early in April, but all must depend on Henry getting leave. It is to be a quiet wedding. . . Evelyn has the licence ready as he may only be able to give 24 hours notice of his return.'

Earlier in the war Evelyn had made her way alone across wartime France and taken ship to Alexandria to bring home her sister's newborn baby, a mission she achieved with success in spite of being knocked unconscious by an officer's tin box falling from the rack on to her head on an Egyptian train. She was married from the house of her cousins, Helen and Arthur Hill at 106 Eaton Square, close to the church of St. Peter, and the reception was at the Warwick Club. Arthur Hill also had a house at Walmer, Kent, which was to prove an invaluable stopping-off point on the way to and from the front.

What was written in the sand for a bride, born in the last month of the Earth-Mouse Year, marrying a man of the Water-Horse Year? A man who gave his recreations in *Who's Who* as Central Asian exploration and big game shooting? Henry's marriage would contrast strongly with that of his parents, whose life together of perpetual blue sky had lasted for thirty-four years. His own, born of wartime and fraught with separation, risk and danger would last fourteen. Evelyn was left in no doubt that written into her marriage lines was Henry's right to go on expeditions; in the intervals between she must not leave his side for an instant.

The year 1917 marked a dangerous phase in the war for the Allies. Russia had been defeated and, although America had entered the war her troops had not yet started to arrive. The submarine campaign was at its height and the French offensive of April 1917 proved a disaster. The front line stretched from the Channel to the Swiss border. Once the initial German thrust

Evelyn Widdicombe in 1913

```
                    LETTER FORM 'B' (WIVES)        In the Field

      (dear,                                    /    /1917
My    (dearest,
      (darling,                                      (overworked
            I can't write much today as I am very (busy
                                                     (tired
         (CORPS      )                               (lazy
         (G.O.C.     )
and the  (G.S.O. I   ) is exhibiting intense activity
         (A.A. & Q.M.G.)
                                              (quite well
               Things our way are going on (much as usual
                                              (pas mal


We        )                 (last night)      (complete )
THE HUNS  ) put up a show (yesterday )  with (tolerable) success
                                              (out any  )

Our                The French     )
The Russian        The Belgian    )
The Italian        The Serbian    )
The Montenegrin    The Roumanian  )
The United States  The Portuguese )  offensive appears to be
The Monagasque     The Japanese   )  doing well.
The Brazilian      The Cuban      )
The Panama         The Chinese    )
The Bolivian       ...............)
                        (obviously   )
The German offensive is (apparently  )  a complete failure
                        (we will hope)

I really begin to think the war will end (this year
                                          (next year
      (flies  )        (vile              (sometime
The (rations) are/is (execrable          (never       (cheery
      (weather)        (much the same                   (weary
                       (............ The Division is (languid
                                                       (distressed
      (hoping soon to come on   )                      (at rest
I am (about due for             )
     (overdue for               ) leave, which is now (on
     (not yet in the running for)                      (off

I am suffering from a (slight) wound (shell shock) (fright)
                      (severe)
               @ ......................................
..........'s Wife has just (presented him with) ..........
                           (sent him         )
What I should really like is ...........................:
                (letter         )            (poultry/cows)
Many thanks for(parcel         ) How are the (potatoes) getting on?
                (good intentions)            (children)
I hope you are (well            Insert here protestations
               (better          of affection - NOT TO EXCEED
               (bearing up               TEN WORDS
               (not spending too much money  ............
               (getting on better with mother
xxxxxxxxxxxxxxxxxxxxxxxxxxxxxxxx(Delete or add as may be necessary)
```

@ Or state disease. If the whole of this sentence is struck out,
  the writer may be presumed to be well or deceased.

towards Paris had been repelled by the 'miracle of the Marne' there were few great changes in its shape; it was largely stalemate. The Germans failed to break through at Verdun in the south-east; the great British offensive on the Somme in 1916 had gained very little ground.

Letters from the Front were censored. There was little to write home about anyway, and somebody had fun drafting a proforma for the purpose.

The 33rd Division were moved back during part of the summer of 1917 and the time spent resting and training. A Brigade Group Gymkhana was held, at which Henry was one of the Stewards. His Field Company came second in the Bare Back Mule Race and third in the V.C. Race. In the latter they had to clear the jumps, pick up a dummy at the far end and return over jumps. The Tug-of-War was a bare back affair with no spurs or whips allowed!

Two months flashed past, making it a fractional anniversary of sorts. Evie was at her cousin's house, waiting for the summons, which came as a telegram 'Meet me Hotel Chatham Paris June 3rd'. Pasted to a Café de Paris menu for Déjeuner le 7 Juin 1917, measuring sixteen inches by a foot, the two documents betoken a few snatched days of delayed honeymoon.

A Divisional Exercise was held, followed by a Horse Show. The Staff were generously 'At Home' to visitors, a tea tent supplying tea for the asking; provided the request was accompanied by a mess-tin. Only animals on the War Establishment could be entered, but of these there were plenty.

33rd (Domino) Division 'At Home'

Division

At Home

Tuesday & Wednesday 17th & 18th July 1917, at the Cross Roads, one & a half miles North of Cavillon on the main Picquigny-Airaines Road.

Horse Show. - 10 a. m. to 6 p. m. each day.

There were events for Pack Animals (ponies and mules), Pairs, Ride and Drive (horses and mules), Heavy Duty, Light Duty, Complete Cooker Turnout, Six-mule Teams, Four-mule Teams, Officers' Chargers over and under 15 hands, Infantry Officer's Chargers 15.2 and under, and Jumping. In one race, the 'Domino' Stakes, a horse made its appearance clad with tartan trews on its front; but, as always, the mule race was the most entertaining, at any rate for the spectators. Those riders who were not left at the starting point to complete the course on foot performed some remarkable feats of horsemanship, all over the mules, several of which would bolt, scattering the crowd in all directions.

Bands played, the Shrapnels Revue Company performed, and the Horse Show was a brilliant success, largely due to the enthusiasm of Major-Gen. R.J. Pinney, C.B., the 'Domino' Divisional Commander. A squadron of the Royal Flying Corps obligingly patrolled overhead keeping the enemy scouts at bay, a duty which did not prevent some of the pilots from exhibiting their skill by looping the loop amid the plaudits of the crowd below.

Earl Haig relieved the pressure on France by an offensive through the

Graves of 212th Field Co., R.E., September 1917

Christmas Card of 212th Field
Co., R.E., December 1917

autumn of 1917 in front of Ypres at Passchendaele. This mournful affair, fought mostly in rain and mud over a period of months, brought great losses and little advance. By March 1918 Ludendorff had driven the English and French back behind Ypres again. As a Field Company Commander, R.E., Henry was involved in zone defences, front line and reserve line posts and wire, reserve keeps and the siting of machine gun positions. Christmas 1917 was spent at the Base Depot, Rouen, and he rejoined 33rd Division soon afterwards.

Railhead was still at Poperinghe and onwards by car to Ypres, where Army, Corps and Divisional Headquarters were all dug in. The days were spent in an endless inspection of defensive systems with the Chief Engineer and the Divisional C.R.E., liaising with the Belgian Engineers, and attending to the requirements of his men. Four letters arrived at once from Evie together with some new trench boots which she had obtained for him.

He had been complaining of a sore heel, and a bout of trench fever was building up. The latter, a disease transmitted by a body louse, had been first recognised in 1915. The Casualty Clearing Station sent him back to the Anglo-American Hospital at Wimereux, Boulogne, where the Consulting Physician was Sir Bertrand Dawson, later Lord Dawson of Penn. Recovering, he was free to walk along the cliffs and dunes to Ambleteuse and back, gradually lengthening the walks until his Medical Board. Three weeks leave followed and Evie, who was a V.A.D. cook at the hospital then at 26 Eccleston Square, met him at Victoria.

They went to Hawkes for clothes, and to see *The Bing Boys are Here* the first day. Then Evie's cousin Owen Batchelor, a 6ft.4in. giant who had come over from Canada with his two sons to enlist, insisted on taking them to Daly's Theatre to see Jose Collins in the musical play *Maid of the Mountains*, which he had seen several times already.[3] He told the authorities they could only enlist his sons if they took him too, which they did. On Sunday they went again to a service at St. Peter's, Eaton Square, and visited an exhibition of war photographs at the Grafton Galleries. One morning of this leave a member of the white feather brigade accosted Henry, gibing 'Why aren't you in uniform and at the front?' It was Evie who was stung to reply with as much contempt as she could muster on the spur of the moment. They both thought of better replies afterwards, but by then it was too late.

All too soon Henry was catching the returning leave train and rejoining 33rd Div. H.Q. three days later. Needless to say they were still just outside Ypres, but hard pressed now. Ypres itself was becoming a salient as the 29th and 33rd Divisions were pushed back in the Lys battle; and the 34th was forced to retreat from Armentières to Bailleul. All three were congratulated by Earl Haig, the 33rd for their determined resistance on 14 April.

A period of 'active defence' was beginning. The much-used railway junctions behind the front line had come under effective enemy fire, and during the period April—July 1918 a comprehensive programme of railway construction of 200 miles of broad-gauge track was undertaken, doubling and quadrupling the existing network; at the same time a complete series of new defensive lines was built involving the digging of no fewer than 5,000 miles of trenches,[4] many of which had individual names. Over 23,000 tons of barbed wire and 15 million steel pickets were used.

Henry spent a fortnight liaising with the French, attached to a French Divisional H.Q., before being posted to command 222nd Field Company. They were busily engaged in digging switch line trenches and Brigade H.Q. dug-outs. The east Poperinghe support line was in the salient and was becoming decidedly unhealthy in both senses of the word; a few words of microscopic writing in his diary convey the gist. 'Roused 3 am to accompany Chef de l'Etat Major to Corps & Div H.Q.', 'v. hot & shelling. 2

killed & 2 wdd' and once more, but only for a day this time 'sore throat and trench fever'; '466 Company gassed' and 'Horse died'.

He found time to organise a Sports Day for his own 222nd Field Company. The events had some originality and included:

> Blindfold Drill Competition (Teams of 8 under Section Sgt)
> Veterans Race (35 years of age and upwards, over 220 yards)
> Wrestling on bare-back mule
> Team Bumping and Bobbing Races
> Gurning through a horsecollar
> Reveille Race
> Officers' Lemon Slicing Competition (Open to Divisional R.E.)

The last event was not the fastidious affair it sounds; done at the gallop with a lance or a 3ft.6-in. cavalry sword, it was also known as Cleaving the Turk's Head.

On 1 June Henry was promoted Acting Lt.Colonel and posted as C.R.E. 46th (North Midland) Division a little further south in the Bethune sector. Being of Brevet rank, the promotion made no difference to his pay and very little to the work he was involved in. There was a music-hall joke going the rounds about the woman who proudly said that her son in the army now signed himself L/C: she did not know whether that stood for Lieutenant Colonel or Lance Corporal—but anyway he was still in the cookhouse.

The Fourth Army Commander, General Rawlinson, received his preliminary instructions on 13 July to prepare to attack east of Amiens on an eleven-mile front. Henry was due for leave, and once again Evie was summoned to Paris where he had booked them in at the Majestic. They visited the Louvre and Nôtre Dame, and dined at the Ambassadeurs; took the electrique to Versailles and back; dined in the Bois de Boulogne, and Henry saw her off at the Gare St. Lazare. The next day's diary entry 'to Whizzbang at Hesdigueul 5.30 to 7.30 pm' could easily be mistaken for some new revue at a Paris theatre, were it not for the fact that one knew that the final offensive was imminent. The Battle of the Hundred Days began at 4.20 a.m. on 8 August with massed artillery opening intensive fire along the entire front. Simultaneously British infantry and tanks advanced to the assault. Douglas Haig:

> 'The derelict battle area which now lay before our troops, seared by old trench lines, pitted by shell holes, and crossed in all directions with tangled belts of wire, the whole covered by the wild vegetation of two years, presented unrivalled opportunities for stubborn machine gun defences.'

After the freeing of Amiens came the battle of Bapaume. The Third and Fourth Armies, comprising 23 divisions, were now relentlessly driving 35 German divisions from one side of the old Somme battlefield to the other, passing on the way localities that they had stubbornly defended two years previously. The war had still not become fluid; there were pillboxes to be sited and concrete shelters to be made. Henry sometimes walked his 'retention lines' and at other times made use of car, cycle or horse. At one time he had a Portuguese Field Company under him. The construction and repair of bridges, pontoon and otherwise, was one of the duties of a Field Company. This sometimes had to be done under enemy fire. With a network of canals ahead of them on the IX Corps front the fact was significant. On 25 September he was reconnoitring canal crossings from a front line position in the Mœuvres sector.

Evie opened her next telegram anxiously, knowing he was not expecting leave. '...admitted 2 Red Cross Hospital Rouen severe gunshot wound thigh Secretary War Office.' Henry's own letter arrived at the same time. It was contained in a small packet, inside a matchbox, wrapped round a piece of copper driving-band from a 4.2" shell, and he seemed more concerned about the loss of his new trench boots than the wound:

> 'Who was it ordered her hubby home on Michaelmas Day and forgot to ring up G.H.Q. and tell them not to have a stunt that day? We are having no end of a success, as you will probably read in tomorrow's paper. While I was still unconscious, some stretcherbearers came along and jumped to the conclusion I was hit in the foot. They ripped my new boot and slashed the sock down with a knife in their haste to get at what they thought was the wound.
>
> I say Evie, today's *Times* has given me a brainwave. Did you see this article on W.A.A.C.s with the American Army in Paris? Isn't it the very thing? Why not go and interview that Miss Blow-me-tight at W.A.A.C. HQ, 49, Upper Grosvenor Street? I'm sure if you put on your Canadian twang they'd take you straight away!'

Henry was x-rayed and operated on at 48 C.C.S. at 2 p.m. on 26 September, and was back in Div H.Q. on the evening of the 27th. Lt.Col. W. Garforth arrived as Acting C.R.E. on the afternoon of the 28th; and the Division attacked at 5.50 a.m. on the 29th. Tied by the leg now, Henry was passed back to No.2 R.C. Hospital, Rouen. The C.C.S. was itself moving forward.

Tomorrow's paper, as Henry had forecast, described the success. So did the following day's; and two years later *The Times* devoted a whole page to what it called a notable anniversary. Haig's Victory Despatch was later contained in a four-page supplement to *The Times*, whose leader said that the three things which impressed Haig most were the capture of Mont St. Quentin by the Australians, the breach of the Quéant switch by two Canadian and four English Divisions, and perhaps most of all, the capture of Bellenglise by the 46th Division. On the morning of 26 September French and American forces attacked on both sides of the Argonne, between the Meuse and the Suippe rivers; on the next day the British and Canadians attacked towards Cambrai on a 13-mile front. Douglas Haig again:

'The success of the northern part of the attack depended upon the ability of our troops to debouch from the neighbourhood of Mœuvres and to secure the crossings of the Canal du Nord... It was necessary to force a passage on a narrow front and turn the line of the Canal further north by an attack developed fanwise from the point of crossing. This was carried out successfully and our infantry, assisted by some sixty-five tanks, broke deeply into the enemy's position.'

Henry's rendezvous with a shell splinter marked the end of his war. By the time he was able to rejoin his division they had advanced forty-five miles, and it was only two days before the Armistice; although he received another mention in despatches on 16 March 1919. For the moment, however, he could only pore over the newspaper accounts.

The 46th (North Midland) Division, provided with lifebelts, bridging materials and rafts and under cover of artillery and machine-gun fire, had stormed the main Hindenburg defences, surpassing all records by taking over 4,000 prisoners in the day and a great number of guns. The latter included two complete batteries of 4.2" howitzers, and one of 4.2" long guns, with over 300 machine-guns and quantities of mortars and ammunition.

One correspondent found himself with a group of officers who were reading a telegram. It stated that the children of Buxton had saluted the flag in honour of the glorious deeds of the 46th.

Where *had* those liferafts come from? What matter if a few lifebelts were missing from a leave boat? Had not the Lincolns and Leicesters, the Staffords and the Sherwood Foresters captured Bellenglise, Lehaucourt and Magny-la Fosse?

Congratulations were the Special Order of the Day; from General Sir H.S. Rawlinson, commanding the 4th Army, to Lt.General Sir W.P. Braithwaite, commanding IX Corps, to Major General G.F. Boyd, 46th Division commander, who issued them down to Battery and Platoon level. Garforth forwarded the Engineer-in-Chief's letter to Henry at Rouen,

Eagle captured from a German Headquarters. Somehow Henry got it home

generously disclaiming all credit: 'I keep thinking what rotten luck you had in not being here for the show for which you made so many preparations.'

Three days later he was transferred, horizontal but chirpy, to No.74 General Hospital at Trouville, opposite Le Havre. The Medical Board in due course instructed him to go on leave and report back exactly three weeks later, on his way back to the front. Taking two days to attend some lectures at Rouen and visit the blast furnaces at Quévilly nearby, he went by car to Boulogne. Evie was at Victoria as usual; they chose her a wedding present and then went to Daly's again.

While Henry convalesced in Devon, Evelyn had a foretaste of the distances she would be expected to cover as his walking companion. Back in London, there was just time for a brisk constitutional, to Battersea and back, before catching the 12.35 p.m. returning leave train, which reached Boulogne at 6 p.m. The Rouen train did not leave till 4.30 p.m. next day, so he walked via the cliffs to his old hospital at Wimereux and back.

Cleared by the Medical Board, he reached Amiens next day at midnight and spent the night at 'Rawlinson House'. Leaving next day he found his Division near Landrecies, which had been captured by the 4th Canadian Division in the battle of the Sambre. The pressure was off by now, and the enemy in general retreat on the whole front. In the south the French had pushed forward to the line of the Meuse. In the north, in the early hours of Armistice Day, the Canadian 3rd Division had the honour of recapturing Mons, where it had all begun, the whole of the defending force being either killed or taken prisoner.

'The troops had been warned that hostilities were to cease at 11 a.m.' runs the official account.[5] 'The firing, however, which had been heavy all the morning, continued until 3 minutes to 11 a.m. when it ceased for a short period and then broke out in a final crash at 11 a.m. Then all was silence. Combatants from both sides emerged from cover and walked about in full view.' The final act of one German machine gunner was thought worthy of a separate footnote: 'At 2 minutes to 11 a machine-gun, about 200 yards from our leading troops, fired off a complete belt without a pause. A single machine-gunner was then seen to stand up beside his weapon, take off his helmet, bow and turning about walk slowly to the rear.'

First there were repairs to be made and G.O.C.'s inspections to arrange. Then Educational and Demobilisation lectures were planned on a variety of subjects, including shorthand. Debates and Concert Parties were organised and a Point-to-Point course laid out. Notwithstanding Eric Bailey's comments, Henry was a useful Glee Club singer and organiser.

King George V visited the battlefields, accompanied by the Prince of Wales, Prince Albert and the Army Commander, to a spontaneous and rousing reception. As soon as possible Henry took a day off to walk the Bellenglise battlefield in company with Captain Priestley, the divisional historian. Billeted as they were in the Forêt de Mormal, the Canadians soon had a Forestry Camp going. There was an electric light engine to be rigged up, the lock gates operated on the Sambre canal to relieve the floods, and so on. The classes all returned to their units for Christmas. Snow fell on Christmas Eve, and we can take leave of them as the officers traditionally served their men's dinners.

Notes

1   Sir Ernest Shackleton was already at Buenos Aires by August 1914. His men were subsequently marooned in Antarctica, and rescued from S. Georgia in 1916 at the fourth attempt.
2   If there is anything more useless than a vote of thanks it must surely be a tardy vote of thanks.
3   Its 1,352 performances lasted from 10.2.'17 to 26.12.'21. Daly's, in Leicester Square, is now the Warner West End cinema.
4   'Douglas Haig's Victory Despatch', Part I.
5   *The Story of the Fourth Army in the Battle of the Hundred Days*, p.261.

7 | Exploring Scotland

No children were born to Evie for nearly four years, by which time she was thirty-one years of age. This was a conscious decision of Henry's. For a year or two he was not sure whether he had acted fairly in getting married at all. There were gloomy silences as he debated the issue within himself; the last thing he wanted at this stage was children. Evie never made an issue of it or stood in the way of his life-style; but the six months leave that my father took before returning to India must have been a severe test of her character.

No plans had been made beyond the fact that he was determined to see as much of Scotland on foot and as cheaply as possible. Evie seems to have met him half way: a woman decathlete could hardly have done more. Henry did not bother to record walks made for pleasure in Scotland any more than he did in India. Evie, however, jotted down their itinerary and, with the aid of a contemporary Baedeker, I traced their route. Baedeker would have classified Henry as a 'pedestrian of modest requirements', but that was an overstatement.

Despite being 'good with machinery' Henry never had much luck with the cars he owned. He did not consider them all that important and they were invariably second-hand. Upon whether the car would go or not depended how long they would spend in a given place and where they stayed. If the car broke down Henry expected to walk while Evie waited. They started their tour by train, but with a vague notion of buying a car if something suitable came on offer. It would anyway have to be sold at the end of his leave. They did buy one in due course and it let them down spectacularly.

The first day in Edinburgh was clearly for Henry's benefit; they explored a shale mine in the Forth, went over the Power House, and learned how the cable tram system worked. The Castle, the Cathedral and the Botanical Gardens were viewed the next day before going on by train to Pitlochry for four days of walking. They took a ten-mile walk to the Tummel Falls and Bonskied House for starters. When Henry climbed Ben Vrackie, 2,757 ft., in the rain Evie climbed Craigour to meet him. That was in the morning; in the afternoon they walked the Portnacraig and Clunie Brig circuit.

Next came a week at Oban. The rail journey took a whole day, with a change at Balquhidder, and they booked into the cheapest hotel, whence they took a coach to Dunstaffnage Castle, and on to see the Falls of Lora, formed by the ebb tide out of Loch Etive. Henry walked 'most of the way' home and they met for a late lunch. In the afternoon (guess what?) Henry went for a long tramp. They cruised the inner islands south to Shuna: and the next day east to Tobermory Bay. They took a train to the railhead at Ballachulish along the old Caledonian (L.M.S.) Railway's line round the Appin peninsula, a route that was closed in March 1966 and the track uplifted. Coaches were available to take them up Glencoe, but they preferred to walk as far as they could before catching the train back the same day. The 100-gun salute that they heard in the distance was H.M.S. 'Caernarvon' sounding off for the Declaration of Peace on 28 June.

Henry had to return to London for a Medical Board on 1 July, but came straight back and on they went to Inverness. The Waverley Temperance Hotel (£1 a day for the two of them) made a suitable base and cost less than half the price of the better hotels. They took the train to Culloden Moor, a station that was closed in May 1965, and walked back across the 1746 battlefield, seeing the Cumberland Stone, the Cairn and the Highlanders' graves. A MacBrayne steamer took them down Loch Ness; the Kessock ferry took them north. They took a train to Beauly and walked on to the Falls of Kilmorack. 'Good walkers may go on thence through Strathglass to (17 m.) Invercannich' says Baedeker. Evie was evidently left contemplating the waterfall. Her diary says simply 'Hal walked on up the valley alone.' Today there is only a hydro-electric dam to contemplate.

At Thurso (two days) they walked to Holburn Head and Dunnet Head on the same day and found *Primula Scotia*. Crossing from Scrabster to Kirkwall, Orkney, they passed the sunken German ships in Scapa Flow. When, by 10 p.m., Henry had failed to find rooms, they finally ended up at the Harbour Master's house. In the five days they were there he explored the Orkney mainland from end to end like an ant on a floating leaf, discovering for himself the Standing Stones and Maeshowe. On 17 July he had a wire from Dunfermline; his offer for a second-hand car had been accepted and they decided to make their way slowly south and collect it.

The next stop was for three days at Wick, where they walked to Noss Head lighthouse and up the Wick river. Suddenly finding it tedious to be travelling by train down the east coast of Caithness, Henry jumped out as the train was leaving Lybster Station (now the local golf clubhouse), yelling to Evie to find accommodation at Berriedale, some fourteen miles down the coast, and await his arrival on foot. They were making for Aviemore, now a flourishing skiing and sports resort with many three- and four-star hotels. The only accommodation then was the Station Hotel which was rated good in its class.

The seven days of their stay at Aviemore are an eloquent blank in Evie's diary. An idea of the walking regimen that Henry had prescribed for himself is given on the day of their departure, when she took the train and Henry left her for two days and 'walked to Blair Atholl via Braemar'. It is worth expanding this entry. From Aviemore to Braemar is 20 miles as the crow flies; but the crow might avoid Cairngorm, 4,084 ft., and Ben Macdhui, 4.296 ft., the second highest mountain in Scotland after Ben Nevis. Henry did not wish to avoid them; he shared his uncle Fred's view that a peak was never so truly a peak as when it was also a pass.

It was late July and there was plenty of daylight, the only thing that mattered. He did not bother with accommodation at Braemar. There were only two hotels, both overcrowded in the season, and he did not know when he would arrive. From Braemar westwards to Blair Atholl is 26 miles by crow, 30 miles by Baedeker's tracks up to 1,500 ft. or 50 miles round by road. Beinn Iutharn Mhor, 3,424 ft., and Beinn a'Ghlo, 3,671 ft., the 'mountain of the veil', lay across the route, an open invitation.

The flivver they acquired in Dunfermline was a 1914 model, of Detroit manufacture, known as the Scripps Booth Light Car. The Scripps Booth Company had been acquired by General Motors in 1918 but the marque was, understandably, allowed to lapse in 1922. This tin lizzie took them happily into Edinburgh, where they found rooms in the New Waverley (Temperance) Hotel, and Evie started on a course of botany, which became the basis of a considerable knowledge of plants and a useful complement to Henry's activities.

Their plans were interrupted by two funerals. Henry's mother Ella died in August, necessitating a month's break in their holiday. Four months earlier she had sold up the family home of Hurlditch Court, lock, stock and barrel by auction, and gone to live in Guildford next door to her second son, Dick, who now had a medical practice. Ella's death made no financial difference to Henry since he had, at his mother's request, stood down from his share of any inheritance from her. The reason for this outwardly strange and unwonted fiat was that Ella understood Henry to be the heir of her brother, with whom she was staying at the time she caught pneumonia and died.

Qysmet se lara nahin jata : no-one can claim precedence in the court of Fate. Ella's request proved misplaced, for Henry did not live to inherit his uncle's estate; and it was part of Evie's Kismet that Henry, an elder son without patrimony, would, in his turn, leave her without life assurance or pension rights.

Ella's estate was not large, however, and Hurlditch was largely mortgaged to her brother. The other death was that of Evie's wealthy cousin Helen Hill, from whose house she was married. Helen, having no children, had promised Evie all her jewellery. Her husband Arthur, not knowing of the promise, gave it all away to those around him and died himself within a few weeks.

They returned to Edinburgh and collected their car, planning to drive south through the Lake District. At Carlisle the car was already giving trouble and they had to spend an extra day (a Sunday) at Lockerbie's Hotel. Somebody got it going again on Monday but at Keswick it would go no further, apparently needing some obscure part which would have to be specially ordered and made. While the work was put in hand they saw enough of the Lakes to last a lifetime. Evelyn was good for the ten-mile circuit of Derwentwater, and the walk to Bassenthwaite. She was not scared of Skiddaw (3,054 ft.). It was possible to go up and down it in four to six hours; but when Henry announced he would walk to Ullswater and back he had to go alone. For the Buttermere trip he agreed to go part of the way by coach.

After a fortnight the car was ready. It dragged itself to Hyde Park Corner, early in October, where it came to an expensive-sounding halt. Something large had fallen from underneath, probably the sump. They got out and disowned it.

8 | North-West Frontier

The idea of having to go before another Medical Board seems absurd. Routine being satisfied, however, Henry returned to India in December 1919, ahead of Evie, and was soon on active service again on the North-West Frontier, back in his substantive rank of Major; it was not until June 1928 that he would regain the acting rank that he had first held ten years before.

'I am glad to hear your name is noted for the Everest Expedn', he wrote to Jack Hazard, the 1924 Everest climber, who had served as his 2nd-in-command on the Somme. 'I have every hope that I shall be nominated by the Govt. of India as Survey Officer, but when the happy day is going to be, is more than I can say!

Yes, I am to go with Kellas if he decides to attempt Kamet in June, but I have not heard from him since leaving England. He proposed to go straight to Garhwal where I was to have all the coolies, supplies etc. ready. It will be the height of the monsoon and none too pleasant.

I wasn't long left in peace in Dehra Dun. Got sent off here as O.C. Surveys 6 weeks ago, just as I was thinking of settling into a bungalow. Had to dump the wife in a hurry at Rurki, and rush off. It's a soft job for me as my subalterns have all the work to do, unfortunately, and I have to content myself with turning out their results on a hand-press. It's splendid country up here and would make a magnificent hill-station — 6,000 ft. A thousand pities the Govt. won't take over all this frontier country right up to the Afghan border; there will never be real peace until they do.

Have just heard from my old Tibet pal, Bailey, who is being lionised at Viceregal Lodge, Delhi, after his sensational escape from Bolshevik captivity in Central Asia. He goes home in April for a year's leave, then takes up the job of Political Agent in Sikkim, whence he and I start on a journey in Tibet, I hope, in 1922 — wives permitting!'

Field Survey Sections accompanied the Tochi and Derajat columns advancing from railheads at Bannu and Tank respectively, and 480 square miles of new map on the 1-inch scale was produced, within the triangle Razmak, Wana and Jandola. Some heavy fighting took place, notably at Palosina Ridge and Ahnai Tangi, as the 4th Gurkhas under Captain Borrowman advanced up the valley of the Tank Zam river.

A trace of each new area surveyed was sent by plane and despatch rider to the reproducing section at Dera Ismael Khan, for inclusion in a fresh edition of the map. Aerial and landscape photographs were sent to the Survey Offices in Calcutta for reproduction, and officers could purchase private copies at 8 *annas* per print. Borrowman made many field sketches, and his caricatures of brother officers were in demand. The surveyors emulated Lewis Carroll:

> The Trig man and the Topo man were working hand in hand,
> They wept like anything to see such quantities of land,
> 'If only this were measured out oh wouldn't it be grand?'
> 'If a million men with Invar[1] tapes Trilaterate the sphere,
> Do you suppose' the Trig man said 'that they would make it clear?'
> 'I doubt it' said the Topo man, and shed a bitter tear.

With Mahsud and Waziristan clasps on their Indian General Service Medals, the Survey Detachment returned to their peace station at Dehra Dun, and ceased to exist as a separate unit in June 1920.

What 'being dumped in a hurry' meant for Evie, was arriving for the first time in a new country without money, finding no-one to meet her, and no message waiting. Plan 'B' had to be swiftly put into operation; after a visit to Henry's bank, where she managed to establish her identity and his whereabouts, she had to dump herself at Rurki, where she stayed as a guest of some cousins. When Henry returned from his 'soft job' on active service it was only to disappear again up Mount Kamet with Dr. Kellas who had arrived earlier than expected. Henry tried to enlist his friend Hazard:

> 'Kellas has suddenly appeared on the scene. He writes to me from the Rockville Grand Hotel, Darjeeling to say that he expects to be at Kathgodam, the nearest rly stn for Kamet, early in July, where he hopes to find his scientific apparatus. He would proceed by easy stages to Niti, where the oxygen cylinders should arrive by early August.
>
> What he wants is a transport officer to relieve him of the onus of getting his stuff from Kathgodam to Niti. Not expecting to hear any more of Kellas this year, I have undertaken a biggish programme of work in the Department this summer; I hope to join K. for his final climb, but

don't see how I can possibly spare the time in July & Aug for running his *bandobast* from Kathgodam to Niti. Let me know as soon as you can. I got demobbed from Waziristan last month & am in Mussoorie fair-drawing the results. Hope you're fit.'

The bungalow Henry was 'thinking of settling into' had to wait until his return from Kamet. For three and a half years Evie had been waiting to use her visitors' book wedding present. In October, 1920, her first home was written into it, Mountain View, Dehra Dun: the Mountain was the Himalayan foothills, the View a good one.

Note

1   Invar (=invariable), an alloy with a low coefficient of expansion.

9 | Kamet, 1920 & Everest, 1921

Dr. A.M. Kellas, a lecturer in chemistry in the Medical School of the Middlesex Hospital, had made many Himalayan ascents and his inconclusive experiments with oxygen on this expedition were the first ever made. A technical expert in the craft of mountaineering, he had reconnoitred Kamet twice before, the second occasion being cut short by the war.

Henry's contribution, on the other hand, was in the form of energy rather than experience. By modern standards their progress would be considered slow and amateurish. Nevertheless, in the event, the height reached was 23,600 ft. equalling C.F. Meade's third attempt in 1913. Only five people had ever been higher at that time, the Duke of the Abruzzi holding the unofficial 'record' at 24,600 ft. on Chogolisa I (Bride Peak) in the Karakoram, in 1909.

The oxygen apparatus was unexpectedly delayed by the shipping authorities' classifying it as 'high explosives'. They soon learned that the heavy old-fashioned cylinders were not the easiest things to divide up into suitable loads, and when Camp 3 was pitched on rock at a height of 20,620 ft., the majority of the porters were showing signs of distress. Next morning the thermometer recorded 28 degrees of frost, their servants (they had no Sherpas) were 'hors de combat', and they had great difficulty in preparing any cooked food. The daily convoy of provisions and firewood ceased to function in the absence of supervision, and the coolie guides became extremely despondent.

While Kellas and his two remaining porters continued to cut steps in the ice cliff Henry retraced his steps and installed his personal servant, who was now recovering, in charge at Base Camp with orders to despatch regular supplies on an invoiced system. Providing similarly for someone in charge at Camps 1 and 2, he quickly reappeared at Camp 3. One has to read between the lines to discover the trifling fact that Base Camp was 5,240 ft. lower down the mountain.

They pitched their small single-fly tent on snow at 22,000 ft. for Camp 4, the porters descending for the night and returning next day with a second tent for themselves and a supply of ready-cooked food. It was mid-September by now and late in the season. The temperature fell to 15°F. below zero (-26°C.) and their blankets were as stiff as boards. After heating a tin of soup, and thawing sufficient snow to fill a thermos with Bovril, the two climbers started forward, with three porters, on the rope, emerging on to the wide flat valley which separates Kamet from East Abi Gamin. The summit showed clearly 2,000 ft. above them, easily climbable had time permitted.

'Wild life by no means ceases at these heights,' wrote Henry. 'Our approach disturbed a pair of ravens who kept hovering round the rocky crannies of the saddle, seemingly resentful of the unexpected disturbance of their nesting operations; while overhead, barely distinguishable without the aid of glasses, a huge lammergeyer circled and soared.'

Henry had been unaware until too late that the large Primus stove on which he had been relying would not work in the rarefied atmosphere over 20,000 ft., while Kellas' small spirit stove took an hour to thaw enough snow to fill a teapot. 'Failure is often more instructive than success', he concluded, 'and I only hope that this expedition, on which I shall always look back with pleasure, may be the prelude to future efforts in the same genial company.' The all-in cost of the expedition, including his own salary, was less than £1,500. This compares, for example, with the cost of £22,000 shown by the ledgers of the Royal Geographical Society as being the expenditure on the 1924 Everest expedition.

Kamet, which was the first peak of over 25,000 ft. ever climbed, would have to wait until 1931 for Frank Smythe to conquer it; it was ironical that Smythe should have been actually climbing it, and at Camp 3, when he read in the papers of Henry's murder in Burma.[1]

Tibetan consent for the Reconnaissance expedition to Mount Everest under Lt.Col. Howard-Bury came through in January 1921. The high climbers were to be George Mallory and Guy Bullock. H. Raeburn and Dr. A.M. Kellas provided additional expertise, Dr. A.F.R. Wollaston was the surgeon and naturalist and Dr. A.M. Heron the geologist. Henry was placed in charge of the survey detachment, with Major E.O. Wheeler in charge of the photo survey, surveyors Lalbir Singh, Gujjar Singh, Torabaz Khan and 16 khalasis. As Henry was the only member who spoke any Tibetan, two good interpreters were taken as well.

MEMBERS OF THE EXPEDITION.

| *Standing:* | WOLLASTON. | HOWARD-BURY. | HERON. | RAEBURN. |
| *Sitting:* | MALLORY. | WHEELER. | BULLOCK. | MORSHEAD. |

Members of the 1921 Mount Everest Expedition

Evie's first child was born at Mountain View, Dehra Dun, in November 1920, and he was four months old when it became necessary to move to Darjeeling whence the expedition would start. They had no ayah or nurse and the baby suffered prickly heat as they waited in Calcutta. The first few months in Darjeeling were spent at the Bellevue Hotel, where a small coterie of expectant mothers, grass widows and expedition wives were soon drawn together, most of them sharing news of each other's babies or news of the expedition or, in Evie's case, both. Lord Ronaldshay, Governor of Bengal, threw a lavish dinner-party for 30 at Government House, Darjeeling, on 12 May. George Mallory took in Evie; Henry took in Mrs. Graham of the Kalimpong Homes.

The survey party left next day, not via Bhutan with the main body but via the shorter Sikkim route, correcting the existing map as they went.

Henry called on his old friend F.M. Bailey at the Residency at Gangtok as he went through. Leaving Torabaz Khan to complete the Sikkim revision, the rest of the survey party crossed the Sikkim-Tibet frontier over the Serpo pass and arrived at Kampa Dzong nine days ahead of the main expedition, and busied themselves re-observing some of Colonel Ryder's old triangulation stations of 1903.

Henry had barely started talking with Howard-Bury when a messenger ran up to announce that Dr. Kellas, his climbing colleague of the previous year, had died of sudden heart failure. This was a bombshell to Henry, who had dined opposite the perfectly fit Kellas only three weeks before. An older man, he had been climbing almost continuously since Kamet. Acute gastritis had caused him to lose a stone in weight but he had refused to turn back.

At Kampa the 100 mules that Lord Rawlinson, now C.-in-C. India, had lent them were changed for those of the local breed. The former were proving a little too fat and sleek for the job. A cuckoo was heard busily calling away at 14,000 ft.

An amusing incident occurred in the kitchen tent one evening. The cooks had put a tin of fish in boiling water, and when they thought it sufficiently hot they took it out and tried to open it, when the tin to their surprise exploded violently, covering everyone in the tent with small pieces of fish. Fortunately no one was hurt, and the sight of it kept them amused for days.

Shekar Dzong was reached on 17 June. The town was perched on the side of a hill reminiscent of Mont St. Michel, with a monastery higher up commanding a view of irrigated fertile barley fields. With marches averaging 15 or 20 miles Henry opted to use existing triangulation points, but it was still necessary for the surveyors to climb the hills on either side of the valley all the way to Tingri Maidan which was reached on the 19th. Tingri was a small trading post 50 miles north-west of Everest and was to be their supply base.

They had now travelled three times the direct distance, or, as a *Times* leader put it, it was as if they had marched from Hastings to Birmingham via Aldeburgh in Suffolk. Splitting up into pairs they set about their respective jobs, Mallory with Bullock, Wheeler with Heron, Henry exploring northwards and westwards with Gujjar Singh, leaving Lalbir Singh to complete his plane-tabling at base.

Henry shot numerous hares, partridge and bar-headed goose for the pot, and once inadvertently offended the Buddhist susceptibilities of a Tibetan who saw him kill a butterfly for his collection. It seemed illogical when, immediately afterwards, the same man requested some of Henry's 12-bore cartridges. Hospitality, when they had it from the Tibetans, included hips and haws of wild roses and apparently edible fungus washed down with powdered brick-tea, salt, soda and butter. They also ate a spinach substitute made from young nettles.

Picking up Wollaston, Henry and Gujjar Singh marched south-west to Nyenam, a point 60 miles due west of Everest, almost on the Nepal border. Their visit was the result of a cordial request from the two *Dzongpöns* (one to watch over the other) of Nyenam that some members of the expedition should visit him. Wollaston describes this uncomfortable journey in a chapter of Howard-Bury's book.[2] When they arrived at Nyenam their 'hosts' denied all knowledge of the invitation. Finally, they said, in effect, 'glad to see you but we hope you'll go' and, so saying, gave them false information about the passes and discouraged the local traders from dealing with them. This was, I believe, the only unfriendly incident in the entire expedition.

They returned via the sacred valley of Lapche, which no European had visited before, below the north-east slopes of Gaurisankar,[3] 23,440 ft. Arriving after dark, they spent a cheerless night on boulders in drenching rain at 14,600 ft. with no fuel except a few green twigs of dwarf rhododendron. The valley was so sacred that they were only able to buy a sheep on promising not to kill it until after quitting the valley. Trailing streamers of lichen festooning the trees bore witness to the extreme dampness of the climate there.

Base Camp was now advanced 20 miles up the Kharta valley, east of Everest, to 17,500 ft. Mallory and Bullock had already left on 31 August, and were followed by Colonel Howard-Bury, Raeburn and Wollaston. After starting Gujjar Singh on an area of 1-inch plane-tabling north of the Kharta Chu, Henry joined Wheeler during his photographic survey of the Kharta Valley. There was a further week of tedious waiting before Camp 1 was pitched at 20,000 ft. on a stony ledge overlooking the Kharta glacier, followed by Camp 2 at 22,000 ft. on the summit of the col at its head.

An icy blast raged on the summit of the col and they named the spot Hlakpa La (Windy Gap). Wheeler's camera and theodolite station on the col was the highest that had ever been made at the time.

Henry and Wheeler were both keen to join the high climbers for the final stages. How would they stand up to the pace of the chosen representatives of the Alpine Club? What experts they were too! Was there ever a climber like Mallory? Or a pairing like Mallory and Bullock? For his election to the Alpine Club in 1909 Bullock had submitted 'one of the best lists of qualifying expeditions ever sent in'; both had been pupils of Graham Irving since 1905.

One is tempted to compare it with a Pro-Am sports event with Mallory and Bullock as the pros and Henry and Wheeler as the amateurs. The analogy is spurious, of course, since Mallory was a schoolmaster at Charterhouse and Bullock a member of the Consular Service on leave. Wheeler himself was son of the President of the Canadian Alpine Club. They were indeed all amateurs and none more so than Henry. The surveyors were made more than welcome. Henry was the first to appear and arrived at one of the very few moments when Mallory himself was feeling seedy and depressed. From Mallory's section of Howard-Bury's book:[4]

'It was impossible to stay in bed with such thoughts, and by the middle of the morning I was sitting in the sun to write home...I looked round and saw, to my great surprise and unfeigned delight, the approaching figure of Major Morshead. I had long been hoping that he might be free to join us; and he arrived at the due moment to cheer my present solitude, to strengthen the party and to help us when help was greatly needed. Moreover he brought from Wollaston for my use a medical dope.'

Mallory's target was the Chang La (North Col), 23,000 ft., and it was now evident that a second advanced camp would be necessary to achieve it. Hence the journey up to 'Windy Gap', which Henry disposed of in about four lines of his report. It actually took them four days, the fourth of which Mallory described:

'On August 18th, with the low moon setting, the three of us with one coolie [Mallory, Bullock, Morshead and Dorji Gompa, the strongest coolie] set forth on the most critical expedition of the whole reconnaissance. Failure on this day must involve us in a lamentable delay... The first few steps on the glacier showed us what to expect; we sank in to our knees. The remedy was of course to put on rackets—which are no great encumbrance, but a growing burden on a long march. We wore them for the rest of the day whenever we were walking on snow.

About dawn the light became difficult; a thin floating mist confused the snow surfaces; ascents and descents were equally indistinguishable, so that the errant foot might hit the slope too soon or equally plunge with sudden violence to unexpected depths. Crevasses forced us away to the right ... and a long traverse brought us back to the glacier at 8.30 a.m.

Our greatest enemy was not after all the deep powdery snow ... In the glacier furnace the thin mist became steam, it enveloped us in a clinging garment from which no escape was possible, and far from being protected from the sun's fierce heat, we seemed to be scorched all the more. The atmosphere was enervating to the last degree; never before had our lungs been tested quite so severely.'

Morshead had met his match. A little later on, with a brief exclamation to say what he intended, he untied the rope, unable to go farther.

'Some twenty minutes later, as we sat on the snow gazing at all that lay about us, Bullock and I were surprised by a shout. A moment later Morshead joined us, to the great rejoicing of all three.

To the tired party even descent seemed laborious ... Major Morshead, who had not been trained with Bullock and me to the pace of such expeditions, had kept up so far in the gamest fashion; but now he was much exhausted. The day ended with a series of little spurts, balancing over the snow-sprinkled boulders along and along the valley, in the dim misty moonlit scene, until at 2 o'clock in the morning we reached our lower camp, twenty-three hours after the early start.'

It was not long before an opportunity presented itself of a less arduous climb, namely Kama Changri, a peak of 21,300 ft. ten miles E.N.E. of Everest. Howard-Bury's prose stands up to the test of being quoted immediately after Byron's epic poetry. Firstly then, from the start of the second canto of Byron's *Lara*:

> 'Night wanes—the vapours round the mountains curl'd
> Melt into morn, and Light awakes the world.
> Man has another day to swell the past,
> And lead him near to little, but his last;
> But mighty Nature bounds as from her birth,
> The sun is in the heavens, and life on earth;
> Flowers in the valley, splendour in the beam,
> Health on the gale, and freshness in the stream.'

Follow *that*, Colonel Howard-Bury:

'The next day, Mallory, Morshead and I left camp at 2 a.m. by the light of a full moon, which made the going as light as though it were day. Except for the distant roar of the stream far away in the valley, there was no other sound, only an intense stillness. Never anywhere have I seen the moon or the stars shine so brightly. To the South, far away from us, there were constant flashes of lightning—the valleys in Tibet, the great gorges of the Arun, the wooded valleys of Nepal all lay buried under a white sea of clouds, out of which emerged the higher mountains like islands out of a fairy sea. In this bright moonlight, mountains like Kanchenjunga—100 miles away—stood out sharp and distinct. Here on this sharp ridge ... sunrise came to us in all its beauty and grandeur. To the West, and close at hand, towered up Mount Everest, still over 8,000 ft. above us; at first showing up cold, grey and dead against a sky of deep purple. All of a sudden a ray of sunshine touched the summit, and soon flooded the higher snows and ridges with golden light, while behind, the deep purple of the sky changed to orange. Makalu was the next to catch the first rays of the sun and glowed as though alive; then the white sea of clouds was struck by the gleaming rays of the sun, and all aglow with colour rose slowly and seemed to break against the island peaks in great billows of fleecy white.'

They stopped on the top of Kama Changri for over three hours. It was extraordinarily warm; for the moment there was not a breath of air, and the sun seemed to shine with an intense heat.

The second visit to Windy Gap took place a month after the first and this time it was reached in two days. Six climbers and eighteen porters spent the night camped there at 22,500 ft., two to each Mummery tent, buffeted by the malicious north-westerly wind. The tents flapped like machine-guns in the gale but were strangely stuffy inside, owing to their small size and narrow entrance. Mallory, sharing with Henry, cut two gashes in his to increase the ventilation, and the two of them slept better than most.

It was the three Alpine climbers, Mallory, Bullock and Wheeler, with the ten fittest porters, who next day descended on to the glacier 1,000 ft. below and emerged up on to the North Col of Everest two days later. Bury, Wollaston and Morshead were not sorry to return to the 20,000 ft. camp which appeared homelike.

During the period of the expedition their incoming mail had of necessity reached them only sporadically. Outgoing despatches, however, went by regular runner.

The Royal Geographical Society were impatient for their map and, in their correspondence with Morshead (now in the Society archives) a note of exasperation creeps in, with the implied suggestion that he do more mapping and less mountaineering.

Owing to the unfamiliar nomenclature of the places, some quaint mistakes got past the sub-editors. Colonel Howard-Bury's own book includes a place called Thrashing in the index. On the page itself: 'We found the people busy thrashing' (their barley). The *Times* correspondent must have had people reaching for their gazetteers with his reference to a place called Yakdung, no doubt confusing it with Yatung in the Chumbi valley: 'The country around Shekar Dzong is entirely fuelless, so without a regular supply from Yakdung it would be impossible to remain and carry out explorations'.

Returning their own separate ways, the whole expedition was back in Darjeeling by 25 October 1921. Henry and Gujjar Singh did three marches northwards from Tingri before rejoining Lalbir and returning, back through the leech belt and over those Heath Robinson bridges, to Darjeeling on the 16th. After over five months' absence, and with a stubble of hair of equal length covering head and face alike, it is not surprising to learn from Evie's diary that 'Hugh would have nothing to say to his father on the latter's return, and was very jealous of his touching or even coming near me'.

'Well, we have all just returned to civilisation after a ripping 5 months trip,' Henry wrote to Hazard. 'We missed the top of the old mountain by 6,000 ft., but have got the whole country pretty well reconnoitred & surveyed, so that the next party to come along will know what they are up against. We had pretty bad weather in July, August & Sept, followed by gales of wind which lifted quantities of snow from the surface and threatened to suffocate the climbers at 23,000 ft. It looks as if May and June are the months for a successful climb, and I doubt if there'll be time to organise an expedn for May /22.'

He had underrated the ability of the Committee to mount another expedition so quickly. With the latter due to start in a few months, and another baby on the way, it became worth his while to rent a house and employ an ayah. Evie moved their possessions into a house called Chevremont as the Surveyor General, Col. C.H.D. Ryder,[5] C.B., C.I.E., D.S.O. inspected the Survey Detachment. The area mapped was 12,000 sq.miles of ¼" original, 4,000 sq.miles of ¼" revision and 600 sq.miles of Detail Photo Survey, at an average over-all cost of Rs. 3.9 per sq.mile. A preliminary map in six colours was available before the last expedition members had sailed from Bombay. Henry's collection of 18 species of butterflies was taken to Bombay, where they were listed by Brigadier Evans; one of them was proclaimed a new species and named 'Lycaena morsheadi'.

Henry's civilian rank went up from Assistant Superintendent to Deputy Superintendent, and he was in charge of No.15 Party (Triangulation). He continued to be a stranger to his son, who was now beginning to speak a mixture of English, Tibetan and Hindi, and to do such engaging things as 'listening with his ear on a full-page advertisement of watches to hear whether they ticked or not'.

Back in England, Colonel Howard-Bury was received at Buckingham Palace shortly before Christmas, before going on to Queen's Hall, where the Duke of York was among the large audience of experienced travellers to applaud the appearance on the platform of the returned explorers.

Henry himself went north of the main Himalaya range again, immediately after Christmas, to carry out a programme of plumb-line deflection observations.

Evie's visitors' book shows that George Mallory was back in Darjeeling in March 1922 and spent a week at Chevremont with Henry, Evie and the two babies before the expedition moved off. This time Henry was to be a climber, not a surveyor, which meant that he would have more time for writing letters. She enjoyed getting the letters; but she was always slightly afraid that the envelope might contain the information that she was now married to a corpse.

Notes

1   *Kamet Conquered*, Frank S. Smythe, Gollancz, 1932, p.137.
2   *Mount Everest, The Reconnaissance*, 1921. Arnold, 1922.
3   *The Times Survey Atlas*, as recently as its 1920 edition, was giving Gaurisankar as an alternative name for Everest. In bringing back the Tibetan names of the five sacred peaks of this valley, the highest of which was Gaurisankar (Chomo Tshering in Tibetan) Henry played a part in proving that they were different mountains. Vide 'Mount Everest and its Tibetan Names', a review of Sir Sven Hedin's book on Everest, by Sir Sidney Burrard, Dehra Dun, 1931.
4   p.238 *et seq.*
5   Colonel Ryder was not knighted, as most post-war Surveyors General were. However, his son made up for this by winning the V.C. in the St. Nazaire raid in March 1942.

10 | Letters from Everest, 1922

We got here yesterday afternoon and all joined in a gigantic meal of beefsteak and onions at about 4 p.m. Heron came to see us shortly afterwards—he looks fit and cheerful, and doesn't seem to bear any malice at being turned down at the last moment though he is naturally disappointed. I'm going to tea with them this afternoon, and am dining this evening with the Cowans (forest-*wallah*) who live next door to the D.B.

We are dividing into two parties from here,[2] the same as they did last year. The two Bruces, Mallory, Norton and Noel all went on to Pedong this morning—the rest of us follow tomorrow. Each party is breakfasting with Dr. Graham before starting, and this morning at 9 we all attended the boy scout parade at the Homes, where Bruce delivered Baden-Powell's message and there was the usual battery of cameras to be faced. Mr. Reid, the Darjeeling stationmaster, has taken 5 days leave and come round here with us; he takes a great interest in the expedition.

At Phari we shall catch up the first party and all go on together after sorting the stores. I've distributed maps to everyone and have taken charge of the scientific apparatus, aneroids, thermometers, theodolite etc, which gives me some light occupation—otherwise I feel I might almost have stayed another day in Darjeeling with you, darling.

Pedong I.B.
Wed 29.3.22   5pm

Mr. Reid promised to give you a copy of the group-photo which he took at the Homes yesterday. We got here after an easy march of 14 miles, and Wakefield and myself have celebrated our emancipation from civilisation by getting Munir Khan to clip our heads all over. Somervell

EXCELSIOR ON ELUSIVE EVEREST
THE GREAT FEAT OF THE CLIMBERS

THE MEMBERS OF THE EXPEDITION AT DARJEELING BEFORE SETTING OUT FOR EVEREST

Front row, left to right : Finch, General Hon. C. G. Bruce, the leader, Strutt. Back row : Crawford, Norton, Mallory, Somervelle, Morshead, Wakefield. Mallory, Somervelle and Norton in first effort reached 26,800 feet ; Finch and Captain Bruce (not in this group), in second, 27,200; and Mallory, Somervelle and Wakefield, in third, are said to have got within a few hundred feet of summit.

Members of the 1922 Mount Everest Expedition

and I have been having lessons in Nepali from Morris this afternoon. I was surprised to find that both Somervell and Morris had been with the 46th Divn in France—S. in a field ambulance and M. in the 5th Leicesters. They had both been transferred elsewhere before I joined the Divn.

The others all had a large budget of English mail before leaving Kalimpong; there was nothing for me, as of course it would be addressed to Chevremont. It seems years already since I left you and I'm longing to hear what you have decided about moving in with Mrs. Seal at Catherine Villas. You might just let me know that you are getting my letters regularly, in case they take to going astray like last year. [This letter started *Meri Jan Khush Raho*, which means literally 'My Own Keep Happy for Life']

Sedongchen D.B.
Fri 31.3.22

It was along today's march that I lost that Rs. 90/- out of my pocket three months ago. [Between the two expeditions Henry was engaged in a programme of plumb-line deflection observations north of the main Himalayan range.] The marches have been rather hot and dusty, and I've been glad of my old thin khaki drill coat, but after today we shall be in higher & cooler country. Paul, the interpreter, has been in the doctor's (Somervell) hands since Kalimpong with conjunctivitis. Darling Evie, I'm longing for that letter which you were going to write the very day I left. I wonder if you have seen anything of Sir H. Hayden, and whether Gujjar Singh has left yet? I'd like to know what has finally been settled about his coolies.

There is a great *tamasha* going on just behind the bungalow, 3 or 4 lamas chanting prayers to avert the hailstorms to the usual accompaniment of drum, cymbals, rattle and trumpet, the latter made of human thigh-bone. Somervell, who is a very accomplished fellow, has been writing down the tunes of the lamas' chants in musical notation. Did you hear that old Raeburn has been off his head since his return to England last autumn? He is apparently under the delusion that he murdered Kellas!

Kapup D.B. (13,000 ft.)
Sun 2.4.22   5 p.m.

A short march of 4 miles today through flowering magnolia and rhododendrons. I wonder if the Bobrinskoys have returned yet and claimed their big box. I suppose Ruth[3] and Dor[3] have departed today? Please let the Gymkhana Club know that Ruth and I are not to be charged subscriptions after the end of March. I forgot to tell Mackenzie before leaving. Will you also ask Hari Singh to oil my gun and rifle frequently; your olive oil will do quite well, and he knows how to do it. This is a queer little oasis in the wilds—it contains only a *dak*-runners' hut, a public-house and this little 2-bedroomed *dak*-bungalow which 5 of us are sharing tonight.

Shasima, Chumbi valley
Mon 3.4.22   6 p.m.

Our wedding day—darling it's just ripping when entering that dangerous 6th year to find a letter waiting for me at the end of a long march.
We started at 7 a.m., crossed the Jelep La, the Gate of Tibet, and marched
through splendid country to Shasima (21 miles) where we caught up
Bruce & Co.

I got here by 1 o'clock, ahead of the others, and just in time to accept
an invite to lunch with the David Macdonalds who live here. Such an
odd mixture of East and West. *He* is ½ Scotch and ½ Tibetan, and his
wife is pure Nepali. There is a family of 9, of whom there were in evidence today 4 daughters ranging from 20 down to 2, and one son who has
just left St. Paul's school, Darjeeling, after 9 years there. The meal was in
Tibetan fashion, with chopsticks, & was followed by a Tibetan dance
lasting all the afternoon from which I've just returned.

Longstaff and Norton are just back from a day's naturalising, with a
collection of birds and tailless rats, which they are busy skinning—I
gather this was the chief reason for their halting here today. I'm glad to
have Hayden's[4] letter, and to know that Gujjar Singh's business is settled
all right. Macdonald is expecting them to pass through here in about
three days time, so we may meet at Phari. Bruce is writing to Bailey to
try and get permission for Noel to visit Gyangtse in July to take cine film
of devil-dances, and this may give me an opportunity of going too.

4.4.22 Strutt and I walked 5 or 6 miles up a side valley before lunch.
We are still among pines and birch trees, and that lovely daphne is still
in flower—not the Tiger Hill[5] variety, but the one which flowers without
any leaves. I like Strutt very much and have been seeing a lot of him, as
he and I usually share a room together. Your telegram sent from Darjeeling at 10.55 this morning reached me here at 11.30. Thank you so
much for it my darling, but I'm quite happy now that I'm getting your
letters. By all means send Ruth a cheque for her birthday, it was very nice
of you to think of it.

That's a gloomy prognostication in Gunter's[6] letter about the Survey
Dept. being gradually reduced to nothing in 10 years' time or so. Makes
it all the more important to hunt for a new job before one is turned forc-
ibly adrift into military duties, which is what I suppose will happen to
R.E.'s. I feel so strange without any definite job, it makes me miss you
more than ever, and when I become a soap-boiler in U.S.A. you are
coming to the works with me every day.

Gautsa D.B. (12,000 ft.)
Wed 5.4.22   6 p.m.

A ripping march of 11 miles today to this little spot where Longstaff and I then spent the afternoon trying for a pheasant on the hillside behind the bungalow. I met on the way one of the 4 English-educated Tibetans, the one trained in electrical engineering. He was going to Kalimpong to collect material for the telegraph line which he is going to extend from Gyangtse to Lhasa, at the request of the Tibetan Govt. I thought it a striking and welcome sign of the times in Tibet, and an apt commentary on Bell's idiotic policy of encouraging the Tibetans to persist in their isolation.

Phari (= Pigs hill)
Fri 7.4.22   10 a.m.

Your *first* letter reached me today though I got your two later letters 3 days ago! I sometimes wonder whether I wouldn't have been wiser to go with Bailey on his less ambitious trip to Bhutan.[7] However the die is cast now. I think there will be less risk of your letters going astray if you address them Mt. Evt. Expedn, c/o Postmaster, Phari; there is no need to register them.

I have paid Hari Singh up to end of April, and I'm asking Cowie to send his pay monthly direct from Dehra Dun, so unless Dehra Dun forgets (which they may do!) there should be no need for you to pay him at all. Today is General Bruce's 56th birthday and I believe we are going to celebrate the event by busting a bottle of 100-year old rum at dinner tonight! I must write to Cowie, Gunter and old Burrard.

I'm sending you Munir Khan's wrist watch—would you have it repaired and post it back to me please? He is a great favourite with the expedition, they all admire his manners.

Your ripping 'wedding day' letter has just arrived, and a roll of newspapers. I think, darling, it will be best to postpone the Pioneer advert for the motor bike [another non-starter] until I get back; Hiltons may have managed to dispose of it meantime. Today you will be moving into 2, Catherine Villas; I'm so glad you decided to go there, and hope the old girl's chatter won't be too distracting!

Camp, Anzang Trak
Mon 10.4.22 2.20 p.m.

We left Phari on 8th and marched 18 miles over bleak uninhabited country to a deserted grazing camp called Lungye; a driving snowstorm came on in the afternoon and we were scarcely able to make a yakdung fire for a cup of tea before turning in. We were all in bed by 6 p.m. The General had sent me on ahead to select the camping ground and was rather inclined to blame me for going too far, though everyone agreed there was no other place. However, I had my revenge yesterday when General Bruce announced that we would do a short march of 12 miles or so, and that he himself would go ahead and select the camping place. Accordingly we all started in a leisurely way about 9 a.m. expecting to reach the new camp by lunch time. On and on we went till after 5 p.m. Bruce had done 25 miles and 4 or 5 coolies have not come in yet! So today we are halting here while young Bruce goes back with a search party.

By the way, your parcels of papers are much appreciated in the mess, as Thacker Spinks have just written refusing to supply the papers which Bruce ordered unless 6 months subscripn. is paid in advance! So it will be several weeks before our regular papers start arriving. The mornings usually start bright and sunny but by 10 a.m. the sky clouds over and the usual howling Tibetan wind starts which lasts till sunset, and as often as not the afternoon ends in a snowstorm.

Munir Khan and General Bruce have just discovered that they have met before, in 1912—13, when M.K. was with Kenneth Mason and they stayed in Bruce's house in Abbottabad on the way to the Pamirs. Munir is looking rather rheumatic and has a cough, but professes to be all right. He rides most of the long marches, and shares a tent with Paul, the interpreter, whose eyes have now recovered. Munir produced your tin of home-made peppermints today from the bottom of my box, and the mess passed you a hearty vote of thanks.

Kampa Dzong
Wed 12.4.22

A jolly 21-mile march and the place feels quite like home to me. We stay here two days to allow the yaks with our heavy kit to catch up. I went over to see Kellas' grave before breakfast—it is quite well cared for. I have written a long letter to Col. Burrard and am sending it with this, by a Tibetan who happens to be leaving for Phari at 3 a.m. There is no sealed mail bag and he is only taking it as a favour.

Munir is busy clipping people's heads with my new shears. He cropped Wakefield (we've nicknamed him the Archdeacon!) and myself 10 days ago, now Mallory, Norton and Longstaff are being operated upon. Bruce is busy dictating his third despatch to Morris on the typewriter; he has been rather in the wars lately, the intense cold tickles up the old wound in his foot, and he also has a stiff knee.

14.4.22. Finch and Crawford joined us yesterday afternoon, having brought the old gas-apparatus along at record speed. They brought along a small budget of *dak*, including yours of the 4th. They overtook Hayden and Gujjar Singh in the Chumbi valley; the latter was travelling ahead and only missed me by one day at Phari, he sent me a note by Finch to say all was well.

Whether or not I shall return to Darjeeling with the expedition depends on Bailey's reply to my letter suggesting joining him at Gyangtse and accompanying him to Lhasa. We ought to have our plans ready in case I return any time after about 20th July. Would you like us to stay out our time at Chevremont on leave till we go home in October (I'd be quite happy reading my H.G. Wells & Einstein & working at Nepali) or would you like Dorothy Mason to get us diggs in Kashmir for Aug & Sep if we can wriggle out of Chevremont? Or would you rather we went straight home in the rains? Of course, darling, these are all castles in the air. The expedn *may* not return till October; my leave *may* not be granted for 18 months; I *may* end by going with Hazard to U.S.A. I feel I've been selfish in making plans to suit my own convenience and duty, and that it's your turn to have a say in making plans when we are on leave.

I've been reading the proofs of the Everest Book of 1921—Mallory has a number of chapters and Wollaston 2 chapters of natural history. This brings it to 300 pages. Then comes a mountaineering *shabash* by Norman Collie, presdt. of the Alpine Club. I understand that my, Wheeler's and Heron's reports are coming last of all in small print, as being too technical for the multitude. 'Malleroy' tells me that the book is already being translated into four European languages. You might instigate Kenneth Mackenzie to order a copy for the club and give you first *dekho* at it.

A noisy lama has been intoning prayers for our success in a corner of the compound all the morning—his monotonous chant drives me nearly silly. Bruce's despatch is just finished. I occasionally hear the quaintest things being dictated to Morris on the typewriter. The other day, in a letter to the R.G.S. he remarked that the had done 'everything possible to help the expedition forward, from interviewing the Viceroy to emptying the *po's* in a *dak* bungalow.' Can you imagine old Hinks,[8] who hasn't a grain of humour in his composition, rubbing his gold-rimmed spectacles in amazement as he reads out Bruce's despatches to the assembled committee?!

Tinki Dzong
Sun 16.4.22   6 p.m.

I enclose a cloth-mounted map with our proposed route pencilled on it for you to follow. Somervell's (32nd?) birthday is today and he produced a plum cake with almond icing for tea. If you happen to be writing to the Lewis', will you ask them whether their chalet in Switzerland would be available for rent next spring, say Feb to April. February is the best month for skiing. Monday, Longstaff is seedy today—I hope it is not the result of Somervell's cake! The coolies and Gurkha orderlies are having their first drill today in the use of the rope, under the supervision of Bruce and Mallory. Finch has been giving us a lecture on the use of the oxygen apparatus; we are to practise it every day from now onwards. Finch is a good fellow and I don't know how all those yarns about him originated last year. We all like him, and I personally consider him far more of a sahib than our local representative of the I.C.S.

Tuesday, Longstaff was too ill to travel this morning, so we practised some easy rock climbing on a cliff behind the monastery. It appears that last week's English mail was late, owing to having come in my old friend the P. & O. 'Dongola'. My last letter from you was dated a fortnight ago.

Our messing and transport are lavish compared with Bury's frugal methods on last year's trip. I'm sure there will never be enough money to last beyond July even if anyone wanted to do so. We are a very happy party, absolutely no jarring elements, and my only complaint is the extreme cold compared with last year. However, there is plenty of warm clothing which I can borrow[9] if necessary.

Gyangkar Nangpa
Thu 20.4.22

We are at a beastly windy spot near where I got that go of poisoning last year. Four enthusiasts are taking light tents and climbing the slopes of Sangkar Ri, the big hill, 20,400 ft., behind our camp. I was tempted to join them, but decided to stay in camp and nurse a sore heel, caused by wearing a pair of coolie-boots which I've cadged from the expedition.[10]

Darling, have you heard the story of the two ladies discussing House of Lords Reform 'Do you believe in a second chamber?' says no.1. 'Of course I do,' says no.2 'My husband is a liberal pe-er.' Bruce propounded this at breakfast.

Shekar Dzong
Mon 24.4.22

We have to wait here while the *Dzongpön* collects 300 yaks for us. He is most affable and obliging, and has been down here discussing plans with Bruce. He recognised me as an old friend of last year, and has invited any of us who like to breakfast with him tomorrow at 11. Munir has been having a go of fever and has had to ride the last three marches, but he is better today. Bruce's present idea is for Strutt, Mallory and myself to reconnoitre the E. Rongbuk glacier & select sites for the two intermediate camps on the way to the North Col (Chang La on Wheeler's map).

If this leave is granted I'd like to go to Canada for the Can. Alpine Club camp in the Rockies during the last half of July '23. It's a social sort of gathering which I think we'd both enjoy together (the Wheelers are sure to be there) and we could join the Hazards afterwards in U.S.A. on our way back to India. The only difficulty seems to be Owen who will inevitably be due to arrive about 1st May '23 as far as I can see! [It was not a bad guess; Owen, their third child, arrived on 4 June '23.]

After the climbing Mallory and I have a scheme for crossing the Arun at Kharta and thence making for Tashirak by a pass near Ama Drime. Then I would either join Bailey, or try and get permission to cross the Kang La into the Walung district of Nepal, whence one would join Freshfield's route W. of Kangchenjunga and back to Darjeeling in about 10 days. I've been developing a spool of Kodak film which has come out well. Noel tells me that each member will be given an album of the best photographs, so I shan't take any more. It seems such a long month since I left you in Darjeeling—we really must marry and settle down after this trip!

Rongbuk Base Camp, 16,500 ft.
Mon 1.5.22

We are camped 12 miles from the top of Everest at the highest point to which transport animals can get up the Rongbuk valley, a mile below the snout of the great Rongbuk glacier. From here we push forward using our own coolie-power. The next two months are going to provide a pretty stiff test of patience and endurance for all of us, but what does it matter darling, when I'm going to be back again in your arms before the end of July? It is still early in the year for high climbing; there were 23° of frost last night and the streams are frozen almost solid. I shall have about 10 days work in Darjeeling packing up kit from the *khamal*, and then I must go to Dehra for 10 days to get some kit for going home in. I don't see why we should not sail from Bombay before the end of August.

Tuesday. We drank Bruce's health in a mouthful of champagne last night for having brought this huge caravan in safety to the base camp on the appointed day. Today we had a 'Europe morning', breakfast 9 o'clock. Strutt, Norton and Finch are just off to reconnoitre the road to no.1 advanced camp. I'm lending Munir our green eiderdown for the higher camps and I shall use the sleeping bag and Hudson Bay blankets provided by the expedition—also a pair of moccasins. I think darling this must really be my last big expedish away from you. The others don't seem to mind the absence of mails half as much as I do, though Mallory's last news from his home was dated 9th March.

10.5.22. Got back yesterday after 4 days reconnaissance with Strutt & Norton, laying out advanced camps between here and the foot of the N. col. A coolie met us on the way down yesterday with mails, the first *dak* since leaving Kampa Dz.! Five letters from you (7–18 April) with heaps of enclosures, also a fortnight's *Statesman* which Mallory had wisely opened and distributed to the mess.

A letter from Bailey says that he has got permish from Lhasa for my triangulation up the Phari-Gyangtse road, and I've written to Cowie suggesting I cancel my leave & spend the cold weather doing pendulum observns. in Sikkim and finishing the △n, which I was unable to complete last winter. We could keep on Chevremont, and Ruth could rejoin us if she liked and stay and look after the babies while you came to camp with me. I've asked Cowie to write direct to you, so that you may know whether to keep on Chevremont for the winter. Darling, I do hope you won't mind this change of plans after the castles which I built in my last letter about going home this very August; but you know how keen I am about finishing off this business before we leave these parts, and darling, wouldn't it be rather ripping to go home with our three (?!) babies in Aug '23.

Munir's watch has come back; the parcel had had a ducking in some river en route, but the water does not seem to have penetrated its guts. I hope your mother's next letter will be more cheerful, she certainly seems overworked. Old Park is really surpassing himself for inefficiency this year; all sorts of letters intended for residents of Darjeeling are being re-addressed here. A mysterious parcel reached me with the sender's address obliterated by its ducking in the river; it turns out to be not for me at all, but a present from the manufacturers, of a square of white pegamoid waterproof sheeting for use as a tablecloth by the expedition.

Mallory and Somervell have started off up the line which we have just reconnoitred; they are going a stage further, to the summit of the North Col. I expect Norton & I will join them in 3 or 4 days time. Poor old Longstaff is no longer the man for these altitudes; he insisted on accompanying Strutt, Norton and myself, but the height and the cold (37° of frost at night) were too much for him and 4 coolies had to fetch him down on a stretcher. I'm horribly afraid of another Kellas case, unless the General insists on his staying down at base. It's a pity that people cannot learn that Himalayan mountaineering is a young man's game; I'm going to give it up myself when I'm 40! [In 6 months time. Shri Tenzing Norgay was 39 when he reached the summit in 1953.]

13.5.22 11 a.m. Strutt, Norton and I are going up the line again tomorrow to join Mallory & Somervell who ought to have established a camp on the North Col by the time we reach them. The weather continues fine though we are getting 25° of frost at night even at base camp, and the wind is damnable all day long, filling one's tent and bedding with dust and litter.

Almost the whole party, except Bruce, Wakefield and myself, have been indulging in stomach troubles; Finch is quite bad and has had to spend several days in bed which is a poor way of training for a high climb. Paul has turned out quite O.K. as interpreter. I've just had my head cropped short for the last time. We want to find a 5th camping place half-way up to the N.E. shoulder at about 25,000 ft., from which one might rush to the summit and back in a day. The N.E. shoulder is just one mile from the summit.

14.5.22 8 a.m. No mail arrived; we are just starting, so must leave this with Bruce to be posted at next opportunity. I shan't have a chance of writing again until I come down to the base for a rest, which may be some while if all goes well.

(From Dr. Tom G. Longstaff)   *Rongbuk Base Camp, 16,500 ft.*
                                               28 May 1922

We are all so sorry that your husband is frostbitten after his magnificent climb to 25,000 feet. I do not think there will be any permanent injury, but it is impossible to be certain. The worst that can happen is the loss of one second toe and the tips of some fingers—*not* the first ones. You may rest assured that I will do everything I possibly can, but at the same time that is very little. I fear he is suffering a lot of pain at present, but he never complains. Yet this is a good sign, the best, of returning vitality.

Major Norton says he was extraordinarily plucky coming down. Norton, Mallory & Somervell were all more or less frostbitten also. It was the wind.

Although he is in no danger, I think it best to bring him back to Darjeeling as soon as we can collect the transport animals. I hope to arrive during the first week of July, but you must not count on this. I have not tried to spare your feelings, but have rather put things at their worst possible. General Bruce thought I ought to write to you, but pray do not be in the least alarmed. I think on the whole he would get better more quickly in your care than mine.

(Written by Karma Paul)   *3 June 1922*

Madame, My best respects to Mrs. Morshead, K. Paul has to write my letter as my fingers are still tied up; they are going on quite well however, and my left hand will soon be out of bandages. I am going to lose the top joints of the middle fingers of my right hand, but you wouldn't divorce me for a little thing like that would you?

Finch & Geoffrey Bruce have also had a shot at the mountain, using oxygen; they camped near our high camp, and reached a height of 27,200 ft. Bruce had three toes badly frostbitten which adds another to our list of invalids. Today the remaining fit climbers, Mallory, Somervell and Finch, are starting for a third and final attempt. [Mallory and Somervell had had only 10 days rest, Finch only 5.] The weather has turned very monsoonish & I doubt whether they will have much more luck than before.

Strutt, Longstaff and myself are starting for Darjeeling tomorrow. I will send a wire from Gangtok to say when I am arriving. I am feeling very fit and well in spite of being temporarily incapacitated by this jolly old frostbite.

MOUNT EVEREST EXPEDITION.

May. 28. 1922.

Dear Mr Morshead,

I don't know what Henry may have told you about ~~himself~~ our climb; he is rather down on himself. But we who were his companions realise that it may happen to anyone to find himself not strong enough physically for a supreme effort of that sort & we have nothing but admiration for his courage & fine spirit in adversity — He was simply splendid we all say.

I think he would have quite recovered from the strain] now if it were not for his fingers. As it is he seems a bit run down; but I very much hope we shall bring him back to you as fit as when he started.

Ever yrs very sincerely,

George Mallory

Letter from George Mallory to Evie

(From General Bruce) 4 June 1922

I am afraid we are sending Major Morshead back in a sad way. As you know he got caught by the frost on the great attempt on May 21st, and had to stay in the tent at 25,000 ft. where they camped. This was much the highest camp ever established.[11] Dr. Somervell assures me that although he must lose the tops of two or three fingers, yet that he will be able to write as well as ever. He is so full of cheer that he will get through this terrible time much better than others. He leaves with Dr. Longstaff and Strutt the day after tomorrow.

In his book, *The Assault on Mount Everest, 1922*, Bruce described the first attempt on the mountain, made by the party consisting of Mallory, Somervell, Morshead and Norton, as a *tour de force*, a tremendous effort unparalleled in mountain exploration. Two laden journeys were made to the North Col, with a day's rest in between. Mallory sensibly wore two felt hats against the glare of the morning sun; Strutt and Somervell also had headgear, while Morshead, Norton and the porters had no special protection.

Mallory has in his section of the book an amusing account of Henry's achievements as a cook. He invented a stew based on tins of army and navy rations, which he called 'hoosch', and adopted as his motto that the foundation of every dish must be pea soup. It followed that any and every available solid food might be used to stew with pea soup. Some solids were found less suitable by experience than others, and there is even a hint that Henry's flotsam and jetsam was not always palatable. Nevertheless, it was 'hoosch' that they ate at Camp IV on the afternoon of the 19th May. They were able to make a start at 7.30 next day. From Mallory's account:[12]

'Morshead, who by the testimony of good spirits seemed the fittest of us all, was set to lead the party; I followed with two porters, while Norton and Somervell shepherded the others on a separate rope... The air remained perceptibly colder than we could have wished; the sun had less than its usual power; and in the breeze which sprang up on our right, we recognised an enemy, the devastating wind of Tibet... Remembering bitter experiences down in the plains 10,000 feet below us, we expected little mercy here.

We had risen about 1,200 feet when we stopped to put on the spare warm clothes which we carried against such a contingency as this. For my part, I added a light shetland woolly and a thin silk shirt...and with these two extra layers I feared no cold we were likely to meet. Morshead, if I remember right, troubled himself no more than to wrap a woollen scarf round his neck, and he and I were ready and impatient to get off before the rest.'

As they prepared to rope up, Norton's rucksack got knocked over and they watched spellbound as it gathered momentum in lengthening bounds down to the Rongbuk Glacier. A number of offers in woollen garments for the night were soon made to Norton; Mallory's own pyjama-legs had been in the rucksack as well. The clothing comforts that each had brought were a matter of personal choice; Morshead's consisted of what he had been able to buy in the local Darjeeling bazaar. He eventually stopped and put on a sledging suit; but he had left it too late.

It is probable that he was already frostbitten when they pitched camp, on a stony slope of 30 degrees, and sent the porters down at 3 p.m. Mallory and Norton shared one double sleeping bag, Somervell and Morshead the other. 'Wherever we lay,' Somervell recalled many years later, in his own book, *After Everest*, 'and in whatever position, there were always a few sharp stones sticking into the tenderest parts of our anatomy. We obtained sleep in snatches of the most fitful and unresting variety, so much so that on the following morning we were quite glad to get up and stand on our less tender feet.'

Mallory: 'I do not propose to emphasise the agonies of an early start or to catalogue all that may be found for fumbling fingers to do; but one incident is worth recording. A second rucksack escaped us, and went bounding down the mountain. Its value, even Norton will agree, was greater than that of the first; it contained our provisions; our breakfast was inside it... Somehow or another it was hung up on a ledge 100 feet below. Morshead volunteered to get it. By slow degrees he dragged up the heavy load, and our precious stores were recovered intact. At 8 a.m. we were ready to start and roped up, Norton first, followed by myself, Morshead and Somervell.'

Somervell:[13] 'We had gone only a hundred yards or so when Morshead announced that he was not feeling at all well, and could not come with us. We knew him...well enough to realise that if he complained of his health he must feel pretty bad; so we went on without him, leaving him to go back to his tent and there to await our return.'

Henry's breakdown could not be said to have robbed the other three of a chance to reach the summit; another camp would have been necessary for that; and all three climbed even higher in 1924. It was, however, in the knowledge that he would have to be got back to Camp IV on the North Col by nightfall, that the climbers turned back at just under 27,000 ft. and, at 4 p.m., reached Henry, who pronounced himself fit to descend.

Inactivity had probably worsened his condition and shortly afterwards, both accounts agree, the third man on the rope slipped. They are too polite to say who it was, but it was clearly Morshead. Somervell, marvellous anchor-man that he was, was caught off balance and Norton could only check their combined weight for a moment. Yet it was long enough for Mallory's quick reflexes. He drove in the pick of his axe, hitched the rope round, and, leaning with his whole weight into the slope, held all three. Somervell:

> 'From then onwards we were much more cautious. This was undoubt-edly necessary, for Morshead, though he stoutly endeavoured to appear normal, was obviously getting worse every minute, and we soon dis-covered that he had hardly the strength to walk. He kept suggesting a glissade, which might have spelt disaster to him, if not to us all. We had to use every possible persuasion to keep him moving and using his legs... It was now dark and we were still some distance from the tents on the Col. A jump of 10 feet down an ice-cliff was successfully nego-tiated, Morshead being lowered on the rope. On we went through deeper snow, pushing and pulling our invalid, who persisted that he was all right, but was obviously not far from death... Fortunately we all real-ised it, or we might have been just a little careless or thoughtless, and given death the victory.'

They reached the tents of Camp IV by about 11.30 p.m., but their troubles were not over. By an incredible misunderstanding they found the camp unmanned, the stove and fuel removed and not a living soul nearer than Camp III. Without liquid to drink, or the means to melt snow, the food was useless to their dehydrated bodies.

With Norton giving Henry the support of his shoulder and an arm round his waist, Mallory leading and Somervell as rearguard, they somehow reached Camp III at noon next day through a foot of fresh snow.

Had Henry been foolhardy, or risked lives other than his own? His companions do not appear to have thought so, even if one discounts the obituarist. Thus Colonel Norton, who led the 1924 expedition and stood alone at 28,126 ft., in the *Alpine Journal* for November, 1931:

> 'Equable and easy to get on with, modest and unselfish to a fault... his great heart constantly urged him to volunteer for every enterprise, yet he 'played for his side' first and foremost. But his two most outstanding qualities were physical hardness and courage: I never met a harder man.

I have two companion pictures of him : first, climbing on a stifling afternoon of damp heat the 4,000 ft. from the Teesta valley to Kalimpong without a halt; secondly leading the party through a 25-mile day over three 18,000 ft. passes in that bleak upland that separates the Tuna plain from Kampa Dzong, with his shirt open to the dreadful Tibetan wind—a heartbreaking man to live with. He seemed oblivious to heat, cold or discomfort, and it was probably only his neglect of almost elementary precautions against cold which led to his breakdown on the mountain.

My tent was pitched beside his and I fancy I was the only member of the party, barring doctors, who realised what he suffered for I could hear him groaning in the night; the moment he emerged from his tent he was his normal cheery self, bearing at least his share of the conversation. . . He was the ideal companion in a tight place, ideal in the mess tent when the day's troubles were over.'

Bruce did not rule out the necessity of an operation on the march home; and Colonel E.L. Strutt, Deputy Leader of the expedition, describes how Dr. Longstaff, Finch and himself brought Morshead back to Darjeeling:

'The long trek of some 400 miles—going our hardest we took 19 days without a rest—must have been agony. He was laid back on a Tibetan saddle on a rough pony, his frostbitten feet stretched out before him in improvised stirrups and his mutilated hands strapped to his shoulders. We were short of animals and porters and Morshead had to walk over several 18,000 ft. passes inaccessible to a laden pony. No one heard a word of complaint; with his knowledge of Tibetan, he was not even a 'passenger'.

Cheery as ever, his one idea was to be fit enough, fingers or no fingers, toes or no toes, to act as transport officer to the 1924 expedition! I know what a blow it was to him when the Mt. Everest Committee reluctantly but wisely refused his once invaluable proffered services. He was elected to the Alpine Club on a purely Himalayan, but almost unrivalled qualification, not so much as a climber as, what is far more, a great mountain-explorer.'

Without wishing to wallow in this episode, the story would not be complete without giving Morshead's own account, published in the *Royal Engineers Journal* for September, 1923:

'The onset of a blizzard at midday compelled us hurriedly to camp and send the coolies back to the North Col. The hillside was composed of flat slabs of rock, the strata having an outward (northerly) dip; and it

MOUNT EVEREST STILL UNCONQUERED

SEVENTEEN HUNDRED FEET TO COMPLETE THE TASK

HEIGHTS so far attained are shown in this DIAGRAM

EVEREST 29,002
+Highest Point reached by
EXPEDITION, June
1922

KABRU
23,800
+ Scaled by
Graham in
1883 and by
Rubenson
& MonradAas
later

GODWIN AUSTEN
28,265 +

GURLA MANDHATA
25,850

KAMET 25,500
TRISSUL +
23,382 + Reached by
Scaled by Dr Kellas &
Dr Longstaff Major Marshead
in 1920

Highest reached 24,600 +
by Duke of the Abruzzi
in 1909

Highest Point 24,000
reached by
Dr Longstaff

30,000 ft.

MT McKINLEY
20,464
+ Scaled by
Lloyd's Exped.n
in 1910

+ ELBRUZ
18,470
Scaled by
D. Freshfield
in 1868

25,000 ft

ACONCAGUA
23,080
+

CHIMBORAZO
20,496
+ Scaled by
Whymper
1879-80

Scaled in 1897
by Zurbriggen
& Stuart Vines

SNOWDON 3,560
for comparison

SEA LEVEL

A N D E S   A L A S K A   C A U C A S U S   K A R A K O R U M   Western H I M A L A Y A Eastern

Heights in FEET

G.F.MORRELL

Panorama of notable ascents up to and including 1922

was a matter of some difficulty to scarp out with our ice axes a couple of level terraces sufficient to hold our two small mountain tents. We spent a tolerably comfortable night, the temperature dropping to −20°F. Next day broke fine and we were roped up ready to start by 7.30 a.m. The first hundred yards sufficed to assure me that for some reason I had not that day the pace of my companions, so rather than keep them back, I felt my duty was to unrope, leaving them to carry out their climb untrammelled. In the result, while I remained smoking my pipe in camp, they attained a height of 26,850 ft., just below the north-east shoulder and within a mile of the summit.

It was about 4 p.m. when Mallory and his two companions rejoined me. Instead of benefiting from my day of idleness, my incapacity had now become almost complete; and, leaning on their arms, I could scarcely find the energy to descend the easy slopes up which I had gaily led on the rope less than 36 hours previously. It was 10 or 11 p.m. and pitch dark when we reached the shelter of the North Col camp, too tired even to hunt out some supper.

Next morning, as we made our way down towards Camp III, we met Finch, Geoffrey Bruce and Tejbir starting on their high climb, with oxygen masks already adjusted and in use. They were being accompanied for the first few miles by Dr. Wakefield who carried a thermos flask filled with hot tea and brandy which remains one of the happiest recollections of my life. Shortly afterwards, we came to a trickle of water which had been melted by the midday sun.

Lying prone, I lapped and lapped until I had absorbed perhaps a quart of this icy beverage. At once my strength returned, and I realised that my whole trouble had been due to the lack of sufficient liquid at the high altitudes. All four of us proved to have been more or less frost-bitten; in the case of Mallory and Somervell the damage was limited to a few skin blisters on the extremities. Norton's beauty has been permanently impaired by the loss of the top of one of his ears, and I had to undergo, five months afterwards, the amputation of the top joints of three fingers of my right hand.'

Major Gen. W.H. Ogilvie, whose name appears in the Chevremont visitors' book between the two expeditions, wrote in the *Royal Engineers Journal*: 'Morshead told the writer that in his opinion the frostbite was due to unsuitable clothing; he received permission to join the expedition so late that there was no time to get proper kit from home, and he had to set off with what could be found in the Darjeeling bazaar. Characteristically, he considered the damage to his hand a smaller loss than the failure to reach the summit.'

Seeing the expedition off to England from Darjeeling station. Henry, on right, has his frostbitten hands and feet hidden

Henry's theory about dehydration had the support of medical opinion. Somervell may have drunk less of that icy water, but he admitted drinking seventeen large cups of tea without stirring from his seat.

Henry continued his correspondence with Hinks of the R.G.S., using Evelyn as his scribe in several long letters. 'I may be home on leave this winter,' he wrote, 'but I shall not come unless my fingers are sufficiently recovered to fire a gun by 1 October. If I am still crippled I propose returning to duty and letting the Govt. of India share my misfortune.' Before the end of October he had returned to duty in Dehra Dun.

He declined Hinks' efforts to persuade him to address the Society on the 'difficulties of surveying in the Mount Everest region.' 'The Everest expedition,' he replied, 'produced no new or startling developments in the art or practice of surveying—the ¼-inch general map was a perfectly normal example of plane-tabling in a hilly country such as we get any year in India, while Wheeler's detailed survey was done by a method 30 years out of date which one doesn't desire to immortalise. I really don't feel that there is anything more to be said on the subject beyond what Wheeler and I wrote for the 1921 volume & I'm sure nobody wants to have that over again "viva voce".'

Notes

1   *Dak* (= Post) Bungalow. Holiday trekkers in Sikkim could book them in advance. Stephen Lyttelton used tell how, in the visitors' book at Tonglu (10,074 ft.), someone had written: 'My only complaint is that the privy is too far from the bungalow'. Below this someone had added 'Sir, you should start sooner'.

2   Because accommodation in the *dak* bungalows was limited.

3   Ruth was Henry's unmarried sister; she was capable of out-trekking most men. Dorothy was Kenneth Mason's wife. Count and Countess Bobrinskoy were Russian émigrés on tour in Sikkim.

4   At the request of the Tibetan Government, Sir H.H. Hayden and Surveyor Gujjar Singh, accompanied by a Tibetan official, were off on a five-month journey in Central and South-Eastern Tibet to examine the mineral resources of the area and make further maps.

5   Tiger Hill, 8,482 ft., a seven mile trek out of Darjeeling, is where the energetic may go to observe the sunrise on Everest.

6   Colonel C.P. Gunter, C.I.E., O.B.E., died in 1965, aged 83.

7   Permission to go with Bailey to Bhutan arrived *after* the expedition had left Darjeeling, '. . . but you have a good companion in Meade' wrote Henry to Bailey.

8   A.R. Hinks, Secretary to the R.G.S. and to the Everest Committee. Two years later he was to cross swords with F.M. Bailey, Resident in Sikkim, who correctly maintained that some of Noel's films of lamas dancing, to Somervell's music, were giving offence in Lhasa. Hinks made the *amende honorable*, however, and apologised on behalf of the Committee to all concerned.

9   In view of what happened later the word 'borrow' is significant.

10   One would have thought it essential to have one's own footwear.

11   In 1965, the successful Indian expedition camped at 27,930 ft.

12   *Ibid.*, p.185 *et seq.*

13   *After Everest*, p.64 *et seq.*

11 | Bangalore in '24

When, in February 1923, Henry took his long-planned leave (7½ months on average pay) there was no more talk of expeditions for the time being. The predicted third son was born at 15 Quarry Street, Guildford, and the summer was spent quietly in Cornwall. Henry was on the platform at the Kelly College Founder's Day and Prizegiving, where he presented the O.T.C. Drill Cup and gave a talk to the boys about mountains.

Joining the P. & O. 'Morea' at Marseilles on 28 September, the family were back in Bombay by 12 October, and made the two-day train journey to the city of Bangalore where he was to take up his new appointment. The children lost no time in renaming the place Bang-the-door.

Three years of station life lay ahead, with Henry firstly in charge of No.7 (Topographical) Party, and later Superintendent, Southern Circle Office of the Survey of India. With the aid of Evelyn's diary it is possible to build up a picture of the busy social whirlpool of Bangalore City in the middle 'twenties. Their first house was at 14 Spencer Road, but with Henry's promotion they moved into a more spacious house at 4 Palace Road rented from the Allens. 'Went to see about the new bungalow being whitewashed, hiring of furniture, and a loader and trolley to move our goods and chattels.'

Henry played some form of sport every day, usually hockey, tennis or golf. The Survey Offices, which were a three-mile walk from his home, had their own adjacent hockey ground, and several times a week there would be regimental matches at home or away. His missing finger-tips presented no obstacle to him. I was more concerned about them myself than he was: 'Shall I run and look in the toybox in the nursery and see if they are there Daddy—then we'll stick them on and they'll never come off any more.'

With the 1924 Everest Expedition getting under way, he was finding it hard to forget his non-involvement. It was not the Committee who had declined his services. On the contrary, they pressed him to take part as Transport and Base Camp Officer; he offered to take leave without pay.

Henry as Superintendent, Southern Circle, Survey of India, with his staff, Bangalore

'You should join not later than 20th March. Acknowledge', ran Bruce's tantalising telegram, only to be overridden the next day by one from a harassed Surveyor General, refusing to spare him; several officers had already been refused even ordinary leave.

A consolation prize arrived shortly afterwards by registered post in the form of a handsome silver-gilt Olympic medal, which had been awarded to each of the 1922 climbers, the first ever awarded for mountaineering; and the news that he had been elected a member of the Royal Central Asian Society.

With three children and their social engagements, as well as the official and private entertaining expected of her, Evelyn led a busy and full life. Twenty-eight children came to Owen's first birthday party. With parents, ayahs and chauffeurs, sixty-eight people had tea. A few days later it was Mrs. Wright's children's party at the Central Hotel. Mrs. Wright raised the ante by providing toys, sweets *and* the town band.

Comments Evie: 'We found the children were quite as happy when they simply played in the garden; our children's toys, old as they were, coming as novelties to them.' There is no doubt that the children were over-indulged. It was always some child's birthday, and hospitality had to be

Hugh and Ian, Bangalore

returned; or failing that, there might be a party at the Residency. The Bingham's party had to be held indoors. It appears that on that occasion I was wicked and came home in disgrace. I offer Mrs. Bingham my belated apologies, and distinctly remember parking one right in the middle of her floor. Frankly, I did not think anyone had seen me do it. With all those ayahs and nannies around, I was soon boarded and was lucky not to find myself back in nappies again.

The most sensational party was a joint one given by Mrs. Pender and

Mrs. Shackleton, which featured a whole toy train fixed to the rear of Captain Shackleton's car, which he dragged round and round the drive filled with children, the two fathers dressed up as costers and distributing toys from the train. 'I loved that party and that kind auntie', said one of us: 'She gave us such nice presents.'

Henry gave a public lecture on Mount Everest at the suburb of Malleswaram, with the Rajah of Nepal presiding. This was followed by another to the Mythic Society at which the lantern overheated and some of the slides started to bubble. About three hundred people turned up to each, and he spoke extemporaneously. The idea was soon seized upon by all classes of the community and Henry found himself in the middle of a series that ran to twenty lectures in two months. The proceeds, of up to Rs. 400 a time, went half towards the Everest Expedition Expenses, no part of which was paid for by the Government of India, as Henry pointed out, and half to the Y.W.C.A. of which Evie was President of the St. John's Branch.

St. Joseph's College, Baldwin Boys High School, Bishop Cotton Girls School, St. John's School, 'a large Indian school', the Y.M.C.A., the Club, the Electric Theatre and the various regiments all had their lecture. A private one was given at the Palace for the Maharajah of Mysore, the Maharani of Cooch Behar and the Palace children, Henry suggesting Rs. 150 for the Funds; they gave 200.

For two of his lectures he had the assistance of Dr. Somervell, who brought a Sherpa with him direct from Everest, and of Jack Hazard, who had both come to tell Henry at first hand about the 1924 expedition and the loss of Mallory and Irvine. Hazard nearly missed his train to Bombay when Henry's car would not start.

The Polo Finals, in which the Mysore Lancers beat the Q.V.O. Madras Sappers and miners, was followed by the V—VI Dragoons' At Home; the R.A. Sports by a Fancy-Dress Dance at the Club, with dresses and smocks run up by the *dirzi* in a day. A set of loose covers for the car could also be measured, made and delivered within 24 hours. Sometimes it was Dinner & Vingt-et-un at home ('I'm afraid I won Rs. 5/- off my guests'). The tempo increases, and Evie has a 'shingle' haircut, as the Season builds up to its climax with Planters' Week and the Planters' Ball. The Races, the Horse Show, the Polo Tournament, Investitures, dances at Flagstaff House, the Tata Institute and the West End Hotel are all jammed in; and somehow there is still time for the Maharajah of Mysore's At Home, the Tank Corps Concert, tennis at the Bowring Institute, 'A film called 'The Gold Rush', not to mention the Sappers and Miners' own Mess Night; and, darling, we must try and attend the 'Farewell to the Wiltshires'.'

Suddenly, it all seems to be rather too much. 'Too many social engagements, and listless with the heat', reads one June entry and I for one am not surprised.

The conversation at the Club is of poor (Revd.) Mr. Jervis who had been mauled by a tiger near Shimoga and died two days later; and of poor Mr. Bostock who had been killed at Polo in Mysore in Birthday Week. The Club Bridge Drive was in aid of Central Church Funds: 'We both lost, and the Funds gained accordingly; but it was a very badly managed entertainment with awful muddles over the scoring.'

Evelyn did not like 'hen parties', but occasionally allowed herself to be roped in to tea at the Zenana Mission House or the Sisters' Quarters at the Station Hospital. She also held a weekly Open House Social at her home for the Y.W.C.A. girls to conduct their country dancing and other classes; exhibited her own water-colour sketches at the Mayo Hall Arts Exhibition, judged classes at the Flower Show and gave away school prizes. Cook's accounts, *dhobi* accounts and general household accounts needed seeing to, and kerosene had to be sprayed on all the tanks to keep down the mosquitoes. Cubbon Park and the Lalbagh were the places to take the children to play in the cool of the evening.

Sometime during all this, a General Strike was taking place back in England. Its effects were not felt in Bangalore; but flexibility was necessitated on other counts.

A sudden terrific storm could prolong an afternoon tennis party into a late bridge and dinner party. Once, their canvas-roofed car had broken down in pelting rain on the way home from one of Henry's lectures. They arrived home to find their drive already full of cars which had brought their ten dinner guests, and 'they received me, in a hat and very wet, instead of me receiving them'. It was not for nothing that those old houses were built with a large colonnaded porch.

'Five guests failed through illness' reflects a different, but ever-present hazard. Fever could strike swiftly, and a temperature of 103.8° would prevent the jolliest guest from turning out. At other times it was a sheer surfeit of engagements. Even by the racy standards of the roaring 'twenties my parents thought that one young subaltern had overstepped the mark when he replied to one of their formal At Home invitations: 'Ta muchly for kind invite—Sorry to disappoint you.'

For about ten days in each month Henry would be away in camp, or on tour. He was liable to leave, or arrive back, at any hour of the day or night with little or no notice. Occasionally, he too went after big game at Shimoga: 'Henry got a panther and a barking deer.' At 10 st. 12 lbs. he carried no surplus flesh, and worked and played hard. He arranged and held a Survey course for gunner officers; and by way of a contrast he joined the 2nd Highland Light Infantry for a refresher course of military duties. The latter meant an invitation to yet another regimental At Home, this one complete with Highland Games.

Once, when Henry's tour was going to take two months, Evie took the three children, and the fourth that was on the way, across to Ootacamund to stay with her tea-planting brother-in-law. Henry drove over to fetch them all back, with the following result: 'Hal thought to try a new road back, seemingly twenty miles shorter, though it eventually made us nearly three hours later than we should have been—an awful road which went on for thirty miles and then suddenly brought us by a hidden turning to the edge of a river, the Kabbani! It was neck high and we debated what to do as it was getting late, and a long way back to the main road. An old Muslim told us we could cross on what looked a very insecure raft made of bamboos tied together. With difficulty we ran the car on to it, and were afraid it might slip; but we finally got across with the axles in the water, and had great difficulty at the other side too.'

When Evelyn went to Madras by herself for three days break she enjoyed every minute of it, but it seemed like three weeks away from the family. She was favourably surprised on arriving back at 6 a.m. to find that 'Hal had the children up and dressed to meet me. He has thought of everything'. Likewise, when the Surveyor General, Colonel E.A. Tandy, arrived for several days of inspection Henry turned out his whole Department to the railway station, and the surprised S.G. was caught still in his pyjamas. A day or two later Evie's At Home 'To meet the Surveyor General' offered tennis, badminton, bridge and clock golf.

On a tour of nearly four weeks Evie left her children with Nanny Bullen and accompanied Henry. They went by Henry's car, so she was taking a considerable risk. They stayed at Seringapatam Travellers' Bungalow (no mattresses) and saw the Dowlat Bagh, the Summer Palace and the tombs of Hyder Ali and Tipu Sultan. In the beautiful city of Mysore (under canvas) they were invited to the Maharajah's Durbar. The bouquet of roses and maidenhair fern is still in the back of her diary. In Mercara they were guests of Colonel and Mrs. Bucknall.

'Mercara is just over 4,000 feet up and the road twists and turns in hairpin bends all the way. We arrived at Peremboo Colly Estate at 2 o'clock and found the Bucknalls were waiting lunch for us. They are the Trelawny's successors and have a boy of fifteen who has never been to school. We stayed on to tea, and then found the car would not start. We pushed it down the steep hill from the estate to the main road, but it would not go even after that. It was now dark, so we had to leave that wicked Morris-

Cowley and go back and ask hospitality of the Bucknalls for the night. We climbed up the hill again and felt rather foolish as we had no evening kit with us and of course, as luck would have it, the Bucknalls had people to dinner.

We got up early and soon after seven, while we were wondering whether to get a car out from Mercara to tow us away, we heard a car arriving and were astonished to see young Wuzzie Bucknall driving it up himself! He had traced the trouble to a speck of dirt in the magneto and got her to go, good lad.'

On their return Evie found that a parcel had arrived from her mother with linen frocks, and sweets, crackers and toys for the children. She set to, and wrote twenty-four Christmas letters to England, posting them on 27 November. They were full of the childrens' sayings and doings. 'Nanny, what big legs you've got—just like the garden roller (a small stone one)', was my tactless contribution. English nannies were in short supply, and more than once Evelyn was told to 'get herself another nanny', although there was usually a reconciliation before it came to this.

At Christmas the casuarina made a passable Christmas tree, its clusters of elongated needles looking like ladies' hair, and there were usually several private ones, as well as a large one at the Cantonment Orphanage, which Evie and her Y.W.C.A. girls used to decorate. The West End Hotel, opposite the Race Course, was the smart place to dine out and dance; and the Amateur Dramatic Society put on competent performances of *Carmen*, *The Young Generation* and Barrie's latest play *Mary Rose*.

In 1925 and 1926 Henry hunted regularly with the Bangalore Hounds, a pack recently started by Captain Bert Buckley of the Inniskillings. The season ran from May right through to February, and a picture in the album shows a Lawn Meet at the Residence of Rajkumar C. Desaraj Urs, a near relative of the Maharajah of Mysore. The hill jackal used to give very long points, and the *Madras Mail* described a typical morning:

'7th milestone, Dumlur Road, Sunday. Scent today was first-rate and we seem to be getting back to last year's form. In the casuarina below Vibhutipore hounds opened on a line but were probably running it heel way as it came to nothing. Back across the valley they opened again once or twice before reaching a casuarina just below the brow of the hill near Channapanhalli. In this they opened with a crash of music, and a jack was viewed close in front of them. They ran down towards Vibhutipore and 'Tatler' nearly rolled him over. He now turned up hill again past the covert we had found him in, then left-handed through a mango *tope*.

In this they put up a second jack and running together they took hounds into the casuarina to the north. Here the pack divided, 10½ couple taking the hunted jack away over the open towards Garuda-charpalya and 7 couple taking the fresh jack out left-handed. The larger part of the pack then turned right-handed into a small casuarina in which their jack ran a circle before he was viewed away in the same direction with hounds close behind him; soon after they ran from scent to view and killed in the open by the rocks at Hudi and within 100 yards of the railway. This was a good hunt of between 40 and 45 minutes with a 3-mile point and all the 10½ couple up.'

Thus and thus passed their seventh, eighth and ninth wedding anniversaries, by which time Henry was thinking of taking extended home leave. He was entitled to four months on full pay and opted to take an additional nine months on half pay. We sailed by the Lloyd Triestino liner 'Aquileia' from Madras in November, 1926. Before leaving, a buyer was found for the wicked Morris-Cowley; when he came to drive it away it failed to start.

'Will it sink? Will it sink?' All the boats that had ever sailed in my bath had sunk; the excitement was unbearable.

At Aden, a few hours ashore enabled Henry to bring back a pocket full of sea-shells; they contained hermit crabs which climbed up his back during lunch. At Naples, he avoided incurring a hotel bill by keeping us all on board ship until it was time to catch the train connection the next day, undeterred by the fact that the cabin staff were all off duty and there was no food, light or service. It would be wrong to infer from this that he was mean; within a week of landing in England he had bought a £500 string of pearls (with ten extra added) for Evie, a gesture which cost him a tenth of his entire resources.

While he absented himself in Switzerland for a month's skiing, Evie had her hands full; all four children *and* the ayah got extremely bad 'flu and bronchitis, running temperatures of 104° while living temporarily in a small pub near Guildford. One child ended up with pneumonia and was despatched to a nursing home for a month. Henry was back to enjoy the end of the hunting season and the point-to-point races in Devon. By this time the ayah had sailed back to India, and Evelyn had secured the services of Emma Kitcat, a Norland-trained Nanny, and daughter of a retired colonel of the Royal Marines, to help look after the children.

12 | Off to Spitsbergen

By April Henry was ready to sling his hook again. Having established us in Vann House, Ockley he went off to Cambridge to meet Gino Watkins of Trinity to help plan and raise money for the University expedition to Edge Island, Spitsbergen in July. He was aware that Irvine, Longstaff and Odell had all, admittedly at a much younger age, been on the Oxford University Expedition to Spitsbergen in 1921. Here, in the company of men less than half his age, was a suitably uncomfortable way of spending the rest of his leave.

The leader, H.G. Watkins, was only twenty years old; it was his first expedition and Henry's last. Evie saw them off from King's Cross.

Hotel Rosenkrantz, Bergen
Mon 11.7.27

I hated leaving you on Saturday. We had a good journey to Newcastle but two horribly noisy children in the carriage all the way whose parents insisted on having all the windows shut. Watkins and I arrived in a state of semi-stupor, but a two-mile walk to the docks revived us. How I hate children and their parents! We sailed at 5 p.m. and the first 20 miles was down the coaly Tyne past the great shipbuilding yards, Armstrong-Whitworths, Hawthorn Leslie etc, all looking very idle and derelict on a Saturday afternoon.

The North Sea was as smooth and blue as the Mediterranean. The 'Jupiter' is a 2,000-ton ship which does the 450 miles to Bergen in 30 hours—quite a good speed. There were four of us in a stuffy little third-class cabin right in the stern. Bergen is 20 or 30 miles up a beautiful fiord. The sun set last night at 10 p.m. and must have risen again about 2 a.m. and at midnight the twilight was so bright that no stars were visible—just like the Orkneys only more so.

Cambridge University Spitsbergen Expedition, 1927. Henry, standing, has Gino Watkins on his right

I'm very struck with the cleanliness of Norway—all the houses seem newly painted in red or white, and the fields and pine trees look green and fresh. I think it must be the absence of coal in the country. All their shipping in the harbour seems to be driven by oil engines, and their electricity (from water power) is so plentiful they often leave their lamps burning all day. We had a jolly day ashore—went by funicular up to a hill overlooking the town & spent the morning walking among heather and pines.

[Posted at Trondheim.] It was only after we were well under weigh this evening, in a little 1,000-ton steamer, the 'Kong Harald', that I discovered that my suitcase was missing. I imagined it to be under a big pile of our belongings which the hotel porter had dumped on deck as there was no room in the cabin. I have since discovered that the silly man overlooked it from my room at the hotel in Bergen. No great matter as it is impossible anyway to wash or shave with four people in this little cabin.

I had to get up early as the cabin was too stuffy for sleep. Apart from this the ship is all right and the food is plain but good. The scenery is like the W. coast of Scotland, and the steamer goes inside the belt of islands so we are protected against the Atlantic waves. Two big P. & O. ships are doing pleasure cruises up this coast, the 'Otranto' & the 'Ranchi'—I noticed the latter, which was on her homeward journey from seeing the midnight sun, had a complete Lascar crew with their usual bare feet and thin cotton clothes! I bought a Baedeker's guide to Scandinavia which says that the population of Norway is 2¼ million, & of Sweden 5¼ million, so the whole of the two countries together only hold as many people as London!

Grand Hotel, Tromsö
Sat 16.7.27

We had 3 or 4 hours ashore at Trondheim; the sun came out and we had some good views. Although so far north, the climate is like the south coast of England owing to effect of the Gulf Stream. We crossed the Arctic Circle on Thursday, and stopped at a place called Bodö where people were bathing in the sea just as at Worthing and the women wearing silk summer frocks. We were met here by Capt. Hoegh, the harbour master, who is the agent for our expedition. It is rather a relief to be in a decent hotel after five days in the third class of a Norwegian coasting steamer. One of our Norwegian passengers, hearing that Woolley was a S. African, wanted to take him into partnership for the sale of Norwegian herrings in Cape Town!

It is so quaint to find midnight as bright as midday. People stroll and gossip in the streets all through the night, and it is difficult to get to sleep. The town is just as modern as any English town—cars, petrol pumps, cinemas, telephones in every bedroom in the hotel.

We have been down to the harbour to inspect our ship, a 70-ton two-masted sloop with steel-sheathed bow, called 'Heimen', with an auxiliary paraffin engine which pushes her along at 7 to 8 knots. Wordie has chartered her once or twice before for trips to Greenland etc. She has been repainted white inside and is bigger than I expected. The Captain and owner is a blue-eyed giant called Lars Jacobsen. He is taking the ship down the coast with a football team, and will be back on Monday, after which we shall begin putting our things on board. She is chartered until 2nd September; we may keep her a little longer by arrangement, but I don't fancy we shall be tempted to prolong our stay.

My missing suitcase has arrived and I celebrated the occasion with a hot bath, the first since leaving Ockley, and a change of clothing.

Tromsö is on an Island about 12 miles in circumference; we took the ferry across to a neighbouring island, where there is a Lapp encampment, with a herd of half-tame reindeer. They are small red-faced people with blue eyes and flat, Mongolian-looking faces, were it not for the men's thick beards. They have their own language and are pure nomads living in tents or round huts of turf. In spite of their little bandy legs the Lapps are wonderful travellers, especially in winter on skis, when they are capable of running down wolves to a standstill.

As regards our return journey, Watkins, Forbes, Woodman and I are going by the coasting steamer round by Hammerfest and the North Cape to Kirkenes on the White Sea. Thence we go south through Finland to Haparanda at the top of the Gulf of Bothnia, and I hope to be in London by 20 September or so, depending on the steamer sailings between the Baltic and England. We called on the Finnish consul who was very friendly and helpful.

Woolley has fitted up his wireless receiver, chiefly to get Greenwich time signals, but we hope to get Daventry broadcasts if we can do so without running our batteries down. The 'Marmite' people have promised us a consignment of their stuff, but it is doubtful if it will arrive in time. Also the *Daily Mail* wants to publish reports, but there's no means of communicating any news to them till after we return. I'm rather alarmed to find that Watkins has bagged his mother's gramophone for use on board; but apparently I should have had no better luck had I stayed at Vann House! Several of the party are also experts on the mouth organ.

The last two members of the party arrived by last night's steamer. Lowndes is a fat cheery red-faced little man with spectacles and a nearly bald head—reminds me somewhat of Dr. Hillyar, and must be 50—so I'm no longer the grandfather of the party. Thank you for forwarding the height computation books, I am writing to thank Harihara Syer for them. Shall be glad to get started as I feel I've exhausted the possibilities of Tromsö. We've got a lovely calm sunny day for our start.

*   *   *

This was a reassuring note on which to terminate his last letter. It was not calm for long, however, and the 'Heimen' had a rounded bottom which, although it made it unlikely that she would be crushed in the ice, also made it quite certain that she would roll in a swell. Her antics are described by Scott:[1]

'The 'Heimen' left the shelter of the fiords and ran into a storm. A heavy swell capped by breaking waves made her pitch until her decks were awash. Water poured into the cabins, none of the stores could be reached, and everything was soaked. Worst of all, the violent movement stirred up the bilges, which were full of oil and seal blood, the drainings of the ship's last hunting voyage. The reek of sulphuretted hydrogen, which is the characteristic of rotten eggs, was so strong that those of the party who had silver watches found them tarnished black within the first few hours.

They stayed on deck till evening to escape the smell. When they went below they found complete disorder; the table was upset and the lockers had spilled out their contents into the water on the floor. But the tired men were beyond caring; they crawled into their bunks and lay with water dripping on them through the hatches. By morning the storm had gone abeam, so the ship rolled instead of pitching. The men tried to eat...because they were tired of trying to be sick with empty stomachs. But the dry bread, which alone was available, had become soaked with paraffin and tasted of all the smells there were on board: so they drank water and prayed for better weather. They found it in the loose pack ice they reached next morning.'

The log and the wireless aerial were carried away in the storm which made it difficult to estimate their exact position. Gino described the latter part of the next day in his diary:

'Jacobsen has been in the crow's nest all day and directs our course from there. At about 9 p.m. he gave a shout of 'Bear!' and came running down the rigging. Immediately there was colossal excitement, preparations to lower the boats and getting out rifles etc. My rifle was in a case and Lowndes and I attacked it with an axe and managed to get it open. Meanwhile the two bears were swimming along ahead. Morshead dashed off to the bows and shot one just as they were getting on to an ice floe. The other got away to the right.

We quickly lowered a boat and Morshead and I got in. We managed to come up with the second bear and I shot it through the head. It was a pretty cold job putting ropes round them and hauling them aboard. They are now being skinned.'

Polar bear meat formed their staple food for many days thereafter. From the outset, work in the field was hampered by cloud and mist. Henry's plane-table, standing just outside the tent, had icicles two-foot-long hanging from under it, something that had not happened even on the Mishmi hilltops fifteen years before. The most that could be achieved was a small amount of mapping in the north-west of the island, and an extension along

Henry and Gino bed down on the ice-cap

the south coast as far as the head of Deevie Bay. They were able to disprove the theory that the interior of Edge Island was covered by an ice-cap. It was found to contain a big valley in which reindeer live, surrounded by a horseshoe-shaped ice ring. The country itself was open and undulating, and would have readily lent itself to easy and rapid survey had they not been beset by both fog and blizzards.

After a week of waiting for the fog to clear, Watkins and Morshead carried their tent to the highest point of the ice-cap where they could make the most of any fine spell. They had almost finished their work when fog enveloped them again, trapping them with no stove and little food. It took a two-day blizzard to drive away the fog; and the discovery in Gino's rucksack of a pile of biscuit crumbs covered with boot grease and dubbin called for a special entry in his diary.

During the few fine spells that occurred they worked a 24-hour day. To say that they 'turned in' even then is to euphemize: it was broad daylight, of course, and they 'slept' in the open, because they were too tired to pitch their tent.

Food was getting short as the month drew to an end. Paraffin had got into Forbes' rucksack and tainted all the biscuits. Since pemmican and chocolate were the only other food they had left by then they found it most unpleasant having to eat them.

There were also some worries as to whether Jacobsen would manage to locate them on that little-known fog-bound coast at Cape Heuglin. In the event he was twenty-four hours late for the rendezvous, having run aground shortly before on the east coast; late enough to give food for thought to a party who were down to ¼ rations and had been looking forward to a good meal. Soon, however, they were on board again and trying to hold down an enormous meal of wild goose on the heaving boat.

Grand Hotel, Tromsö
Fri 2.9.27

We got back here in pouring rain yesterday and I was never more thankful for a bath and a change of clothes. For the whole month I'd not taken off more than my coat and boots. It has been a most interesting trip which I would not have missed for anything. Our great trouble was with fog and mist and I only got five days' work with the plane-table in the whole of our time, so I fear the R.G.S. won't feel they've got much value for their money.

Five of our party have already left for home. I was tempted to go with them, but decided that the extra time spent out of England would save me a year's Income Tax. I wired you yesterday saying I hoped to be home about the 14th. It's impossible from here to find out particulars of the steamers from Helsingfors [now Helsinki] or Stockholm and I don't know whether I'll land at Newcastle, Hull, Grimsby or Tilbury.

If possible I will phone you from London—otherwise I shall just walk across the fields from Ockley station; I shall only have a rucksack, as Michelmore is taking all my equipment across to Newcastle and railing it for me. I was so glad to get your ripping letter of 16–18 July which had missed me by 24 hours when we sailed. We got 4 polar bears (mine was the first) and 2 seals. I'm leaving the skin to be done in Tromsö.

Since we were here in July the sun has gone a long way south, and we are getting 3 or 4 hours of darkness and seeing the stars again at night, after seeing nothing but the sun and moon chasing each other round and round the sky for 6 weeks. Also we can see the *aurora borealis* which is quite new to me and very wonderful; we all stayed out in the street watching it till long after midnight last night. The Tromsö streets are full of people walking up and down in the twilight until at least 1 a.m., and conversely nobody gets up before 9 or 10 in the morning.

I shall have to go to town for 4 or 5 days, but I'll have a day or two at Vann first. In case you have forgotten what I look like, here is a passport photo which I had to get done here today for my visa for Finland.

No letter has come, so I'm arranging for it to be sent to poste restante Helsingfors.

Taking a coastal steamer, the 'Vesteraalen', round the North Cape, they disembarked at Kirkenes in the evening, walked through the woods all night, and caught a motor boat up the Pasvik river. A postal charabanc drove them southwards to railhead at Rovaniemi, whence they travelled by train to Helsingfors and awaited a suitable ship, a cable from Copenhagen giving two days notice of their return.

Strolling round the garden of Vann House in the dusk, Henry and Evelyn found a row of small crucifixes; the boys had been to Sunday School that day and had crucified their sister's dolls.

Note

1   *Gino Watkins*, by J.M. Scott, Hodder & Stoughton, 1935, pp.65, 66.

13 | Director in Burma

Henry decided to return to India overland, using the Simplon-Orient Express (*le train de luxe*), alone, as an alternative to the usual stereotyped sea passage. He received more than one offer of employment in the City, but was not prepared to be weaned away from his open spaces in favour of a city desk. He was due to attend a course at the Senior Officers' School, Belgaum shortly after arriving back, following which he could expect promotion.

With Nanny Emma and the children, Evelyn moved from Vann and joined one of her former Darjeeling friends, Mrs. Best, at Toll Gate House in Merrow for the winter of 1927–28. I am not sure whether the recompense for this considerable invasion was financial or spiritual. Each child needed to be equipped for two different climates, and it was useful to have contacts with mothers of other children a few years older or younger, to provide sources and outlets for second-hand children's clothes. With four children, each needing three pairs of pyjamas for winter and three for summer, it meant for instance that Evelyn had to stock twenty-four pairs of children's pyjamas; and this was before 'drip-dry' techniques were invented.

Henry left London in thick yellow fog, with flares blazing here and there at street corners, the taxi to the Continental Boat Train at Victoria moving at a slow crawl with full headlights on. Most of his travelling companions were heading for the more Capuan delights of Brussels, Paris or the Riviera and he saw no other luggage labelled, like his own modest suitcase, 'Bombay, via Paris, Constantinople, Aleppo, Damascus, Baghdad and Basra.'

Paris, 8 p.m.
Sun 27.11.27

You haven't been out of my thoughts for a moment since we parted this morning, & I'm going to miss you dreadfully for the next 4 months. A comfortable journey so far, the channel like a millpond and the boat not crowded. At Calais I found a coupé reserved for me all the way to Zagreb; an upper bunk lets down in case of a 2nd passenger, but so far I've had it all to myself.

There is a wait here of 2 hours at the Gare de Lyon while the carriages are re-shuffled and shunted. I spent an hour walking briskly across the Seine, and then thought I would start a letter to you before the train moves on. I didn't feel hungry all the morning, but had a big and late lunch in the train on leaving Calais at 3, which will last me till tomorrow's breakfast.

The *wagon-lit* attendant on this most romantic of trains took charge of passports and tickets, producing them as required during the night. Dawn was breaking as they plunged into the darkness of the Simplon tunnel, and Venice was reached at five in the afternoon just as the wintry sun was sinking. First impressions were of endless mud-flats covered with acres of belching factories and a forest of electric poles and cables of the most hideous variety. Twenty minutes later the train was backing out again over the same causeway by which it had arrived. By then dusk had fallen, dulling the crude outline of man's industrial handiwork, and a myriad twinkling lights were reflected star-like in the placid surface of the lagoon.

He could have broken his journey and seen more of Venice, but his programme allowed for a day's halt at Zagreb in Yugoslavia, where his old friend and climbing companion of 1921 was then British Consul.

(In Arabic script) *Toqatlian Hotel*
Khalifah: Niqola Medowich
Constantinople-Pera
Thu 1.12.27 6 p.m.

Guy Bullock was waiting with his car at Zagreb stn. when I arrived at the anti-social hour of 3.40 a.m. He'd been dining out that evening, but in any case he says he always sits up reading till 2 or 3 a.m. After a cup of coffee we both went to bed again and I didn't wake up till 10. They both had lots to say and I couldn't get a minute to finish off my letter to you.

Coming along in the train today, one could have imagined oneself back in northern India; the country is pure oriental, ramshackle villages crowned with a whitewashed mosque, Arabic characters on the railway stations, barefooted urchins staring at the train, even the goats and pariah dogs and the smell of burning dung. I've seen nothing of Constantinople yet except from the windows of the hotel bus, but for the last hour of the journey the train was skirting the shore of the Bosphorus, with the sun setting over the sea of Marmara and tingeing the cliffs of the Asiatic shore.

This is supposed to be the best hotel in the place, and my room looks out over a side street, but never could I have imagined such a din of klaxon horns and tram gongs as goes on all the time in the main street just round the corner. Paris is like a funeral compared to this place — thank heavens I'm off on Saturday morning. I'm missing you every moment darling, and longing for your first letter in Bombay, which you'll be posting today. You will be comfortably established in T.G. House by now.

Friday: Today is the Turkish Sunday, shops all closed, but I've had a most interesting day with a French-speaking Turkish guide to show me all the buildings and sights, including the great mosque of St. Sophia, the Seraglio Palace and various museums, all finer than I had imagined. The town appears less oriental than the countryside, largely owing to Kemal Pasha's edict forbidding the Turkish men to wear a fez and the women to cover their faces, so they all now look like Europeans. They are shortly going to adopt Sunday as the weekly holiday instead of Friday. Religion has gone out of favour in Turkey just as much as in Christian countries. In none of the mosques I visited today were there more than a handful of worshippers, where according to my guide there used to be thousands. This is only very partially accounted for by the drop in the city's population from 1½ million in 1914 to 800,000 today.

Pera, the residential quarter, is rather like a bit of Paris, full of hotels, cinemas and restaurants. Galata, the poorer quarter across the 'Golden Horn' reminds one more of Bombay or some such eastern city. The third district consists of Scutari and Haidar Pasha on the Asiatic side of the Bosphorus, to which I catch the 8 a.m. ferry tomorrow morning.

In spite of the fact that the next section of the line was officially styled the Anatolia-Baghdad Railway, the terminus was no further than Aleppo in Syria. Contemporary brochures were already optimistically dotting-in the forthcoming 650-mile extension to Baghdad (via Mosul), and thus with the already built section onwards to Basra. From Calais as far as Trieste the only bookable sleeping accommodation had been first class. Changing now to second class he found the accommodation was 'identical' and saw little object in paying the higher fare.

The bi-weekly train crossed the Anatolian highlands in the neighbourhood of Mount Olympus and emerged two days later at Aleppo. During the second night it crossed through the Taurus mountains. 'As it whisked in and out of the twenty or more tunnels one could catch glimpses, by the light of the full moon, of the chasm of white limestone through which the railway threads its way.' This was the Cilician Gates, the famous pass known and trod by Cyrus the Younger, Alexander the Great, St. Paul and by the armies of the First Crusade.

Beyrout, Syria
Wed 7.12.27 9 a.m.

I never dreamed one could feel so utterly lonely and miserable as I do without your presence. How I'm ever going to survive these next months I hardly dare imagine. It seems more like 10 years than 10 days that we parted in London.

Quite a comfortable 2 days in the train; I played mild poker to while away the time. My fellow passengers were a Syrian merchant from Aleppo, a Persian rug-dealer from Paris, a Jewish businessman from Constantinople, & a pleasant young Turkish lawyer. Everyone here speaks fluent French, and many speak English as well. English £1 & 10/- notes are accepted gladly everywhere; in fact they are habitually carried by travellers of all nationalities in the Middle East, as being the only currency universally changeable without violent fluctuations in the rate of exchange.

At Aleppo on Monday morning I found a large Dodge car ready to start at once for Beyrout. We arrived here at midday yesterday, having stopped for the night at a place called Homs, because the Syrian roads are considered by the police to be unsafe for single cars after dark. It was 250 miles over a bad and very dusty road, and my companions were a major of engineers in the Turkish army, and a middle-aged lady, teacher at an American Mission at Bangkok, Siam who had chosen this curious route to return from holiday in U.S.A.

This place is the capital of French Syria, and the climate is like Malta only colder. It is the place where St. George is reputed to have killed the dragon, and the bay on which it is built is still called St. George's Bay. I believe there is a well somewhere in the town in which he washed his sword! I'm so tired of motoring on these dusty eastern roads, that I'm taking it easy here today and have given up the idea of going on to Palestine, which would mean another 200 miles each way. Tomorrow I catch the desert car from here direct to Baghdad, where I shall have time to write to you again.

A weekly motor convoy run by the Nairn brothers, two New Zealand ex-servicemen, used to leave Beirut for Baghdad every Thursday morning, a service started four years previously. The road was not an all-weather one and rain, when it came, could turn it into a sea of mud and cause stoppages of up to a week, and long detours as they neared the Euphrates. On the other hand, Norman Nairn had once completed the 606-mile journey in under seventeen hours to win a bet.

> *Hotel Victoria, Damascus*
> *Thu 8.12.27   7 p.m.*

We left at 10 this morning and reached Damascus in time for a late lunch, a glorious drive over the Lebanon Range, 8,500 ft., down the other side and then up over the Anti-Lebanon, 5,000 ft. The road was good most of the way. There is also a metre-gauge railway which climbs the ranges by rack-work. Looking back from the Lebanon Hills there is a lovely view of Beyrout spread out below and the blue Mediterranean beyond, while off to the left is the summit of Mt. Hermon, covered in snow.

I've been spending the afternoon looking around Damascus; its chief attraction is the large area of green vegetation, figs, olives, casuarina, vines, due to the Barada river, which rises in the Lebanon hills and waters the city before losing itself in the desert. The Barada is the Abana river mentioned in the Bible story of Naaman the Syrian.

I am travelling with a Danish professor of Archaeology on his way to join Mr. Leonard Woolley in excavating at Ur of the Chaldees in Lower Mespot. We start at 7 in the morning and stop for dinner at Rutba Wells tomorrow evening, then on again through the night reaching Baghdad about 10 a.m. on Saturday, distance about 550 miles through the desert. They have given up halting at Rutba for the night as the accommodation is too limited, and it is quite easy to sleep in the car.

The Nairn Co. forgot to wake Henry next morning until after the first-class bus had left Damascus, so he travelled in a second-class open car four hours later. The company admitted it was their fault and reimbursed him the difference of £7. At the Iraq border the 'rule of the road' changed from the Continental to the British. In view of the large number of cars now using the desert route the correct observance of the rule of the road was of more importance than might at first sight appear.

At Rutba Wells eight other cars arrived within the space of an hour or so.

An excellent dinner was soon available, and those drivers who were staying overnight were careful to empty their radiators. There could be ten or twelve degrees of frost at this time of the year.

Speeds of 50 to 55 miles an hour were maintained over long stretches giving an average of about 30 m.p.h. The customs post at Ramadi indicated that they had still sixty miles to go. An hour later they were crossing the Euphrates by boat bridge at Faluja, and finally the Maude bridge over the Tigris took them into the heart of the ancient city itself. 'Stephana Drower kindly met me at the Customs House with her own car, so I had no difficulty in finding the house. She is very nice, and full of enquiries for you. I've only just had time for a bath, shave and change of clothes, and haven't met Drower[1] yet except through the bathroom window.'

South Gate, Baghdad
Wed 14.12.27

I've been thinking so much of you on your birthday. It's annoying to think that if you had only known the Drowers' address, you might easily have sent me a letter here, as the air mail via Cairo only takes 9 days. As it is, I've still got 10 days to wait for news of you.

The Drowers are both very nice and I could not have better guides to Baghdad. On Monday night they had a little dinner party and bridge afterwards—Sir Edward Ellington, the Air Vice Marshal, Mr. & Mrs. Bourdillon (late I.C.S.), the acting High Commissioner etc. The house is built native style, in two stories, round a central courtyard. The front opens straight on to the main street, and the back looks out across the Tigris. Prices are dreadful compared to India; they pay Rs. 500/- a month rent and as much again in wages for what is quite a small establishment. Staff are of all nationalities, cook Goanese, butler Arab, sweeper a Persian Jew etc.

King Faisal returns by air from Cairo tomorrow and the town is being decorated with triumphal arches. H.M. is not very popular[2] among the Iraqis as they regard him as a foreigner, but Stephana Drower says he is very pleasant to meet. Sir Henry Dobbs, the High Commissioner, and family, return from leave on Friday. I shall miss them, as I leave by the 8.50 train to Basra tomorrow morning. I break journey twice on the way in order to visit Babylon, and Ur of the Chaldees. This letter should reach you about Christmas day, but you will have to wait 2 or 3 weeks for my next, which will be posted from Bombay.

I'm surprised to find how cold all this country is in winter; hard frosts every night, and even by day I'm glad of my thick clothing. The majority of the Iraqis are every bit as fair-skinned as a European. This was even more the case in Syria, where I often saw blue eyes and fair hair on the most undoubted orientals. I have taken no photographs on this trip, but the 3-*anna* stamp on the envelope has a picture of the 30 ft. high arch of Ctesiphon, 20 miles from here, which I visited this afternoon. It is the remains of an old palace. Mrs. D. thinks the ½-*anna* stamp represents a mosque at Kerbala. This country uses Indian coinage but has its own issue of stamps.

> *British India Steam Navigation*
> *s.s. 'Varela'   Persian Gulf*

Three weeks Friday since we parted. All my arrangements have gone off without a hitch, and now I'm on the last lap. Drower came to the station to see me off. Reached Hillah at midday, and spent the afternoon seeing the ruins of Babylon[3] and the supposed Banqueting Hall in Nebuchadnezzar's Palace where Belshazzar is said to have seen the moving hand trace out the message of doom: 'mene, mene tekel upharsin'.

Then I caught the night train to Ur Junction and spent a most interesting day with Dr. & Mrs. Leonard Woolley.[4] The great ziggurat, and the mound which represents the ancient city of Ur, show up against the western skyline a mile and a half from the station. They were unearthing a chariot with teams of oxen, and copper-helmeted soldiers who had been sacrificed before a Sumerian grave of about 3,500 years B.C.

There is a rest house at Ur with electric light and an Indian *khansama*. The Iraq railway also has an excellent system by which one can hire a kit-bag with blankets, pillow, sheets and *razai*, so I've not had trouble without a valise. When the train reached Basra docks I had exactly used the last *anna* of the cash I brought from England, but as the ship did not sail till 4 p.m. I had time to go into the town and cash a Thos Cook travellers' cheque. Basra is fifty miles up a creek called the 'Shatt el Arab' formed by the junction of the Euphrates and Tigris, and it was rather pretty as we steamed past mile after mile of date palms in the sunset light. We anchored at Mohammerah [called Khorramshahr by the Iranians] for two hours after dark last night to pick up mails, and this morning we are due at Bushire on the Persian coast. The next stop after that is Karachi, so if I go ashore there for 5 minutes I can report having returned to India and can draw my full pay again from the 22nd.

I've got a splendid second-class cabin all to myself, with three great bunks as big as beds. The ship is just under 5,000 tons and she carries

British India Steam Navigation's s.s. 'Varela' of the Fast Gulf Service

mostly deck passengers and Arab ponies for Bombay. There is also a draft of about fifty 'other ranks' of the R.A.F. on transfer from Baghdad to Karachi. We connect with the mail steamer leaving Bombay on the 24th, so this ought to reach you about the day I start work at Belgaum.

Bristol Hotel, Karachi
Thu 22.12.27

I've been strolling round the town all day, feeling utterly lonely and wretched without you my darling. I enquired at the P.O. if there were any Survey parties here this year, and they say that Glennie with No.14 party was camped here, but has gone off to Makran, only Mrs. G. and the baby here whom I don't know. Reuter's news on board ship was full of the cold weather and winter sports in England—wish I was there!

My total expenses, including sleeping car, food and hotels, visas and the cost of sending my heavy luggage round by sea, is about £94, about equal to the cost of a first class 'A' passage by P. & O.

Senior Officers' School, Belgaum
Tue 14.2.28

After your last cable, I shall assume that you and Audrey are coming out alone on the 'Naldera' via Marseilles, leaving London on March 15th. This means that next week will be my last letter to you in England. I shall address one letter to you *on the ship* at Port Said, and after that you must enquire of Thomas Cook's young man in Bombay whom I shall warn to meet you. It's ripping to think that my course is ½-finished and that you will soon be on your way to join me.

I simply can't think what to do about an ayah for Audrey on arrival in Bombay; there isn't one to be had in Belgaum, and I doubt if any of the Bangalore ayahs would be much use in Dehra. My present *chokra* is anxious to come to Dehra Dun—he has worked in Quetta and Hydera-bad. Don't you think we could carry on with his help till we get to Dehra? My lecture was quite a success last Thursday, and I am being asked to give a repeat performance at the Belgaum Club.

I was out on Sunday morning, in the country 10 miles west of Belgaum, when a *shikari* whom I'd never seen before came up and said that a panther had killed a cow near his village that night; he'd already built a *machan* and only wanted someone to come and sit in it! So out I went. The panther came along before dark, but spotted the *machan* and was too wily to give me a shot till after dark when he came again. There was no moon and I only had a borrowed torch which I tried to fix on to my gun barrels, but it wasn't satisfactory and I missed. However, I went out again last night to the same place with a better torch arrangement and got him with a dose of buckshot. He is a male beast 6 ft.9 ins. long to the tip of his tail. I've had him skinned by a *mochi* and am sending it to Van Ingen's in Mysore as soon as it's fit to travel. Saturday morning I went out as usual after small game, and got about 20 head to two guns.

Next Sunday we go off to Chikodi, fifty miles on the Poona road, for a couple of days' 'mountain warfare' practice. This is followed by five days break—a sort of 'mid-term holiday'; I'm going to drive with a friend to Karwar on the coast, and possibly Goa as well. Several people are taking forest blocks and trying for tiger[5] or bison, but I don't feel that five days is long enough to make it worth while.

Tomorrow evening I'm due to dine with the doctor Major Walker and his wife and go on afterwards to a dance at the Mahratta Mess. I'd sooner have dispensed with the latter entertainment, as I am quite out of practice in dancing, and also we have our own fortnightly guest night the next evening which includes dancing till 11 p.m. If you were here, darling, it would be different!

At least Evie was met at Bombay this time—by 'Thomas Cook's young man' bearing a letter for her:

I've asked Cooks to try and get you either an ayah or a bearer who is prepared to go to Dehra Dun. I also wrote to Perumal but he has not answered; even my *chokra* has let me down at the last minute and says he must return to Bangalore; and Abid Hosein could not get to Bombay in time to be of use.

Darling, you are to go straight to Poona, where I have taken a room at the Poona Hotel. I shall arrive by car [it was an open Vauxhall now] about 8 or 9 p.m. so you had better dine without waiting for me. I'm told all the hotels in Poona are bad, but we must have a day or two honeymoon there. I've been very surprised and disappointed at not getting any letter from you this week, only the R.E. Journal redirected in your handwriting; I call it a bit thick, when only the week before you had been telling me off good and proper for writing too short letters to you. At least I've never missed a whole mail!

I wrote for rooms at the Alexandra Hotel, Dehra, but no answer yet; I hope they have not gone out of business. I have not done anything about rooms in Mussoorie.[6] We can do that by phone from Dehra, which I hope will be cool enough for you and Audrey to stay in with me until the end of April. Evie mine, I'm just counting the hours till you are with me, and can hardly bear to wait these last five days. I hope you got my letter at Port Said and that you managed to get a cabin to yourself. It is ridiculous being stuck 3 in a cabin on the outward journey at this time of year.

Evie's diary: 'I sailed in the middle of March, 1928, leaving the boys with Colonel & Mrs. Kitcat [Nanny Emma's parents], and they all came to see me off at Portsmouth. Hugh gave me a wintry smile, though the other children did not seem to realise my going—a heartaching job.

I took Audrey, the youngest, with no nurse, she was extremely good and easy to look after all the way to India. At Bombay I had to stay one night, a very hot and trying process getting luggage through the customs etc. with Audrey clinging to me like a monkey. The din of coolies was deafening and the heat intense; we made our way to Poona where we met Hal who had come by car from Belgaum.

After three days Hal had his car loaded on to a train and we left the same night for Dehra. We had a 4-hour wait at Kalyan, which was hot and noisy, and two nights in the train. At Dehra we stayed in the Royal Hotel for a month, after which Hal took Audrey and me up to the Savoy Hotel, Mussoorie, returning for occasional weekends. Audrey took ten days to acclimatize, but afterwards got back her rosy cheeks.' Henry wrote to Evelyn:

> 4, *New Survey Road, Dehra Dun*
> *Wed 16.5.28*

I hope you got the English Mail and the batch of *Times* which I sent you on Monday. I'm now living in a suite of rooms in Hunter's[7] house; Phillimore[7] has a room or two on the other side. I'm sure there would be room for all our family provided Graaff doesn't bring out a wife of his own, or object to having our big family. We must discuss that with him on his arrival; I'm only cabling to ask if he will put up us two and Audrey till October.

The heat is nothing to worry about; I played tennis at the club yesterday, and today I've been roped in to play in the Survey hockey team. I've taken to sleeping on a camp bed on the gravel outside the house, but one is awakened before six every morning by *koels*. Bomford's cat has taken up with a gentleman friend somewhere in the bazaar and only comes here at irregular intervals; I'm afraid she won't stay here with no one in the house to look after her. The Griffith's chauffeur joined me yesterday, but there's damn-all for him to do as I never use the car during the week. It has to live under the Survey clock tower, as there is no available garage either here or at the Club.

*   *   *

Back in England the boys went to the Parents' National Educational Union school down the road. 'Are you Chinese?' someone asked me on my first morning. 'I don't know, I'll ask', I replied, unsure of my own nationality at the age of six.

The cold winter was followed by an exceptionally hot summer. The boys lived on the beach out of school hours, and Emma wrote regularly to Evie, sending snapshots taken with her 'Vest Pocket Kodak' and notes of their heights and weights.

In September, when Emma brought them out to rejoin their parents at Dehra, Henry was pleased to see how brown they all were, and to learn that all three had been taught to swim. (He was so brown himself that he once overhead two officers in the mess debating his ancestry.) He was less pleased when he took over teaching the two eldest arithmetic. He used to come out of the lesson fuming and saying how stupid they both were. He sometimes fumed at the servants as well, which would worry Evie. 'Hasn't Daddy got a loud voice!' said one of us plaintively as someone was bellowed at. He was quite capable of cutting the Surveyor General's wife, in front of Evie, if he thought the former deserved it. Sartorially intransigent, he seldom wore a hat even in uniform, and did not possess such a thing as a *topi*. He would take us all on long expeditions into the environs of Dehra Dun.

Henry's promotion to Lt.Col. came through in June 1928 and he was made Deputy Director of the Geodetic Branch, with charge of the Forest Map Office and No.2 Drawing Office.

In the visitors' book appears the name of the archaeological explorer and writer Sir Aurel Stein, then aged 66. He too had been frostbitten and had lost all the toes on his right foot in 1908; part of his collection of manuscript fragments from Central Asia now forms the Stein Collection at the India Office Library. Also H.R.H. the Duke of Spoleto, from Turin, about to lead his Karakoram Expedition off to the Baltoro Glacier; and Dr. Wilhelm Filchner, the German explorer and scientist, who later took the trouble to write to the Survey of India when he read of Henry's death. The Survey had a tradition of lending its equipment and surveyors to assist such explorers, thus adding to the knowledge of, and improving the maps of, the remoter regions. The ubiquitous Kenneth Mason's name appears, as does that of the Surveyor General, Brigadier R.H. Thomas, the latter giving as his address 'Simla, Calcutta, Delhi, etc., etc.'

Sometimes there were tents pitched all over the garden to accommodate the visitors; the children would climb the guy ropes and slide down their roofs. Graaff Hunter's fiancée, Gwen, arrived at about this time, and recalls: 'Evie was the most remarkable person, she could cope with *any* situation. "Don't worry about space;" she said at one of her crowded dinner parties "I will get in the grand piano, if needs be."'

Six months later another upheaval was necessitated when, in April 1929, Henry was appointed Director, Burma Circle, of the Survey of India. Evelyn stayed behind to have her fifth child, while the advanced party of Henry, Nanny and the other four children set off on their journey to Maymyo via Calcutta, Rangoon and Mandalay. It was the hottest time of the year and Henry ordered a large block of ice, for the railway compartment floor, on which to stand the drinks. In Calcutta we had iced drinks at Firpo's restaurant on Chowringhee, while Henry called at the Survey Offices at 13 Wood Street; in Rangoon there was time for a visit to the Zoo and the Lake in Dalhousie Park, the Shwe Dagon Pagoda, and to have lunch with Henry's cousin Leonard, of the Bombay Burma Trading Co., before catching the Flotilla steamer upstream to Mandalay.

The Irrawaddy Flotilla (& Burmese Steam Navigation Co.Ltd., 1865, to give it its original title) had come a long way by 1929, and the river fleet was at the height of its prestige. The biggest vessels were the double-decked side-paddlers of the new 'Siam' class, built at Denny's and re-erected at Dalla dockyard opposite Rangoon, 326 ft. in length, 46 ft. in beam and drawing only 6 ft. fully laden. Designed with a spoon-shaped bow to thwart the shifting sandbanks, their powerful triple-expansion engines enabled them to tow a laden cargo flat on each side, as well as carry 4,000 deck passengers, with their bedding and food, the six-hundred-mile passage upstream from Rangoon to Mandalay, in only five or six days in the low-water season. With a combined width of nearly 150 ft., it required skill to avoid the rafts of teak logs floating down on the stream to Rangoon without grounding.

When Evelyn followed a few weeks later, the city of Meerut presented an extraordinary sight. It was the anniversary of the Sepoy Revolt, which had broken out there is 1857. Troops and police were everywhere and trouble was expected.[8] Mahatma Gandhi was on the same train as Evelyn and was particularly kind to her, clearing a passage through his teeming supporters for her and her small bundle of humanity. A fortnight later, on 25 May, as the Mahatma was in Bombay addressing the All-India Congress Committee, Evelyn was welcoming the first visitor to the new house at Maymyo. This was Captain Rawdon Briggs[9] of the Burma Sappers and Miners, who had first met Henry in the Guards Division in 1915; two years later he would lead the search for, and find, his colleague's body.

With the arrival of Evie and Nigel in Maymyo, Henry's complete family were under one roof for the first and last time; within six months it would be necessary for Nanny Emma to take the eldest boy home to boarding school.

Maymyo, some forty miles north-east of Mandalay, on the edge of the Shan plateau, was blessed with an ideal climate and a singular idyllic charm. The days were sunny and the nights cold. At 3,000 ft., its air scented with eucalyptus and pine, it was the official hill station, complete with Government House and a G.O.C. Its name embodies its origin, for the Burmese word *myo* means a place or village, and Colonel James May, liking the place, built the first barracks there in 1886; in much the same way as Captain Hiram Cox left his memorial in the town of Cox's Bazaar in Bangladesh.

The house, called Upperfold, was on East Ridge Road, and stood in a large compound of some three acres with its own tennis court. Two miles away were the town and the Survey Offices, where Henry and his colleagues, Major Kenneth Mason of No.11 Party in the South and Captain G.F. Heaney[10] of No.10 Party in the North, were engaged in making the very maps which the Japanese were to use in the invasion of Burma eleven years later. I am glad to say that the Japanese versions displayed formal

Lt.Col. Henry Morshead, D.S.O., F.R.G.S., on his appointment as a Director

Hugh, on Good Sort, at
Upperfold, 1930

acknowledgement to the Survey of India, in Japanese characters at the foot
of each sheet, in the customary manner of cartographers.

Just as the social round at Dehra had been less arduous than at Bangalore
City, Maymyo was a smaller and quieter place than either. The town did,
however, have the usual amenities of such a station, including a Club with
tennis, golf and polo facilities. Henry took up the latter game again and one
of his three ponies had the Prince of Wales' feathers branded on it, which
made it something very special to the children.

Immediately across the road from the house were the Game Reserve
forests. The undergrowth here was thick but far from impenetrable, and in
places contained a large amount of eucalyptus plantation; it was criss-
crossed with a series of 'rides' maintained, as the name implies, for the
enjoyment of riding. Most of the regular 'rides' had names, such as
Boundary Ride, Switchback Ride or Peacock Ride; Pathin Ride we used to
call Mafat Ride. Some were signposted, but as there were 180 miles of them
it was still quite easy to get lost. It was not considered in any way
remarkable for the two elder children, aged seven and eight, to ride long

Audrey, on Devsi, with
Emma, at Upperfold, 1930

distances into the forests. In fact, to return home early from a ride was to
invite a scornful rebuke from their father.

Parties were few, but Emma was a tomboy and kept the children
occupied; and occasionally there would be an all-day picnic, on one of
which the car had a puncture and ran out of petrol simultaneously. On
another, one might come upon a plantation offering pineapples at 50 for a
rupee, and fill the car with them. Amid great glee a hot-air balloon was sent
up at one of our birthday parties, to descend miles away when the flame in
its small gondola burnt out. 'One-Tree Hill' loomed on the northern horizon
in thicker jungle. Picnics there were more exciting, and someone was alleged
to have seen a bear on the path. I asked Emma, who is now Mrs. Douglas
Dalzell, for a character sketch of Henry at this time:

'One morning you boys forgot to take your *topis* to the Army School,
who insisted on them, and the car had to be sent back to school with
them. Your father was at home at the time, and fairly blew his top as to
what he would do to the two of you if you ever forgot again. I put them

Children's party at the Maymyo Club, 1930, Owen on the slide

in the car before breakfast the next morning & neither of you transgressed again!

Once we had settled in at Maymyo your father thought he had better have a try at learning basic Burmese, so he had lessons twice a week I think—anyway it ended with the teacher having the book thrown at his head and your father declaring he had never heard such a stupid language and was not going to learn any more of it. He and your mother used to go out for long walks in the late afternoon; how she ever survived with her flat feet I don't know, but she never refused.

Very energetic and restless, he was not one to sit around. He could not bear to be idle for long and always had something planned for his leave, Spitsbergen etc., though your mother hated it and was all tense until he got home again. He was very careful over money, would insist on investing anything spare and then complain there was no money in the bank for everyday use. They preferred evenings at home to going out anywhere, neither of them cared for dances at the Club, and having no T.V. in those days we used to read in the evening, sometimes have the gramophone on, and early to bed! Just a very good stable for one and all of us.'

Notes

1   Sir Edwin Drower, K.B.E., Judicial Adviser, Iraq, 1922—46.
2   The Hashemite Amir Faisal was nominated as King by the British, whose Mandate in Iraq lasted from 1920 to 1932. The monarchy was overthrown in the July 1958 coup, in which King Faisal II and the Crown Prince were killed.
3   These were five miles from the station, and had been laid bare by the excavations of Dr. Koldeway and his staff of German assistants, during the fifteen years prior to 1914.
4   Later Sir Leonard Woolley.
5   The tiger population of India is estimated by some people to have fallen from about 32,000 in 1928 to fewer than 2,000 at the present time.
6   Mussoorie was half a day's journey away, and clearly visible from Dehra, perched on mountain ledges at 6,500 ft.
7   Dr. James de Graaff Hunter, C.I.E., F.R.S., Sc.D., had just succeeded Col. R.H. Phillimore as Director of the Geodetic Branch.
8   See *Indian Quarterly Register*, Vol.1, 1929.
9   As Lt. General Sir Harold Rawdon Briggs, K.C.I.E., K.B.E., C.B., D.S.O., M.C., he was back in Burma in 1946 as C.-in-C. Burma Command.
10 Brigadier G.F. Heaney, C.B.E., R.E., became the first Surveyor General of India after Partition, and President of the Indian Institute of Surveyors.

14 | A Crime and Some Detective Work

Why should someone leading such a very ordinary life be murdered, I puzzled? Who stood to benefit? That bit about his temper concerned me; could it conceivably have had something to do with his mysterious death in the forests? I had felt the weight of his hand myself; but I had also received an apology before the sun went down, and an invitation to play chess or any other game. The Burmese language and script were enough to try anyone's patience. The writer Maurice Collis, who came to Burma in his early twenties, found it monosyllabic, tonal and without grammar in the accepted European sense.

In all my researches I had found nothing to impugn my father's character. On the contrary, the opposite was the case. In my early life, his character was iterated to me verbally by his contemporaries as being a shining example of his Corps motto, '*Quo Fas et Gloria ducunt*'; in 1953 a man came to my door to ascertain whether I could possibly be the son of his 1917 company commander, whom he had never forgotten. Yet someone had seen fit to murder him: it all seemed so *unlikely*.

I wanted another opinion, and decided to write to one of the names in the visitors' book. Four young Americans had come to stay with us the month before we left. One of them, now Professor J.N. Hazard[1] of New York, was a cousin of Jack Hazard, the previously-mentioned 1924 Everest climber. I traced his address and asked him if he would oblige with a United States view of the 'set-up' in our Maymyo house. He wrote back by return:

'Jack told me of the disaster in Burma soon after we had left. We were a group that had just graduated from Yale with our B.A.'s and were on our way round the world at a slow pace. Jack had given us a letter to your father, and we stayed several days. Since we filled the house a tent was set up on the lawn for you and your brothers, and you slept out there while we had your room.

You had a very pleasant English girl [Emma] of about our age as your nanny or companion. The house was a large English type one and we might have been right in England. Indeed, it all seemed very English, for the British carried their culture with them. The master of the ship was English and his Chief Engineer was Scottish, as was the case almost everywhere.

Your father was a pleasantly informal man, although very much a British officer. All was neat and well ordered. He presided at the head of the table, as we expected he would, with grace but with a no-nonsense attitude. You children were well behaved, as I recall, perhaps because he would not have expected otherwise. His moustache was in the best British Army tradition. Of course he was interested in maps, as that was his primary concern, and he outfitted us with maps of Burma up to the Chinese frontier, to which we were headed. Our plan was to join Harold Young, the American Missionary, who later became chief interpreter for General Stilwell, at his mission station just over the frontier of Burma in China.

I recall our walks with your father round the community, possibly along the very route over which he rode that fateful morning. There was no indication of hostility to us: indeed all along the trail into China we were welcomed with outstretched hands by the tribesmen who had been taught by Harold Young to shake hands.

I would enjoy a return visit to Burma, but they make it difficult. We have returned to many of the Indian, Indonesian, Malaysian and Chinese places we visited, but not to Burma. I envy you the opportunity to make a nostalgic trip, but I hear that the quality of life has deteriorated badly, and it may be a sad return in every way. If you do reach your old home, I shall be very interested in news of Mandalay and Maymyo.'

The departure of Henry's whole family to England was now only weeks away, after which his sister Ruth would arrive to keep house. Meanwhile he had to go to Rangoon and Prome on business for three of those weeks, and, in his letters to Evie in Maymyo, he is still making plans and changing them:

Rangoon 6 p.m.
Fri 12.12.30

Your letter of 9th arrived just after I'd written to you. Thos. Cook can only offer me a 3rd berth in the old 'Bhamo' sailing on 28th March, and I'm thinking of going round the world via Japan & Canada; by travelling 2nd class I could do the whole journey for under £150. It would take 10–12 weeks, so I'd be home by the middle of June.

Henry and Evelyn, with the four youngest children, just prior to their departure for England in 1931

The Barrons (Burma Rifles) suddenly hailed me from their car as I was walking round the Royal Lake before breakfast this morning, and I drove round the town with them. They are spending three months leave touring in Burma. This afternoon I went to have a look round Mingaladon Cantonment and some of the surrounding rubber plantations. It's 12 miles from Rangoon; I went by train and came back on the front seat of a bus for 4 *annas*! Even Rich couldn't have done the journey cheaper! Last night Leonard & I went to see 'Lord Richard in the Pantry' by Rangoon amateurs at the Boat Club—a rotten play, badly acted, not half as good as our Maymyo show last October. The Elliot Taylor girl was in it, and I met Betty Armstrong in the audience.

This was how Evelyn was expected to spend Christmas 1930, subject of course to last-minute alterations, in the small unfashionable hill-station of Kalaw:

'For our Kalaw trip your programme is as follows: leave Maymyo by 10.10 a.m. train on 24th and try and get a Xmas concession return ticket. Arrive Mandalay 1.55 p.m., lunch at station refreshment room, depart 2.25 p.m. in same through carriage, arrive Thazi Junction 6.2 p.m., dine and sleep at railway rest room. We go on to Kalaw by 8.15 a.m. train on Christmas Day.

If I can I will meet you at Mandalay, but it looks as if I shall arrive at Thazi *after* you, at 2.45 a.m. on the 25th and burgle my way into your bedroom. Mosquito nets are provided at the Rest Rooms, but it would be as well for you to bring a valise with a sheet and one light blanket. I'm warning the Kalaw Hotel to expect us on the train at 3 p.m. Xmas Day for five days stay. P.S. Has our car been repaired yet? One of the letters you forwarded was from F.M. Bailey.'

Rly Rest Rooms, Rangoon
Sun 14.12.30   7 p.m.

Yesterday I had a long afternoon at the Races with Leonard and the Foucars. Leonard was busy starting the races, but joined us in the paddock for a few minutes between races and gave us tips. I won about Rs. 12/-. It's the last word in up-to-dateness, electric totalisator etc. We dined together and went to a talky-cinema (Owen Nares and Edna Best) after which we adjourned to the Gym. Club for the last few dances of the evening, and so to bed at 1.30 a.m. At 7 this morning Leonard drove us to the 11th milestone, where his horses were waiting, and I rode 'Why Worry' on which he won the jumping at the Rangoon Horse Show last year. After lunch we all went swimming in one of the big Rangoon lakes—water pretty green and filthy, but it's the only swimming place available just now, as the Kokine baths are under reconstruction.

I leave for Prome by Tuesday night's mail, arriving on 17th, address c/o No.11 Party, S. of I., Prome, but don't post anything after 21st. I noticed 'Fifi' dancing at the Gym. last night, and met Mrs. Lacy Nicholls and sundry other friends at the Races.

The letter before Christmas was mostly about the arrangements for the family's return to England: 'The Kings have a lovely house at Prome, and they are looking forward to seeing you on your way through on 23 February. It belongs to Mr. Kermode (alias Thunderbox sahib), Indian Forestry Service, who is on tour all the winter and whom I met at the Forest Service Ball in Maymyo. The steamers fit in very well; you will all have to be on board the mail steamer in Mandalay on Friday 20 February and will

145

sail at 6 a.m. next morning. You reach Prome on the afternoon of the 23rd, and Rangoon on the evening of the 26th, giving 1½ clear days to catch the S.S. 'Chindwin', and they will let you stay on board the I.F. boat in Rangoon till you embark.'

On the same day as this letter was written, 22 December 1930, the Rebellion to overthrow the Government began in Lower Burma. Saya San had been secretly crowned King of Burma a few weeks before in Tharrawaddy, and had reviewed his army, poorly-armed as it was with shotguns, swords and a belief in invulnerability formulas.

Burma was a prosperous country, but little of its wealth was in the hands of the Burmese. Resentment was felt against the wealthy foreign community of English, Indian, Chinese and Japanese businessmen. The Indian Government tactlessly treated Burma as a mere province: Henry's appointment, for example, was Director, Burma Circle, Survey of *India.*

An armoured train was provided between Maymyo and Mandalay, but no incident occurred. The river steamer duly interconnected with the liner: the 'Chindwin' was a Henderson Line steamer, and 'Paddy' Henderson's line also operated the Flotilla Company. At Prome Henry disembarked and waved goodbye on the afternoon of the 23rd; he felt it was pointless to prolong the goodbyes for another three or four days and Evie may well have agreed.

Under suitable headlines the *Rangoon Gazette* for Tuesday 19 May 1931 carried the following statement issued by the Commissioner of Police, Mandalay Division:

'Shortly after 9 o'clock on the morning of Sunday the 17th May, 1931 the Subdivisional Officer, Maymyo, received a telephone message from Mr. Syed Ali of the Maymyo Electric Supply Company to the effect that a riderless pony with blood on its neck and saddle had just come into the compound of his bungalow on Manor House Road from the direction of Elephant Point. He at once collected a dozen policemen and with a Sub-Assistant Surgeon went by car to Mr. Syed Ali's house, where he found that though the pony was not in any way injured, it was obvious from the large amount of blood upon it that a serious accident had occurred.

Meanwhile it has been discovered that *the owner* [my italics] of the pony was Lieut. Colonel Morshead, D.S.O., R.E., Director of the Burma Circle, Survey of India, and that the riderless pony had been seen coming down the hill along Inlya Ride towards Switchback Ride and Elephant Point. As the search along the rides however proved unsuccessful, the

Subdivisional Officer, at 12.45 p.m., telephoned for assistance to the 10th-20th Burma Rifles, and parties of them under the direction of the Commanding Officer carefully searched a wide area of jungle to the south of Inlya Ride for the rest of the day, but without success.

The search was renewed by the Military Authorities at dawn next day and about 7.30 a.m. Captain Briggs, R.E., with a party of Dogras discovered Colonel Morshead's body lying in the jungle about 150 yards to the north of Inlya Ride about 2½ miles from Inlya (village). A post-mortem examination held by the Civil Surgeon, Major McRobert, made it clear that Colonel Morshead had been killed instantaneously by a gun-shot fired at very close range into his chest, whilst a second shot, fired from a greater distance, had made superficial pellet wounds on the back and side of the left shoulder. An examination of the place where the body was found suggested that the shots were actually fired while the Colonel was on the ride and that his pony afterwards carried him into the jungle.

Various theories have been advanced as to the cause of the murder. It is impossible to say as yet what the real cause is. There is, however, no evidence at all to connect the attack with rebel activity. Two arrests have already been made and a reward of Rs. 1,000 has been offered for information leading to the discovery and conviction of the murderer.'

On the same day Henry's brother Owen, who was the King's Librarian at Windsor Castle, was breaking the news to Evie:

'I was rung up just now by Sir Clive Wigram who had been charged to convey to you the deepest sympathy of both the King and Queen. Their Majesties were horrified to read the first report and had earnestly hoped that it would have been mitigated by subsequent tidings.

I was particularly to say that the King will as far as he is able make it his personal endeavour to secure to you the maximum assistance for the children; and that you were not to hesitate later on to bring to notice any obstacle which might be surmounted by a timely word from him. In the meantime His Majesty is receiving Lord Irwin today and is going to speak to him about your position.

I have written to H.M. so you need take no action.'

'My brother was a gallant fellow, and no stranger to death;' Owen had written in his dutiful expression of thanks the same day, 'for his widow it is a hideous calamity. She had just come home to put the two eldest boys to school: there are two sons below them and a little daughter. As far as anything can comfort her in the presence of such a tragedy it will be the assurance of that personal concern which Your Majesties have ever shown in the proud sorrows of those who follow Your Majesty's service overseas.'

Some further details of the search itself were given in the following day's *Rangoon Gazette*:

'The civil police, the Governor's bodyguard, the 7th Bengal Mountain Battery, and fifty of the Burma Rifles went out at once to search the rides, and were helped as to the direction in which he had gone by a lady rider reporting that she had seen Colonel Morshead near Elephant Point making towards Inlya Ride. It was not sufficient to search the rides, as it was known that Colonel Morshead was in the habit of riding through the jungle between the rides.

The whole battalion of the Burma Rifles was called out about 1 p.m. and members of the Club joined them to form a cordon to beat through the rides and the jungle. Some woodcutters along Inlya Ride were questioned, and said they had seen a riderless pony galloping along that ride, but they knew nothing more. The rain came down heavily at 5.30 p.m. and the searchers were drenched. The Burma Rifles and the police were out till 9 p.m.

On Monday morning the Dogras were out at 5.30 a.m. and were to be relieved by the Burma Rifles, but the body was found by the Dogras at about a quarter to eight. It was found in the jungle, about 200 yards from Inlya Ride. All marks were destroyed by the heavy rain.'

Letters from Henry continued to reach Evie for three weeks after she knew he was dead. The penultimate one told of the near escape of his colleague Captain Heaney, who had been shot at by an employee of the survey; could the same thing have happened to Henry, I asked myself? The last letter was written an hour before his death.

'Heaney was not actually hit—Ali Ahmed fired three shots at long range with a scatter-gun, after having been told off for misbehaviour, & one of the pellets went through the top of Heaney's hat. The man has been given 3 years R.I. for attempted murder, with commendable promptitude on the part of the civil authorities. He was a bad fellow whom I took over from the Frontier Circle 18 months ago at Phillimore's request— spent all his time messing about with village girls instead of doing his work.

About your coming out for the winter, Ruth [Henry's sister] says that the 'California' & 'Tuscania' will be sailing from Liverpool to Bombay in October and that the rush for bookings is always great. You ought to get in touch with the Anchor Line offices near Dent's clock shop in Cockspur Street. The fare is £30 single and probably £50 or £55 return, but there is no return steamer after March. I think certainly bring out

Sir Owen Morshead in 1944

Audrey—she may as well use up her Govt. passage money. I feel it will be nice for you and I to have the house to ourselves for the winter, and I'm not saying anything to Ruth about staying on. It is probable that No.11 Party and possibly 21 Party will be kept back from the field next season owing to retrenchment; in this case my touring won't amount to much. Mrs. Bowden, or someone, would I'm sure look after Audrey while you are touring with me.

The days here all get filled up; I've started regular polo again this week. Monday night I dined with the Leach's[2] to meet Mr. Wyatt Smith (Br. Consul at Tengynah). Tuesday the Masons came to tennis here, and Ruth & I dined with them at Inlya Lodge. Wednesday, I brunched with Barton to meet Mr. Grose the D.C. Myitkyina. Thursday we had our first heavy storm with gusty wind which has made the air much cooler ever since. Friday night I dined at Govt. House—rather a senior crowd, but I was glad to find Clague and Harvey both staying there; Marshall is that rather nice P.M.G. whom we met at dinner with the Lynch's last year, and the Breithaupts are our old friends from Bangalore, she with the game leg and he Comdg. the Madras Pioneer Bn. now in Mandalay. I played bridge after dinner with the Marshall's (I.C.S.) and Mrs. McCallum, whose husband has just been succeeded by Clague in Taunggyi. Heath (B.B.T.C.) has gone to the Civil Hospital in great pain with gall stones and is to be operated on at once, I believe.'

Upperfold, Maymyo
Sun 17.5.31   6 a.m.

On Thursday 14th I started my third year as Director, which means a rise of Rs. 50/- p.m. in pay; on the other hand I have to pay Rs. 100/- more in income tax than last year. Under this year's budget my income tax is equivalent to almost 2/6 in the £1. I haven't cashed a cheque in the whole 3 months since you left, but I have been living on my T.A. and on the various debts which have now all been refunded to me— Rs. 100 from Mrs. Leach for looking after her horse, Rs. 300 from Mrs. Murphy etc.; Rs. 2,000 of Barton's refund I paid into the bank, so I ought to have a wage balance there when my pass-book is written up at the ½ year.

I had your friend Mr. Tilley the electrician round this week and had the electric light removed from the apex of the verandah roof, where one could never reach to replace a dead bulb, and had a new light fixed on a 'goose-neck' bracket. The Bulkeleys have returned to Rangoon; she is off on a 4 months return trip to England next week, and I've taken over

Tewfik for the rains. I very nearly bought Cane's old pony 'Mannequin' from the 52nd this week, but she is dead lame, and Hayes tells me she will always be hopelessly unsound, and not worth risking any money on.

Col. West has been promoted Maj. General and is going home to a job at the War House. I have had a busy week. Monday night Ruth & I dined with Barton. Tuesday we had the Masons and Powers (Burma Rlys) to T. & T. here, and Ruth dined with Barton at the Club. Wednesday evening I got let in for a Toc H. meeting at the Soldiers' Home—padre Park, Blaikie, Kay-Mouat, Sergt. Ingles etc—I wasn't greatly impressed and don't feel it's my line. Thursday we went to tea with the Sherratts. Friday we had a dinner party of 10 here. The Holbertons (Pine Lodge); Mr. Hopwood (Ch. Conservator of Forests) and his niece Miss Rowland [later married to J.H. (Elephant Bill) Williams]; Mr. R.R. Brown; Batten (B.B.T.C.) and Mrs. Worthington. Mrs. Oberlander (Namtu silver mines) got ill at the last moment and could not come.

Yesterday we had tennis here—McLean, Mrs. Worthington, Ruth & I. Last Sunday I had to go to the anniversary meeting of the United Club in Band Road—speeches by Sir J. Maung Gyi[3] etc; Mr. R.R. Brown, Syed Ali & I were the other 'guests of honour'. I'm wanting you so badly, darling. Hurry up and book your passage to Rangoon!

*   *   *

The air was soon full of rumour and conjecture; it was still circulating seven years later, when Lt.Col. H. Westland Wright took over the then equivalent of Henry's appointment in 1938: 'Early during my stay I heard, unconvincingly, that your father had been killed by a tiger in a 'Forest Ride': further, the ride was indicated to me as being one that terminated about a mile from the house we lived in, Broomhill, by the lake. I was also warned not to go walking in that ride! So, you see, nothing authentic. My wife, on the contrary, heard (only hearsay) that your father had been killed and that his body had not been found, but no mention of any tiger.'

Leonard Aspinal, of the Bombay Burma Trading Company, who was in Maymyo at the time, also remembers the tiger rumour circulating at a very early stage concurrently with those of murder. The rumour of the tiger was of course absurd, but the place pointed out to Colonel Westland Wright was very accurately described indeed.

Twenty-five days after the murder, on 11 June, under the headings 'MYSTERY SOLVED?' and 'ACCUSED'S STATEMENT', the Rangoon Gazette had an account which contained the following:

'The accused (former) Gurkha, it is stated, has made a statement in which he alleges that Colonel Morshead was accidentally shot in the following

Funeral of Henry Morshead

circumstances. He (the accused) was out shooting, when he accidentally shot Colonel Morshead. Colonel Morshead remonstrated with him and, while Colonel Morshead was attempting to pull the gun away from him the S.G. (small game) shot from his left barrel was discharged and Colonel Morshead received the fatal wound.'

Drawing the attention of the India Office, Whitehall, to the unsatisfactory nature of the reports circulating, which were syndicated to the press in England, Owen requested that the Government of Burma be asked for the results of the official enquiry. The matter was still *sub judice* and their reply was forthcoming on 21 August:

The press reports, it said, were based on unofficial attempts to reconstruct the facts. It was true that two men, an ex-Gurkha and a Burman, were arrested on suspicion when it was discovered that the former had been shooting at the time that Henry Morshead met his death in that part of the forest in which his body was found. The only ground for suspecting that the Burman might have been implicated was the fact that the Gurkha was using his gun. On investigation, however, the case collapsed. The police were satisfied that the Gurkha left his village of Inlya at about 6.30 a.m. and returned at 9.30 a.m., and that to have visited in this period a place where he satisfied them that he had shot a jungle fowl and the spot where the body of Henry Morshead was discovered (two miles from where the fowl was shot), he would had to have covered at least 7½ miles. This they considered impossible having regard to the nature of the ground. He was, therefore, released together with the Burman who, being ill, had not left the village during the day in question.

I knew the nature of the ground myself and, in my opinion, to cover a 7½-mile triangle between 6.30 and 9.30 a.m. was perfectly possible whatever the terrain. Was it really impossible for an experienced *shikari* to average less than three miles an hour?

I took pen and paper and drew a map from memory, of Maymyo and its surroundings, with intersecting arcs to calculate the possible positions of the shot bird and the body, from the known positions of Maymyo and Inlya village. There were variations of up to half a mile in the distances, according to which account one read; but there appeared to be only one combination, one triangle, of village, bird and body, which satisfied all the known data; and the more I studied it the more equivocal and vacillating the official view seemed. Why had the police adopted this 'non-possumus' attitude?

The report from Whitehall continued: 'The line of investigation then pursued was to verify the whereabouts of the licensed gun-holders on the date of the occurrence and the movements of any that might possibly be ill-

Grave of Henry Morshead

disposed to your brother such as any dismissed by him from the Survey Department for slackness in their duties. The enquiries led to no result and the authorities are forced to the conclusion that the case must remain a mystery.'

Reverting to the telegrams published in the press, the Gurkha was neither an employee or ex-employee of Colonel Morshead, nor was he a sepoy as stated in one paper. In the light of the verified accounts of his movements, he could have made no admission of the nature alleged in *The Times, Star* and *Evening Standard*, that he had struggled with Colonel Morshead, or even that he had seen him at all. There is also of course no evidence in support of the idea that Colonel Morshead struck him with his riding whip. The basis for this suggestion was to be found solely in the fact that when arrested the Gurkha had marks on his right ear and cheek. These however were caused, he declared, by a fall. The police authorities accept this explanation both because the Gurkha's statement appeared in other respects to be true, and because it is the opinion of all who knew him that Colonel Morshead was far from being quick-tempered and was the last person likely to have gone deliberately up to any person and struck him in the manner suggested.'

Owen found *The Times* particularly helpful, keen to correct rumours, and to publish the final official report. He also arranged for Professor Gleadowe (who later designed the Stalingrad Sword) to design a small memorial plaque for the cloister wall at Winchester College.

A year later Evelyn enlisted the aid of her friend Mrs. Philip Fogarty in Maymyo in obtaining a certified copy of the actual police report, from the District Superintendent of Police, Mandalay, R.G.B. Prescott. Not surprisingly, this merely stated in five pages of foolscap what Whitehall had précised into one. In a sense it was even more unsatisfactory, making use of expressions like 'rather impossible' for the suspect to be able to 'walk' the required distance through the jungle. Might he not possibly have run? I was always interested in the opening remarks of this report. They bore out the original press reports that the riderless pony had not gone back to Henry's own house, Upperfold:

Copy of Final Report in F.I.R. No. 103/1931 of Maymyo
Police Station, Mandalay District, under Section 302, I.P.C.

— — — — — — — — —

In this case the late Lt.Col. H.T. Morshead had left his bungalow 'Upper-fold' at about 7 a.m. on 17 May 1931. The same morning at about 9 a.m.

his [my italics] horse appeared at the gate of 'Manor House' where Mr. Syed Ali and his *mali* discovered that the saddle was covered with blood. The *mali* at once informed Mr. Syed Ali who telephoned the Sub-divisional Officer (Mr. H.F. Oxbury). Suspecting that there was foul play the S.D.O. organised search parties etc., etc.

From the fact that the horse returned to another house I deduced that he must have been riding someone else's horse. This did not surprise me in the least. In his last letter he referred to 'looking after Mrs. Leach's horse' and to 'taking over the Bulkeleys' horse Tewfik for the rains'. If the Leaches or the Bulkeleys lived at Manor House, and Henry had been riding one of their horses, then it had merely returned to its own home. Alternatively, it might have passed by Manor House on its way to Upperfold. Mr. Syed Ali reported it as *a* riderless horse, so presumably it was not his.

Perhaps Kenneth Mason[4] had expressed a view? Only a few days before his death Morshead had been discussing with Mason the possibility of organising an expedition to triangulate Kungka Shan,[5] a 25,325 ft. peak in China, a fortnight's march from the Burma border, and Mason had been President of the Committee of Adjustment following Morshead's death. I wrote to his daughter Helen and asked if he had left behind any papers relevant to Henry. She replied by return enclosing a couple of pages from her father's as-yet-unpublished memoirs:

'Dorothy and I rented a comfortable house on the edge of the artificial lake. My old friend Henry Morshead, whom I had known all my service in India was my immediate senior officer. We looked forward to a pleasant time, for we had much in common as mountaineers, and like me he was sad to be posted so far from the Himalaya. 'Punished and exiled like me, for being too keen?' was his query to me on arrival.

Then suddenly came tragedy. Henry was in the habit of riding for exercise in the morning. On Sunday 17 May he started out riding to visit me after [early] breakfast. About eleven o'clock [It was about 11 a.m. when it was learned who the rider was] a riderless pony with a blood-stained saddle galloped into the cantonments, *and was identified as having been lent to him.* [My italics] Troops turned out at once and we searched the jungle between his house and mine till late in the night, but without success. We began again at four o'clock in the morning and about nine found his body in thick jungle where it had been dragged after the murder. Vultures overhead led us to him.

It was clearly established that a roving band of armed Burmese rebels had been in the jungle two nights before. It may be that Henry challenged them. It is certain that a gun had been discharged into his body at close range and that he had fallen from his pony in one of the clearings and had been dragged into the thick undergrowth.

Morshead's death was a great loss to the Survey, and a bitter blow to me. His wife Evelyn was in England on leave, with five young children, and his sister Ruth was keeping house for him in Maymyo. I had to break the news to her, and arrange his estate and affairs, as well as take over his official duties temporarily as Director. An enquiry was held, and though there was not the slightest doubt about what had occurred, his wife only received the minimum pension—£80 a year as far as I now recollect—on the grounds that Henry had not been killed *on active service* [Mason's italics]. I did all I could to get this ruling altered without avail, and I got little encouragement from the Surveyor General, though the appeal went to the Secretary of State. Before the year was out I became unofficial godfather to their youngest son, Nigel, whose other godfather [Leonard] was killed in a riding accident.'

Vultures, forsooth! So the body which had courted discomfort in life had become the food of necrophagous birds. At least Evie had been spared this; but here was further confirmation that Henry had not been riding his own horse. Mason described it as murder but offered no definite clues. Ruth too recollected it as being a borrowed horse. Certainly many newspapers, and even the police report itself, refer loosely to 'his riderless horse'. But was it actually *his* horse? The police report made no comment on this vital piece of evidence. The possibility of its being someone else's horse was not even mentioned. Yet this was the first clue that the actual evidence suggested.

Largely as a result of the Rebellion, the statistics of important crimes in Burma (excluding murder), in which firearms were carried, had more than trebled over the same six months of the previous year. For the fortnight ending 25 May the trend was even worse, 223 against 36 the year before.[6] The largest increases were in the south of Burma, and Indians were usually the victims. Martial law had even been considered, but rejected[7]. The Government, therefore, had every reason to be embarrassed if Henry's were to be found to be a 'political' murder; but nobody ever seriously thought it was political. Yet, in declaring the crime a mystery without apparently investigating all the clues, the Government seemed to have a reason that outweighed its own embarrassment.

One was left to conclude that, if not political, it had been done either by one or more game poachers or, equally, by one or more dacoits; that it could have been either premeditated or opportunistic, although the location made it look more likely to be the latter; or that it might possibly have been a case of mistaken identity. The first, more distant, shot from behind could

Evelyn in 1934

Evelyn in 1974, with a
nephew

(conceivably) have been accidental. The second could only have been intentional. After the first shot Henry could probably have galloped off; true to himself, instead, he turned to face his assassin and took the second barrel from point-blank range.

What of Evelyn's financial position? Henry's will was proved at £6,753, all of which he had saved himself. In those days, prior to 1 December 1952, the pension of an officer's widow was subject to a means test. Evelyn's pension of £80 per annum lasted until 1939 when it ceased on account of means. There was no lump sum benefit even after thirty years' service. His death would nowadays have been treated both as being on active service and with greater generosity. For example, widows of short-service private soldiers killed in an I.R.A. ambush at Warrenpoint in 1979 received lump sums of £5,603 plus pensions ranging from £1,714 per annum. Even an unseated Member of Parliament gets severance pay.

It did not take a genius to see that here was no embarrassment of riches. With five children to educate, Evelyn had become a poor relation overnight. Among her papers I found a document penned by Henry:

'Having, in 1919, at my Mother's desire and against my own judgement, waived my claim to a son's share in her estate, and having decided against any form of insurance, I hereby place on record that, in the event of my death at any time leaving my wife Evelyn in pecuniary difficulties, I confidently rely on such of my brothers and sisters as may at the time be alive, jointly and severally to contribute to her a sum of money equal to that which I would have been entitled had I not waived my claim.'

What was Evelyn supposed to do with this well-intentioned but futile adjuration?

Mr. J.L. Stow, Headmaster of Horris Hill, immediately offered reduced fees, a generous act that was maintained for four children over a period of many years. Winchester, Wellington and Downe House did the same; one son won an Exhibition, another was awarded a Kitchener scholarship; and Henry's uncle for many years paid Evelyn an allowance to cover the education of his 'heir', the eldest child. None of these things were as of right, however, and they put Evelyn in the unenviable position, for her, of having to accept charity on her family's behalf. Indeed, when her eldest child was killed in action in the war she repaid his tiny estate of £200 in a spontaneous gesture to his school's Appeal Fund. She also tried to reimburse Downe House, but the Headmistress Miss Willis, in an equally gallant gesture, refused to accept it and returned the cheque. It was lucky that she did, because when Evelyn's allowance ceased it was without notice or notification. The only intimation was a letter from the bank manager pointing out that she was more overdrawn than usual.

The two youngest children were never told about their father's death, but were left to find out gradually; they were still confidently expecting him to turn up in time for Christmas, 1932.

It was seven years before a family car appeared again, and the houses that Evelyn rented invariably compared unfavourably with those of our well-heeled school friends, one of whom observed that it only required two doors to be left open in our house to see from the street into the lavatory. A school contemporary at Winchester with whom I felt an affinity was John Leigh Mallory, the climber's son. We were both in the same house, which my great-uncle Freddie had founded; and our Housemaster was the same Graham Irving, the climbing expert, who had first introduced George Mallory to the Alps. Every schoolboy knew his father's story, and John consequently diffused a rather sad aura. Of impressive physique and devoid of nerves, he inherited the ability to climb the outside of any building and, if suitably dared, would balance across the handrail of the nearest rickety bridge in his best Sunday clothes.

Notes

1 Nash Professor Emeritus of Law in Columbia University (New York).
2 She a good tennis player and he Chief Secretary.
3 Sir Joseph Maung Gyi, Home Member of Council under the recently introduced diarchical constitution, was Acting Governor of Burma between Aug. 1930 and Jan. 1931, in the absence on sick leave of Sir Charles Innes. He attended the funeral.
4 Gold Medallist of the R.G.S. and later First Professor of Geography at Oxford and Fellow of Hertford College.
5 Kungka Shan was climbed for the first time on 12 July 1981 by a team led by Chris Bonington.
6 *Rangoon Gazette*, 11 June 1931.
7 *The Times*, 20 May 1931.

 **15** L'Envoi

For my own part, I inherited neither the desire nor the opportunity to explore or climb mountains, let alone hunt and shoot big game. My one and only climb was to the top of Apharwat, the 13,000 ft. hill behind Gulmarg in Kashmir; on the summit I found a man whom I knew, on leave like myself, from his unit of 14th Army over 1,000 miles away. 'Oh, not you!' we exclaimed simultaneously.

I did, however, share Henry's latent interest in eastern languages, and a visit to the scene of his death was 'brewing up' within me. It would be my first visit to India and Burma since World War II, and I was prepared to take 1980 as a sabbatical year if necessary. People might yet be found who would express opinions more readily today than at the time, for reasons of fear or reprisal.

As a family we had seldom discussed Henry's death. What more was there to say or speculate upon? If the officials and family friends on the spot could not solve the mystery, what was the point? Still, I was armed with more information now; and I had had my scepticism rekindled as I sifted through Evelyn's papers. Once before, twenty years after her pension was suspended, I had made further enquiries about it on her behalf. Sure enough, the rules had been altered without notification to former pensioners. Her pension was re-instated at £180, backdated to 1952, and increased by degrees to £1,540. It was time to bestir myself again, and to continue the investigation.

A box containing some of Henry's belongings never reached England after his death. Would it, I wondered, have contained any evidence? Any letters addressed *to* him perhaps? Possibly money was involved; from the evidence of his last letter a large loan had apparently been made to someone called Barton, whose name was also in the visitors' book. Henry's sister might be worth consulting; at the age of eighty-eight there was a chance that Ruth might still remember something.

Before flying east I decided to drive west, down to Devon, to see her and explain my plans. Earlier in the year I had 'moved house' for her from one small hotel to another. Her entire worldly possessions fitted into the boot of my car in two small suitcases.

Ruth had lived a large part of her life in India and, not having her own house, had often stayed with Henry and Evelyn, sometimes for months at a time. I, in turn, had stayed with her in her chalet at Gulmarg, 8,500 ft., during the war. Her stamina had been so renowned locally that it was difficult for her to find walking companions of her own sex; she made light of the punishing 5-day trek to the sacred cave at Amarnath. She was, in this respect the counterpart of her brother; but, unlike Henry, she did not like riding and had no riding kit.

'Henry was your brother, and you were there, actually living in his house at the time. Tell me what *you* think happened? Did you worry when he did not return? What was the atmosphere like at the time?'

I suppose if Ruth had any theories to offer I would have heard of them before now, and I hardly expected the meeting to produce much. Henry was frequently away, and not returning when expected. That was nothing unusual.

'I remember waking next day to the sound of marching feet. Your father was heavy-handed; he must have made an enemy somehow.' she added.

'Did you ever discuss the subject with Evelyn?'

'No, she was too upset for that.'

It is a great mistake, people say, to try and recapture old memories. I have decided to ignore their advice. After all, Henry's story ends fifty years ago and needs bringing up to date. What of the McMahon Line today? What of the Survey of India now? Are there buildings still standing that I will recognise? Above all, are there people still alive who remember a fifty-year-old murder? Perhaps if I delve too deep they will murder me too... *Tayyib, bismillah, yallah bina...* Well, in the name of God, let's go.

Foreign Office clearance has been obtained, to help me penetrate officialdom should it be necessary. No visa is required for India or Pakistan, but for Burma I am allowed only seven days, in spite of my application to the Burmese Ambassador. I am going to have to move fast when I get there. Inoculations, travellers' cheques: have I forgotten anything? I open the book my son has given me to read on the plane. It is Robert Morley's *Book of Worries*. I close it again.

Flying over Baghdad and Kuwait and along the Saudi coastline, the bright, reddish glare of gas burn-offs strikes the newcomer. What a lot of them there are, and I make the usual novice's comment: 'What a waste!'

Arriving at Bahrain airport at 1 a.m., I decide not to incur a £40 hotel bill for the balance of the night. Pity all the soft seats are on the *departure* side of immigration control. Each day this ship is late is going to cost me at least £50. Parrot-like, I try out a well-rehearsed phrase in my most 'posh' Cairene dialect. Do you understand me? 'It's beautiful' he says in English with a grin. As dawn breaks I have another go, this time asking the way to Gray, Mackenzie & Co., the ship's agents. I wait outside for them to open up. It turns out that the somewhat disreputable, but obviously thriving, establishment outside which I am waiting is their liquor service depot. I am redirected.

Two nights are necessary at this hotel, waiting for the P. & O. Strath Services' m.s. 'Dwarka'. A thunderstorm is raging outside and a violent north wind (*shimal*) is rattling the windows. Glad I'm not on the 'Dwarka' now; she must be shipping it green. Next day I take the island tour, tacked on to Sacha Distel's band. A new French-owned hotel is pointed out by the guide. Next stop is a dilapidated dhow builder's yard. 'Ci, c'est l'hotel nouveau français?' The bus erupts, and it is one-love to the Englishman. We learn about the Dilmun civilisation that was here in 2,700 B.C.; this evening, by way of contrast, I am watching the *Muppet Show* in Arabic on the hotel's T.V.

I get down to Mina (port) Sulman as requested by 9 a.m., together with several hundred expatriates from the Indian sub-continent all waiting to board. I am chatting with them in my World War II Hindi. They are vocal at the way they are kicked around in the Gulf States. Certainly there is nowhere to sit; and we do not embark until 2 p.m. I leave my belongings unattended beside a boy called Anwar, and go for a long walk round the docks. Mr. Mushtaq of Gray, Mackenzie's shows me to a comfortable cabin. Hell, I gather the ship is still on its outward journey, away from India, and will not be leaving here till 11 a.m. tomorrow. I may have to miss out Pakistan on this trip. I am just dozing off to sleep when pandemonium breaks out. It is Hogmanay, and the ship (of course) has a Scottish Chief Engineer and First Officer. Every ship in Bahrain is sounding off the New Year and wanting to have the last blast.

A memorable sight as we leave Bahrain is a two-mile long skein of wild geese in weaving single file, only eighteen inches above the water. 'They are very disciplined' says my companion. 'Discipline and terrestrial magnetism' I concur. The steward presents Captain C.E. Willoughby's compliments and I am invited to drinks in his cabin. As I am the only first-class passenger on board at this stage, he has time to answer my questions.

'Dwarka', 4,851 tons, was built by Swan Hunter's in 1947, and is the last British passenger ship sailing the Gulf. She carries 1,000 people including her crew of 125, most of them deck passengers, as Henry found on the

'Varela'. Willoughby knows of the latter, which was one of the 'V' class steamers that used to run the weekly Fast Gulf Service in the days when the Gulf was run rather like a British lake. 'Dwarka' tries hard to stick to a three-week sailing cycle out of Bombay, but is clearly forced by circumstances to operate on a day-to-day basis. She is nearing the end of her life and it is doubtful whether she will be replaced. I have surrendered my passport to the purser with a couple of spare photographs. He makes no promises but will try and get me a temporary shore pass where possible.

We reach Kuwait in two days but cannot get alongside for a further 36 hours. This means we will not leave till tomorrow, a whole week since I flew over the city. It suits me actually, as I want to savour my return and am in no hurry. Moored alongside us, under a full moon riding high in the heavens, is a freighter named 'Gulf Moon'. Ahead lies a whole day ashore in Kuwait.

My taxi-driver's name is Suliman Saghah al-Zafari and he owns his taxi. We try for the spectacular Kuwaitia Towers revolving restaurant, which can be seen from miles out to sea. The six-hundred-foot-high theatre-nightclub does not open until the evening, so we settle for something less ambitious. He takes me to the Kuwaiti Museum and the curator there thinks Henry's Islamic coin is some form of temple token. An interesting curiosity catches my eye. It is a 'blown-up' photographic enlargement of a 1926 permit, complete with photo, authorising its Kuwaiti owner to 'seek work in Bombay'. The boot is very much on the other foot nowadays.

I am trying to run myself a hot bath. The water is gloriously hot but there is only a trickle from the cold tap. I have an unusual problem. The plug leaks faster than the cold tap runs. How do I get the bath *cold* enough to get into? I notice a third tap and try it, and brown sludge emerges. I go to sleep listening to the combobulating of the antiquated Doxford diesels, sending her along at 12–14 knots through the night, and wake up as we are entering Doha (Qatar). I take a pre-breakfast walk on deck in my dressing-gown *à la* old-style P. & O. We shall be here till lunchtime, but there is no taxi service so I am unable to get much beyond the harbour area. Each port is a law unto itself as to whether it permits you to get ashore.

Life on board has settled into an agreeable routine. Several passengers joined us at Kuwait. Three senior Indian Air Force officers, returning home with their wives and children after two years' service in Iraq, fill a whole long table in the dining room; at another sit the ship's officers. Captain Willoughby presides under the Queen's portrait, with the Chief Engineer and the First Officer, successfully maintaining the imprint of the P. & O. The Christmas decorations were dismantled last night. On my left are Mr. & Mrs. M.S. Khan from Karachi. His hobby is translating *Roots* into Urdu.

He has already translated Goldsmith's *Vicar of Wakefield*. For the drinkers there is a snug little bar which opens as soon as the ship leaves port. I did not get ashore yesterday at Dubai. We were told the ship would be leaving at 11 a.m. but it did not get clear until 3 p.m. Lifeboat drill is blaring out in four different languages one after the other. It does this after each port, from every loudspeaker, and there is no escape from it.

No wonder the ship is late leaving. The delay is caused by arguments over what constitutes reasonable hand luggage for bringing up the gangway. The idea of those leaving a duty-free emporium like Dubai is to get the maximum amount of what is undoubtedly merchandise for resale, up the gangway, rather than into the hold where it would have to pay duty at the other end. The quayside is full of gesticulating, shouting people giving orders to other people who take no notice. A fork lift truck charges them deliberately and everyone scatters and reassembles.

The junior ship's officer on the gangway is lenient and usually gives in, but he is adamant about one enormous bale. After much pleading it is eventually slit open and appears from my viewpoint to contain 6 carpets, 12 umbrellas, and about 15 shirts. Suitably divided out by the gang it still comes up the gangway. Within half-an-hour a bazaar is going full belt between decks.

The gas burn-offs can be seen well out to sea, some groups of them giving off as much light as a medium-sized town. We went through the Straits of Hormuz during the night while watching the film 'Ice Station Zebra' in the ship's library, and are now in Mina al-Qaboos (Oman), all gathered round a transistor set, listening to my cousin Mark Tully interpreting the Indian election results on the B.B.C. World Service. This is our last port before Karachi; we are only here for three hours and no one is allowed ashore. The Captain has sent a cable to the ship's Karachi agents to book me on to a Delhi flight, but he is going to have to change it because we are running late.

*   *   *

It is 3 p.m. and we are 200 yards from the dockside. The sound of the waiting, welcoming throng can be heard as a distant murmur. Time-lapse has made me as elated as they are. The noise is increasing to deafening proportions as the tugs push her in; now people are clambering up the outside of the ship, ignoring the gangway. A face appears at my cabin window.

Saying goodbye to my companions I launch myself into the crowd and through immigration control. The taxi is an ancient British-made Ford 8 h.p., *mazbut wallah* according to its two owners, but it has already run out of petrol and is having to be pushed most of the way to Gray, Mackenzie's through the Karachi rush-hour traffic. When we find a petrol pump I am invited to pay for the petrol. I decline. Fortunately Mr. Mirza knows I am on the way and has not closed his office. He has booked me on a Pan Am flight at 00.40 hrs. tonight and has cashed me a traveller's cheque.

I enquire at the P.O. whether I can phone Delhi, but the line is too intermittent. A cable would arrive later than I would. A kindly Parsi couple, seeing me looking for a taxi, are offering me a lift; they tell me that the hotel I am looking for, the Bristol, still exists but that I will find it run down and empty. The owner is reluctant to serve me. I explain and he understands. He offers me a chicken kabab, and I have an hour to wander in the dusk while it is prepared. It is beyond my capability to explain to him why I am *glad* the hotel stands unchanged, except by time, beside the downtown railway tracks. Nowadays people go by air. I am eating alone in the ancient vestibule, listening to the cicadas clicking, my first night back for 35 years. Two ginger and white cats with sticky fur are crunching up the chicken bones as my taxi arrives.

What clean bilingual efficiency at New Delhi airport at 2.50 a.m.! What clear audible loudspeakers! I can't ring Mark Tully at this hour; but at 4 a.m. I take a taxi to Tully*kothi* and leave my suitcase on his doorstep. The temperature is 5°C. and it is too cold to hang about. I walk to the railway tracks where an impatient monster is waiting for the signal to change. Returning, my case is still on the step. I walk to the nearest Moghul tomb, never far away in Delhi. This one is the double-storied tomb of Khan-i-Khan Mirza Abdur Rahim Khan, Regent to the 4-year-old (3rd) Moghul Emperor Akbar (1556–1605) and adviser to his successor Jahangir (1605–1627). Hundreds of pigeons are circling and settling, circling and settling on the venerable brickwork of its dome and minarets. Down below, in the *bagh*, early joggers are out. By this time my suitcase will have been taken indoors (or stolen).

I am shown in by *khansamaji* and given tea. Thank heavens I did not ring from the airport; I gather Mark did not get to bed till 2.

Sabah al-khair! Good Morning! The Tully household is coming to life. Four children and aunt Gwen are at home. Margaret appears. Soon other people are coming and going, correspondents, journalists, politicians, friends and the children's friends. The dog has had suspected rabies, injections are necessary and the children are late for school. I tiptoe past the seated figure of Mark furiously typing and have a bath.

My day is spent chasing a chimera between the British High Commission (blue Rolls Royce and a smart Gurkha on the gate) and the Home Affairs Departments. It appears that no permit is necessary for my purposes; but I am enjoying traversing New Delhi from place to place. The city lay-out impresses me even more than before. Connaught Place seems larger, the Lok Sabha exactly the same. The driver of my scooter-rickshaw points out the two Lutyens Secretariat Blocks.'I know,' I reply rather smugly: 'I used to work in that one.' There is more English writing than I recollect seeing in 1945; street names are written bilingually and navigation is easy. Some of them are names of great beauty: Raj Path—the Road of State, Jan Path—the Road of Life.

In the evening Mark and Margaret have an engagement. More people arrive; we introduce ourselves and chát. Miraculously our hosts are back in time to sit down to a meal. There must be twelve of us and the conversation is bilingual. Tully*kothi* is clearly a valued local institution. The phone rings three times for Mark during the first course; the answer is always a cheerful affirmative. In the end he takes a plate of food upstairs to the office. I am leaving for Dehra Dun by the early bus tomorrow, and before I get back he will be in Pakistan.

Margaret cuts me some sandwiches and rigs up a camp bed in an office. I lie there, sedated by the chatter of the telex machine in the next room, listening to the sound of Mark's voice again; only this time it is on the World Service once more, from London on my transistor; possibly the very commentary I saw him preparing just now.

I am boarding the Express Bus from the Kashmir Gate Terminus, for the six-hour drive via Meerut, Rurki and Muzaffarnagar. We stop in a pleasant *bagh* by a river (the North Ganges Canal actually) and crows are eating the remains of my lunch. The road starts to climb the Siwalik Range and to grow scenic. Henry built many of these bridges around Dehra; they used to be pointed out to us as children. Colonel Dalal is waving a greeting at the terminus and driving me to the hotel he has chosen.

The local Congress-I Party H.Q. is opposite and a *tamasha* procession is setting out in celebration of their election landslide victory. Bamboompita . . Bamboompita . . Bamboompita . . goes the rhythm, dancers gyrate and speeches are declaimed from the platform. I am back in the hotel, reading two books that Dalal has lent me, after lunching with him and his authoress wife Nergis. A former officiating Surveyor General and Archivist, he has the history of the Survey of India at his bidding. Tomorrow is Sunday, but Dalal will arrange for me to meet the present S.G. on Monday. Meanwhile he has given me a letter of introduction, and a present, to take to his opposite number, Col. Hla Aung, former S.G. of Burma, whose address I will have to find out when I get there.

'The activities of surveyors like your father form the basis of our negotiating position with the Chinese,' Dalal had said. It appears that the 'controversial' McMahon Line of 1914 has stood the test of time and, although never formally accepted by China, is still India's de facto N.E. boundary, delimited if not demarcated. 'McMahon was able to put the finishing touches to his famous red line after hearing the results of an extensive survey made by Bailey and Morshead', wrote Dorothy Woodman in her book *Himalayan Frontiers*. Indeed, the Line follows their very footprints over five degrees of longitude.

*   *   *

The music that is being played in the foyer appeals to me. I look at the name on the record and it is 'Asha Bhosle, live at the Albert Hall', with Rahul Dev Burman, in June 1978. Sirdarji Chug who runs the President Hotel has sensed that I am on a mission. A joss stick is burning in my room; nothing is too much trouble. He personally takes me to tea at the Club, which is larger than I remembered. Last year the State of Uttar Pradesh went dry and the Club's two bars look forlorn, but tennis, squash and card games are in progress. There are billiard tables and a dance hall with a sprung floor.

How to spend Sunday? Sirdarji runs the President Travel Service as well as the hotel and will have an all-day taxi waiting for me. In fact, while I'm visiting he will through-book my entire flight programme if I know my own plans. I do and he does.

How does this confounded camera work? The first two pictures are of my feet. I am outside the Doonga House Hotel, which used to be our house at No.4, New Survey Road. The road is now called Ugra Sain Road or just Club Road will do. The front lawn is a grove of lychee and jackfruit trees. A huge jackfruit, eighteen inches long and weighing 30 pounds, had once fallen here during the night, a yard from my bed. The world's largest known fruit, they are not normally supposed to fall, but the beds were in a different place the following night. During the war the house had been a home for grass widows, called Mulberry Manor, and it was said at the time that a certain amount of 'monkey business' used to take place there. (A wise monkey is a monkey that doesn't monkey about with another monkey's monkey.)

My lunch consists of *barfi* eaten in the taxi as we orbit the immaculate Forest Research Institute, its botanical gardens and the Indian Military Academy, all dating from Henry's day. Being Sunday, what we can see is rather restricted. Nobody has heard of a house called 'Mountain View'; but St. Joseph's Academy looks spotless and newly built. I pay off the driver with a handful of four different currencies mixed up with spare lavatory paper.

Major Iqbal Siddiqi shows me into Maj.Gen. K.L. Khosla's suite on the new Hathibarkala Estate and leaves me chatting with him and his Deputy,

Colonel G.C. Agarwal. Their interest and encouragement are more than mere formalities. Orders are given to search files for anything about Henry, and to post them on to me if necessary. The S.G. arranges for me to be shown round, and gives me an introduction to H.C. Sarin, the well-known Delhi mountaineering personality. For good measure he draws me a map of how to find him.

At the time of partition there were six Directors: this has now gone up to nineteen. The Survey of India emblem is still used, but the motto has been changed from 'A Montibus ad Mare' (from the Mountains to the Sea) to 'A Setu Himachalam' (from the Cape to the Mountains). James Rennell and William Lambton would have been proud to know that their names are on it. We inspect the bust of Col. R.H. Phillimore, the archivist, which was unveiled here in 1974. On the way out I prevail upon Siddiqi to give me some background on Maj.Gen. Khosla himself; the printed word conveys inadequately the urbane friendliness of the present holder of this high office.

Mr. V.K. Nagar is waiting for me at the Geodetic & Research Branch. The buildings date from 1870, and I soon find myself in Henry's office. Right outside is the Basevi memorial clock-tower under which Henry used to garage his car. The clock-tower is named after Capt. James Basevi, who died in 1871 while conducting observations in Kashmir at 16,000 ft. with the recently arrived pendulum apparatus. Over there is the de Graaff Hunter Observatory where we, as children, were taken to look through the telescope. A marvellous museum of old theodolites and survey equipment, portraits and manuscripts waits to be explored. The young Librarian who shows me round, Miss Charanjit Mamik, clearly enjoys her work.

The taxi has climbed to 6,500 ft., dodging the many road-repairing lorries careering up and down the hairpin bends, and deposited me outside the Savoy Hotel, Mussoorie. With its multiple annexes connected by covered walkways, it has the largest ground area of any hotel in India, never mind Mussoorie; but business appears slack both because it is January, and because the locals prefer the smaller and more intimate hotels.

A guide offers his services, but Henry's 8-inches-to-the-mile map makes this unnecessary; nothing has changed. No taxis are allowed in the Mall, so I traverse it eastwards on foot admiring the view of the plains below. The 500-foot cliff above me on my left is the feature known as the Camel's Back, visible for miles around. I come to a new chair-lift, not marked on my map. If I cared to wait half-an-hour I could go up to the summit, but time does not permit. A turning leads off to Grey Castle, but someone tells me the old nursing-home is now a ruin. Farther on is the guarded entrance to the Survey of India, Castle Hill Estate, and, a little further still, the bazaars of Landour cantonment. The older hotels and houses retain their English names. While waiting for my taxi-driver to re-appear I pop into the Public Library. Even the books are unchanged.

I am settling my now rather complicated bill. Siddiqi has arrived with some treasured mementoes from the S.G., and Sirdarji has lent me a travelling rug; he says I will need it and can return it to his Delhi office. I claim my couchette, and the train is already imperceptibly moving as a man from the hotel rushes down the platform with a carrier bag that I have left behind in the hotel. That is worth ten rupees of anybody's money.

This blanket is saving my life: I could have done with two. But what is all this hammering on my compartment door in the middle of the night? *Yeh kya ho raha hai*? (What is going on?) We are at Saharanpur Junction and I am apparently in someone else's berth. This train is going to Lahore? I'm out in a flash. The front half is going to Delhi, and further up the platform is a man who has my name on his list. The system is working. In fact I'm beginning to think it is working uncannily well. Is providence lending me a hand? My project is gaining in coherence and momentum all the time.

I am sitting in the garden of the tomb of Humayun (1530–1556), father of Akbar, and Aurangzeb's great-great-grandfather, listening to a paradise of birds. Delhi is famous for them. There must be several hundred crows in the tree opposite, from the sound of their community roost, although not one is visible amongst the thick foliage. The seat below is to be avoided. Parrots, hoopoes, mynahs and sparrows go about their business, and wheeling high above are tier upon tier of kite-hawks soaring on effortless thermals.

Sarin rings back; I am to visit him tomorrow. President Travel rings back; my tickets are ready. Mark's secretary Lorna is taking all my messages. Mark himself has been to Pakistan and back while I have been away. I chat to Peter Nettleship of B.B.C. External Services News, who has dropped in. I find he went to Maymyo three years ago, following in Theroux's footsteps. He is describing a certain Rest House. I finish the description for him. It is easy; he seems to be describing our house. Peter is as pleased as I am. 'How beautiful!' he says.

I am really keyed up now; how stupid of me not to have re-read Theroux's book *The Great Railway Bazaar* before leaving! Mark has a copy somewhere, but we cannot find it. After fifty years, a war and a Japanese occupation, is it conceivable that our house still stands? It could just be. If so, I wonder how many families are now living in it. I shall soon know. Boy, am I glad I decided to go and see for myself!

A crow carrying a whole *chapati* flies past, and sweepers are burning small fragrant bonfires of fallen eucalyptus leaves, as I walk along the smart suburb of Friend's Colony to meet Harish Sarin, President of the Indian Mountaineering Federation. His home is a veritable museum. Pictures and mementoes on an international level abound, some of the most treasured being of 1965 when an all-Indian expedition placed no fewer than nine men on the summit of Everest.

Sarin was a wrangler of Emmanuel College, Cambridge, and I notice among the photographs his youthful figure in the college team pictures of the 1930s. A spectacular tiger-skin, of record dimensions, is set at precisely the artistic diagonal, adorning the wall of the open-plan room. His wife brings in coffee. She has made their son promise never to shoot another one, she says. Sarin played a large part in sponsoring Sir Edmund Hillary's Jet-Boat Ganga Expedition, and a lot of Hillary's book is about him. While I am exploring Sarin's treasures he is looking up references to Henry in his own books, and I find he has endorsed Dalal's envelope to Colonel Hla Aung with a message of his own: 'I think it was you who came to the Himalayan Mountaineering Institute, Darjeeling for a mountaineering course which we had arranged. I was then in the Defence Ministry. You may remember me. If so, I am thrilled to make contact with you through a friend Morshead—his father was a great surveyor and mountaineer. H.C. Sarin, New Delhi, 16 Jan 1980.'

Sarin generously insists that I take such books as interest me. 'But I'm leaving Delhi at 7 a.m. tomorrow.' 'Well, read them on your travels and return them to my Calcutta office on your way back.' I accept, but which office? He suggests the Tinplate Company of India of which, amongst other things, he is chairman.

I have been to President Travel, handed back the rug, and collected my tickets and a carrier bag complete with Concorde label. The latter, I feel, qualifies me for a meal in the Moghul Room at the Oberoi Intercontinental. It has the most extensive Hotel Shopping Centre facilities I know of, including clothes made to measure overnight. The waiter, Paul Dean, turns out to be a friend of Sateesh Jacob, a member of Mark Tully's staff. He points out a table where Bob Friend (the Tokyo Correspondent), Mark and Sateesh were sitting one evening recently when Bob left his wallet behind with all his papers and $2,000 in cash. When he returned in a panic the restaurant was closed; but he was recognised in the foyer by Paul, who had already handed them in, and was able hurriedly to identify their owner to management. Bob quickly peeled off $200 for Paul and still caught his plane.

Margaret calls me at 5 for my 7 o'clock Indian Airlines flight to Calcutta. It is 19°C. here at Dum Dum airport. Two men are watching intently as I rearrange my kit and extract some cooler clothes, while waiting for my flight connection. I display the contents of my case for their benefit, lifting things out one by one and demonstrating them. The contents largely

Kanchenjunga, 28,145 ft., seen from Darjeeling

comprising dirty clothes, they soon take the hint and walk away. A cow walks along the forecourt eating paper and cardboard. Powerless to help, I watch it eat about a dozen pieces.

*   *   *

A permit, easily obtainable on arrival at Bagdogra airport, is necessary before I can visit Darjeeling, 7,000 ft. The official has not noticed from my passport the fact that I am revisiting my birthplace. The 'toy' railway from Siliguri still runs (at a loss) but takes twice as long as the tourist bus. I am sharing half a taxi for the 56-mile 3-hour drive. This hotel, the (Oberoi) Mount Everest, is the oldest and largest in Darjeeling, and is where most of the climbers stayed. A coal fire is being lit in my bedroom as a matter of course. I gather from Mrs. Chand, the manageress, that Karma Paul, the interpreter to the 1922 expedition, still lives in Darjeeling.

Mrs. Chand arranges for a member of the hotel staff to show me round before it gets dark. Climbing to the top of the ridge behind the hotel we soon find 2, Catherine Villas, now the home of a police inspector. The backdoor overlooks a *khud* with a view over Lebong, 5 miles away, which has the smallest and highest racecourse in the world. Almost next door is the house Chevremont, now occupied by an educational establishment. The whole ridge is Cooch Behar property, and at the narrowest point we come to the site of the Rockville Grand Hotel, destroyed by an earthquake and landslide in 1935; only its annexe remains. The old Bellevue Hotel, now a students' hostel, is pointed out; a new Bellevue has been built lower down the slopes.

There must be a hundred Land Rovers and Indian-made Jeeps here on the summit of Tiger Hill, 8,482 ft., in spite of its being off-season. A 4.30 a.m. call, warm clothes thrown on over our pyjamas, a murmuring goes up from the crowd as the curtain-wall of Kanchenjunga starts to turn pink in the eerie dawn. Two minutes later the higher but more distant Everest lights up, an inspiring start to the day.

Walking briskly along the contour towards the Himalayan Mountaineering Institute in the mid-morning sunshine, I pause for a moment in Chowrasta. Darjeeling today has a population of 45,000, which includes Sikkimese, Bhutanese, Gurkhas, Sherpas and Tibetans, as well as Indians. I find myself staring at one of them. He is staring back at me. I ask him, 'Does he know where I can find old Karma Paul?' He does indeed, he *is* Karma Paul, and I have homed right in on the 86-year-old Tibetan Christian.

We are back at Paul's flat, off Nehru Road, and his daughters Tshering and Sonam are serving us coffee, as he recalls the events of sixty years ago. 'Your father passed his Tibetan exam first time, and won the Government prize of Rs. 500/-. I used to give him lessons at the old Bellevue over there.' He still has in his possession the testimonial Henry gave him. Paul later went on Everest expeditions with Ruttledge, Shipton, Tilman and others, and was the first to interest Tenzing in Mount Everest by introducing him to Eric Shipton in 1935; he rates a picture in Bruce's book on the 1922 expedition, and a painting in oils at the R.G.S.

The curator, B. Sain, is showing me round the Mountaineering Institute, where one of the attractions is to view the mountains through Hitler's telescope. I am more interested in a showcase containing a Sikkim *dak*-bungalow visitors' book, lying open at the year 1921. I am pointing to Henry's signature in it: but he is pointing to another signature *on the same page*—that of his own father, M. Sain, a well-known local artist. Most of the décor at the Institute is by M. Sain, who at the age of 92 still lives in his Darjeeling studio.

We have descended 6,000 feet, through the Darjeeling tea gardens of Peshok and Lopchu, and my 1953 Land Rover has pulled up at the control point at Teesta Bridge at the junction of the Rangit river and the Teesta. Gangtok, 40 miles north, is in a prohibited frontier zone, but my permit is valid for Kalimpong, two marches from Darjeeling on the old Everest trail. Now we are 'climbing the 4,000 ft. from the Teesta valley to Kalimpong

CHEVREMONT,
DARJEELING.

16. 1/22

Karmah Paul has worked with me as Tibetan *munshi* at sundry times since April 1921. He is well-educated & intelligent & has a very pleasant manner;— I can thorough[ly] recommend him.

H. T. Morshead
major R.E.

D⟨y⟩ Sup⟨t⟩, Survey of India.

Karma Paul's testimonial from Henry

without a halt'; only this time it is not 'a stifling afternoon of damp heat'; and I am not on foot, as were Colonel Norton and Henry.

The Dr. Graham Homes, a large and flourishing school in Kalimpong, can have changed but little in 60 years, but I am heading for the Himalayan Hotel. A busy holiday season is over, and there are no guests resident. A strikingly handsome portrait in oils hangs in the hotel lounge, 'such an odd mixture of East and West'. Of his family of nine 'there is in evidence today' one daughter, Mrs. Vicky Williams, who runs the hotel. Her father David Macdonald, author of *20 Years in Tibet* and *Land of the Lamas*, was once British Trade Agent in Yatung and Gyangtse; he assisted in the escape to India, from the Chinese, of His Holiness the 13th Dalai Lama in 1910. Both families, Grahams and Macdonalds, offered hospitality to all the early Everest expeditions. They will always have a presence in Kalimpong.

Back in Darjeeling, Mrs. Chand points out Tenzing in the hotel foyer, and I waylay him for a moment. He has a house close by, and runs his own travel company. He quickly reels off the names of the 1922 expedition.

Seeing me dining alone, three friendly Japanese invite me across to their table. They, apparently, had poor weather for their visit to Tiger Hill this morning. And what am I doing here? Born here? Ah, so! Your father a climber? Ah, so! One of them is chairman of the Mountaineering Institute in Kobe, and insists on full particulars for verification back home. We exchange visiting cards; theirs are in Japanese, mine is in Arabic.

*   *   *

Here in Bangalore, I have specially asked for a room in the old part of the West End Hotel. It dates from 1905, is palatial and, consequently, doomed to be redeveloped this year. There is a huge bathroom, an even bigger dressing room, and a bedroom with its own wide, roofed balcony 42 ft. long all to myself. Did *they* stay in this very room, I wonder?

The numbers in Spencer Road have all been changed. I guess No.14 now forms the centre section of this school. *Age barho* (move on)... Stop, stop...that gate on the left with the sentry. It says on the notice board 'Regional Centre for Technology Transfer'. Bangalore has become a technological boom city; the sentry says 'no photographing please'. Yes, he thinks it probably was once a private house. I *know* it was. I have a photograph of it when it belonged to C. Desaraj Urs, a relative of the Maharajah; the hunt used to meet here.

We skirt the edge of the sun-baked golf course. Now we are in Palace Road and this house, although now numbered 2 and not 4, is definitely where we lived in 1925 and 1926; it contains the offices of Greaves Cotton Ltd. The former Mysore Government Office, a still-impressive large red

2, Palace Road, Bangalore, in 1924

2, Palace Road, Bangalore, in 1980

building, now houses the High Court of Karnataka, but has itself been upstaged by a bran-new State Parliament Building of faced stone. Behind them both, as ever, is Gubbon Park covering three square miles, with its statue of Sir Mark Gubbon, first High Commissioner.

If Maymyo is my Mecca, the Lalbagh here is my Medina. Its enormous size, 95 acres in my childhood, has been expanded to 240 acres of superb and timeless (well, 1760) beauty. Even in the off-season for its exotic scents and blooms, it impresses. I cannot afford much time; from this huge selection of specimen trees I select a giant and read the name on its label:

Fam: Coniferae   "Agathis Robusta"
Hab: Austral   F.M. Baiely (sic)

Remarkable!... Is it destiny that of all these trees I should choose one named after Henry's great friend? Or do I just attract coincidences? My brief visit is illuminated by the event.

I select a second tree: Your Majesty, the "Arancaria Cookii" which you planted on 22.2.61 is doing fine and is about forty feet high.

Somewhere among them must be the water flower trees, whose fallen blossoms contain water which children can squirt out. One more label will I read — the one on that amazing object, whose bulbous multiple trunks seem to end in a few self-effacing stumpy branches: it is an exceedingly rare baobab tree (Fam: Bombacaceae, native of Africa), said to have been planted upside down by God in a hurry, and its trunk is actually a water reservoir. Its 8-inch-long fruits, enclosed in a woody shell, are relished by baboons, and by people with Henry's digestion.

I am taking tea with Colonel A.S. Iyer, Director, Southern Circle, and his Superintendent T.R. Viswanathan. This office is a new one, but apparently Henry's old office block stands empty and locked up, shortly due to be demolished. Colonel Iyer sends for the key, and our footsteps echo down the empty halls to a hexagonal room at the far end. 'This would have been your father's office,' says Iyer, 'overlooking the old hockey ground out there. It's all built over now.' My mind is peopling the rooms with figures from the group photo in Henry's album as we retrace our steps, returning, via the Bangalore Club, to Iyer's own house for more tea. He has not joined the Club himself; like Henry, he has to keep going away on tour. I am lucky to have found him in his office.

This dear old hotel suite is giving me the utmost nostalgic bliss. I order tea and have it on my first-floor balcony. Two mynah birds converse unseen among the leaves; a bright green flash is a parrot's flying display, and crows eat the remains of my airline biscuits. Audacious, cunning and ever wary, they know to an inch exactly how near they can approach.

For breakfast I choose a south Indian vegetarian dish. The day heats up. One bird sounds like running water; the coppersmith I hear again. Most suites here have two rooms; mine is a corner suite with three, and a ground area the size of a house. In the new development, by the Taj Group, it will become a disco, coffee shop or a Polynesian restaurant and earn its keep. Meanwhile I am revelling in the luxury of it. It is still January but the hotel swimming pool is already attracting custom; I shut the windows (monkeys can climb in) and go down and join the swimmers.

*　　*　　*

The Great Eastern is the oldest hotel in Calcutta, and a landmark for two centuries. It is run by the Department of Tourism of the West Bengal Government. The basic room price of £9 compares with £40 in Bahrain, and the room is bigger and the service better. A Leather Industries Expo has taken over the first floor, and a Bengali is holding his astrology and palmistry forum in the lounge. I take a walk down Chowringhee, now called Jawaharlal Nehru Road. The *maidan* is the same, and, although there are two or three times as many people on it as in 1943, there are fewer beggars. A small shop called Firpo's Bazaar stands on the site of the famous restaurant. I go on to return Sarin's books, walking briefly through the business quarter, Clive Street, Bankshall Street, Lyons Range, old haunt of box-wallah and counter-jumper, as opposed to the competition-wallahs of the Civil Service, and the Services.

The phone is ringing in my hotel room: it is Captain Rajkumar Titus, Survey Officer to H.Q. Eastern Command, on behalf of the Army Commander, to whom I have been given an introduction. 'Your father's name is a household word in the Survey of India', the voice is saying. Tomorrow is Republic Day, a National Holiday, the next day is a Sunday, so he will call for me at 11 a.m. on Monday.

The floor show at Maxim's is good, a singer and a five-piece group. I order a second Tom Collins. The carp-like river-fish of Bengal called *bekti* is still the most delicious-tasting fish in the world. I have a third Tom Collins, and recall two aquatic sisters at the Calcutta Swimming Club who were nicknamed Hilsa (another equally delicious fish) and Bekti... Goodness Gracious me... The dancer is coming among the tables... Long hair drifts across my face, and I plant a kiss somewhere about waist level.

Saturday 26 January is Republic Day, and many Calcutta streets are closed to traffic. Stripping myself of all valuables except my watch, and three low-denomination notes buttoned into a rear trouser pocket as a deliberate challenge to pickpockets, I head for the densest part of the crowd lining Red Road. Hemmed-in on all sides, I settle for a distant view of SAM-

III surface-to-air missiles, on show for the first time in Calcutta. There are earlier SAM-IIs and Russian PT-76 tanks used in the Bangladesh war of 1971; six recoil-less guns go by among the many Army and Navy bands. Over 1,000 Services personnel, 2,000 para-military and cadet corps and 1,000 school-children are taking part. I leave before the procession is over. My pocket has been duly and expertly picked, but I still have my watch.

Who are all these distinguished-looking people gathering in the foyer on Sunday? An attractive secretary from the host country explains: the Association of Commonwealth Universities have a seminar, commencing today, under the auspices of Calcutta and Burdwan Universities. She is sure they would not mind my joining them on the sightseeing part of their business, and offers to introduce me to Sir Hugh Springer, their Secretary General, who kindly agrees.

There are two coachloads of us, including wives, and it appears that every man except myself is Vice-Chancellor of a University. Had I known this beforehand I should have been less brazen; at least I am wearing a tie. Seven British Universities are represented, and it looks as if Cambridge are going to be represented by a supernumerary B.A. (War Degree) Third Class.

After inaugural addresses at ministerial level we are taken to the Victoria Memorial, where there is an excellent museum of pictures, busts and manuscripts, including one of the largest pictures in the world. It is of Edward VII, as Prince of Wales, in the Elephant Procession at Jaipur, and was presented by the Maharajah thereof. The foundation stone was laid in 1906 by George V when *he* was Prince of Wales. Here is the 3-foot theodolite, constructed by Troughton, which reached Calcutta in 1830 and was used on the Great Triangulation 1835–73 . . . and here is a whole room full of Perso/Arabic scripts: *History of the Reign of Alamgir. . Counsels of Luqman. .* Persian Translation of the *Upanishads. . Shahnahmah* (Grand Epic by Firdausi, the Homer of Iran). . *Bhagavad Gita. . Diwan-i-Hafez. .* Document written by Ibrahim, son of Tamerlane. . Notebook and letters of Tipu Sultan. . . 'Please come now, sir, the bus is being delayed.'

India is gripped by cricket fever. The Test rubber with Pakistan is already won, and the final Test is on Tuesday; unfortunately I leave tomorrow and shall miss it. Never have I seen so many games of cricket going on at once as there are on the huge Calcutta *maidan*, every hundred yards or so, such that a batsman could be caught by a fielder in a different game. 'Our fourball were just about to putt, when a fifth ball arrived on the green — yours.' someone had once said to me after a gigantic slice from another fairway. 'We had to mark it before we could putt.'

Mother Theresa addresses us before showing us round the orphanage at

Nirmal Hriday, and several handkerchiefs are seen discreetly wiping an eye, before we move on to take tea in a Students' Health Home and Hospital. Now we are watching a brilliant staging of Tagore's ballet *Tasher Desh* (Kingdom of Cards) by Rabi-Tirtha. The dancing hands rivet the attentions and fascinate with their sinuous hyperextension. Does my effrontery know no bounds? Yes; dinner is to be in the Raj Bhavan (Government House), and the coach is wheeling in through the gates, as I slip quietly away before protocol is offended, eternally grateful to Sir Hugh Springer and the A.C.U. for their liberality. I hope I did not push it too far. Remember the Winchester College motto, Morshead: 'Manners Makyth Man'.

A picture of James Rennell, first Surveyor General of Bengal, hangs on the wall opposite me. I am at 13 Wood Street, once the office of the Surveyor General, now that of the Director, Eastern Circle, Colonel B. Sarin (no relation to Harish) and his Deputy, Lt.Col. G.K. Roy. R.H. Phillimore recalled (in a letter to his nephew David) how when His Highness Shamsher Jung, Rana, Bahadur Ruler of Nepal was in Calcutta for the visit of Edward, Prince of Wales, he presented ceremonial *kukris* to Phillimore and Bob Thomas in this room: 'We had a shock when the old man challenged the huge map in our spacious Hall; for to our dismay he had noticed that it showed Nepal accidentally coloured in British Red. I had to concoct a hasty excuse that it was an ancient map, and that current maps had long been put right in that matter.' Truly, the British Empire was acquired by accident.

Similar examples of 'cartographical aggression' occurred several decades later, on Chinese maps of Ladakh and the North East Frontier Area. When Nehru complained to Chou En-lai in 1962, he got the same reply—that they were old maps which they had not had time to change.

Suddenly we notice the time. I have to catch an afternoon flight to Rangoon, and Captain Titus' staff car is racing towards Fort William. Saluted smartly every few seconds, we reach the eyrie of the General Officer Commanding in Chief, Eastern Command, and General Eric Vas, P.V.S.M.,[1] welcomes me in. I regret to say that I do most of the talking, but flatter myself that this is on account of his sympathetic interest in my plans. It is going to be a mad rush back to the hotel for my case, and onwards through dense traffic to Dum Dum airport:

> 'For the wind is in the palm-trees,
>   and the temple-bells they say:
> "Come you back, you British soldier;
>   come you back to Mandalay!"
> Come you back to Mandalay,
> Where the old Flotilla lay:

179

> *Can't you 'ear their paddles chunkin'*
> *From Rangoon to Mandalay?'*
>   Rudyard Kipling

Indeed I can but, alas! it will have to remain a memory; the Flotilla was almost entirely scuttled in 1942. . . and my plane is over two hours late.

I wonder, while waiting, where I will find myself sleeping tonight. A moment's panic: my yellow fever vaccination certificate is mislaid: I find I have foolishly used it as a bookmark. Also I have lost my voice. There is something rather diverting about the concept of someone with pharyngitis trying to speak a foreign language—unless of course it is yourself.

The taxi driver in Rangoon has little English and I have no Burmese. We get on best in Hindi. He has taken me to the Strand Hotel, a comfortable old-style building next door to the Burma Airways office, all ready for tomorrow morning. It is also near an arm of the sea, hence the name. It is too late to contact Colonel Hla Aung and I have an infected throat anyway. The receptionist has, however, located him in the telephone book, and she appears to be telling him about the foreigner with the strange voice, who carries a letter and a parcel for him which he is going to leave here; and who will be back in five days time hoping to meet him.

Accommodation in Rangoon being short, this arrangement will ensure that I get maximum time in Maymyo and have a room to come back to here. I hand her some dirty clothes as an earnest of my intention to return, take an antibiotic (I *had* thought of everything) and retire.

It is 11.15 a.m. and I have been sitting in Rangoon airport for an hour. Every now and then I take a walk round, consulting the oracle of the Tourist Burma counter, the Burma Airways check-in and people generally about my flight, scheduled for 11.30. Nobody has a clue. It is a question of whether rather than when. I take the opportunity to confirm my flight back to Calcutta. This internal section of my through-booking is not recognised here, and I must pay cash over the counter and reclaim later. Aha, but if they are taking my money it suggests there must be a flight some time. 'I know where I'm going,' I find myself humming, almost singing, 'but there's no one going with me.' This has to be done alone.

We are cruising at 900 ft., and I think it was 2.15 p.m. when we took off in this twin-engined Fokker Friendship, two seats each side of the aisle. A short stop at Heho (for Inle Lake), and tea is handed round. There is no time to visit the lake, however outrageously picturesque; an aerial view must suffice. I am the only non-Burman on board. The soil has gone from ochre to terra cotta with grey rocky outcrops. White pagodas crown the hilltops, and the Shan Hills loom on the horizon.

I am negotiating for a jeep at Mandalay airport. Not much actual negotiating. Yes, yes, whole car please, whatever you say, 120/- Kyats in advance, I'm not waiting for other passengers. 'I know where I'm going, and I've got a bottle of 'duty free' for whoever is living there.' It might even be tonight. But what are the chances of solving a fifty-year-old mystery in five days?

We are speeding across the twenty or so miles of rice plain, climbing the 3,000 ft. *ghats*, and are now only two miles off. I ask him to drive slowly. Dusk is descending. The bazaar I recognise, the Catholic church goes by. Wonderful! Those must by the Survey Offices, exactly the same, just as Dalal said I would find them. The road seems familiar; but no, we are turning up a different drive to ours ...

*   *   *

Candacraig, Maymyo

This place fully bears out Peter Nettleship's enthusiastic description. It is not our house but I *have* been here before. I appear to be the only guest, and there is time before supper for a walk in the starlight. I *must* find it tonight. I know I'm near but it is dark; there is no moon and the house I am looking for is down a fifty-yard drive. There are also cowpats to avoid, as I have just discovered. After half-an-hour I give up and turn back. *Al-hamdu lillah.* That row of lights and that overhung roof silhouetted against the night sky. I must have walked right past it. I venture a few steps down the drive. *Al-hamdu lillah.* Tomorrow I will see it by daylight. *Now* I can orient myself. It is only a few hundred yards from where I am staying. I take another look before retiring to bed; it is still there, and I have four whole days ahead of me.

No wonder it took me so long in the dark; Forest Lodge, Fern Lodge, Pine Lodge and Upperfold are nearly identical, all built in the same 'colonial' style as Candacraig itself, although the last, designed in 1904 as a bachelor 'chummery' for the Bombay Burma Trading Co., is considerably larger.

I take a taxi to the botanical gardens and the Harcourt Butler Lake. Right beside it is Inlya Lodge, where Kenneth and Dorothy Mason lived. Now we are on the shiny tarmac of the *bund*, constructed by World War I Turkish prisoners-of-war; here my pony once bolted with me, fell badly and had to be destroyed. The tranquil beauty of this place is stunning; my childhood memory has not let me down.

'Is there an old swimming pool down there below the *bund*?'

The driver is surprised that I know of it. Indeed, I came face-to-face with a water snake in it at the age of eight. My clockwork seaplane had sunk in

Upperfold, Maymyo, in 1930

the deep end. . . I make my way down the overgrown path and examine it minutely—a static tank half full of scummy water that holds me spellbound. The changing-rooms and diving-boards have long since disappeared, but not without trace to an eye that knows where to look.

'This is where they measure land' answers the driver. He has become interested in his passenger and offers to go inside to seek admittance for me as I have no introduction and no appointment. No problem either; I am shown straight in, to the office of U Mya Thein, Officer-in-charge, No.1 Survey Party and Principal of the Survey School, Maymyo. I am seated in my father's very office beside the man who is doing his very job. And where does he live? Holy Cow. . . at Upperfold, our very house! This is intoxicating stuff on my first day here. Tea is brought in as we chat. I dismiss and thank my jeep taxidriver. Mya Thein is driving me back to lunch with him and his wife at Upperfold.

I am strolling round the garden chatting and photographing. The flower beds of cannas lining the drive have gone, and grass has encroached on the carriageway, but who maintains a three-acre garden nowadays? Those beautiful teak floors, teak staircase, and even the children's safety gate at the top are exactly as we left them fifty years ago; the window I climbed out of in my sleep; the landing on which we drank our Ovaltine. The rooms are few and large, and the structure wonderfully intact, even some of the outbuildings.

Upperfold, Maymyo, in 1980

Mya Thein is off on tour this afternoon; a day later and I would have missed him altogether. He has kindly invited me to roam the garden whenever I like. Unbelievably a solitary tennis post, 1929 vintage, still stands, delaying its entropy, beside the grassed-over court; the same walnut tree which looks dead but isn't, and the tree we used to swing from. The pagoda stone on the garden path is still recognisable, its sundial broken; but the custard-apple seed which I planted has either not grown, or grown and died. The large bamboo clump has been cut down; but the magnificent Flame of the Forest tree (*Let-pan-bin*) has spread its umbrella-shaped crown halfway across the old tennis court.

Candacraig is now run by D.P. Kalansuriya, a Sri Lankan 8th Army veteran of the Royal Indian Army Service Corps, who saw service in Cairo, Tobruk and Benghazi, and has now taken Burmese citizenship. At his suggestion, on this my second day, I have arrived at the door of Dr. I.D. Alexander, a veteran of the 1942 evacuation of Burma when he had charge of hospital arrangements. His sister lives in Kingston Vale, with British citizenship while he has Burmese. Politics being what it is, they are doomed never to meet; he cannot leave the country and she cannot enter it. I take a photograph of him for her.

Dr. Alexander is driving me round to the house of Albert Bernard, who used to run Candacraig for 16 years before his recent retirement. He was even in charge of catering there back in the 'twenties when it was a

The old tennis court

chummery. The bachelors must have dined well judging by the calibre of the testimonials collected by Bernard in his long life; he is now 86. We find them gathered round an outdoor fire built round a huge old tree-stump. Green tea is served, Burmese-style, and we talk and talk, all about his various jobs and old times generally. Yes, of course, he knew Colonel Morshead; can even remember serving meals to him. At the time we were at Upperfold he was cook to the Fogartys over there at that house called East Ridge. He says he has even got newspaper cuttings about the murder. A cold night breeze blows a shower of sparks from the blaze, and Albert sends 'Sonny' (aged 39) inside to fetch a couple of pullovers, for himself and me. Sonny is a teacher at the school I should have attended myself (the Government English High School) had I not come home to England. I recall my parents debating the issue.

I am invited to go round there again tomorrow morning, any time I like, and stay to lunch. Back here at Candacraig the house has filled up. All are youngsters planning to stay one night and move on with their rucksacks. One or two I recognise as having been on my flight from India. From the conversation they seem to fall into two categories: those who have just come from Katmandu, and those who are about to go to Katmandu. The visitors' book is international; Theroux's book is partly responsible for this place starting to rival Nepal. *Another day gone.*

For years it has been Bernard's hobby to collect strange stories and oddities, mainly from the newspapers, the concentrated headlines of which make for strange reading: Ox with horns as long as its body—Man wakes up at his funeral—Hen's egg with watch face on it—Saved by his false teeth. Here is one about a sick joke played on a Council Meeting—Telephone hoax of Councillor's death prior to Meeting & in he walks. Many of the cuttings concern longevity and he has clearly been interested in this subject for years. Bernard interrupts me to tell me a joke:

'Have you got anything for grey hair?'

'No, Sir, only respect.'

I carry on searching: Five-year-old girl becomes mother—that was one from *The Daily Mirror*; One-year-old swims ashore after falling into lake from boat—that happened in Canton; 145-year-old man in Constantinople. I come at last to the cuttings on Henry's murder. They duplicate my own; I hardly expected otherwise, since I believe I possess every cutting that ever existed on the subject.

'If it was a poacher he would have been after wild pig, barking deer—they have small horns—or *sambar*—they are the biggest deer of all, almost as big as a pony. Or it could have been jungle fowl, doves or green pigeon. I brought down 28 green pigeons once with two barrels. I was using Mr. Nunes' gun. He was in the P.W.D.—lived at Fernside.'

The conversation turns to people Bernard has met.

'Mr. Cuffe was your father's predecessor. The right side of his moustache was white and the other side black—from smoking.'

Bernard has cooked for varying numbers from 1 to 20 without notice, and regimental and farewell dinners for up to 45 people.

'For General and Lady Slim's Victory Dinner on October 11th, 1945, I had 15 assistants and cooked for 200.'

Lord Mountbatten and Peter Townsend have shaken his hand in congratulation. Here is an appreciative note from Mrs. L.M. Fergusson—must be the wife of Bernard Fergusson of the Chindits; and one from Mrs. Anne Prescott—she must be the wife of the District Superintendent of Police, Mandalay; and here is one from Evie's friend Mrs. H.S. Fogarty.

Bernard is saying grace, and I meet each of the family in turn as they bring in dishes, vying with one another to honour their father and his guest. He has been a lifelong teetotaller and is now reaping the rewards of it in his robust good health. He has, however, shrunk in size, and I would scarcely have credited his former 14 stone had I not seen his early photographs. 'The happiest years of my life', he confides, 'were the ten years I was officers'-mess contractor to the Royal Artillery—the 7th, 10th and 2nd (Derajat) Mountain Batteries, you know.' He is helping me all he can, but there are still no actual clues for me to work on.

The ninth and last member of the family arrives as I am leaving. He is Father Victor Bernard, 34, a Catholic priest, Salesian of Don Bosco, from Kyaukme in the Northern Shan States. A bottle of eucalyptus oil, for my throat, is pressed on me as I leave, and I am to come back whenever I like.

*   *   *

I walk out into the Reserve Forest behind Candacraig. A large belt of it has been felled and not re-afforested; what is left is barely waist high, with the result that visibility is now several miles. Further out still the jungle is much denser. The Rides appear to be bullock-cart tracks now. I rejoin the road opposite Upperfold and take the short cut through the Nursery Garden; it looks private, but I know it as a right of way. Doubling back, I make for the old Club House and find it gone. One of the few casualties of the war, it was burned to the ground, and only a flat bare patch among the bushes marks the site of its tennis courts, ballroom, library and lounges, where the 'Maymyo stare' would scrutinize the newest arrivals in the station.

Looking in at the Golf Club hut I enquire about green fees. I know there is a young New Zealander at the guest house who wants a game, and this is one of the finest courses in Asia. Crossing the old polo ground I find the remains of the practice pit. Hit the ball here as hard as you like and it comes back at you from a different angle. A nippy nine-year-old won a bottle of whisky here, in the musical chairs, but was soon deflated; 'I let you win' said an adult, as the boy went up to collect the prize. My, how aromatic the air smells. Then I remember that I have a eucalyptus handkerchief just under my nose.

It is the wrong season for the *padauk*, or rain-water flower. The Burmese say that when the *padauk* has flowered three times the rains come. Instead I search, unsuccessfully, for a mimosa plant (*mimosa sensitiva*) which grows close to the ground and whose leaves close up when touched. Perhaps that too is out of season; but the grass is soft and dry, and the slanting sun still warm. Lying down beside the fairway, my head propped on a tree-stump, I am dreaming of the tinkling cow-bells of a returning herd getting closer. 'Grandfather sleeping', says a young voice behind me. I wave a hand without getting up, and hear giggles.

On the way home I get lost and walk miles, through cantonments of soldiers mustering for an evening parade, slightly embarrassed by my swinging camera. 'Left Right, Left Right' say I and get back grins. I ask the way of an Indian; he dismounts from his bicycle and, deep in conversation, walks me all the way to my door. *Bang goes my third day.*

I am breakfasting with the New Zealander who wanted a game of golf. 'Ring the club house', I tell him, 'and they will contact a local resident called

John Fenton

Dr. Game.² His handicap was once a bingo 4—he has spare clubs and will enjoy a round. I will join you if you like; I shall be over at that house called Upperfold taking photographs, or with the Bernards.'

Sonny Bernard has offered to accompany me to the old garrison churchyard to look for Henry's grave. A short way down the road a car pulls up. It is Dr. Game with the New Zealander, looking for me. What about the golf? Where are we off to?.. Dr. Game becomes interested...

'Jump in... There is someone I think you should meet.'

Blessed Fortune!... In two minutes we should have been out of sight. With no prior notice we are driving round to the house of a dear old Anglo-Burman aged 91 called John Fenton, who lives in Manor House Road. The moment he hears my name he knows who I am and what I have come about. He is offering to tell me what he thinks happened, *provided I won't be offended by what he has to say.*

'Of course not, that's what I'm here for.'

He is as glad to tell it as I am to hear it. The New Zealander realises that this is the end of his golf game and retires gracefully.

'No need to take notes, my father will write you a statement', explains the eldest son, Walter. Indeed, he has already started writing within three minutes of my setting foot in his house. I am chatting with Walter and his brother Reginald, who both apparently know the story. 'It concerns a relative of yours', says Walter as we wait.

'Do you remember wrestling with me once at a party?'

It begins to come back to me; 'Now you mention it, yes.'

'They all said to me afterwards "that was Colonel Morshead's son you were wrestling with". I remember him coming to address us when I was at the Government English High School.'

The statement is ready; I read the first few lines and feel as if I've been pole-axed. Am I dreaming? Or having a nightmare?... My mind is racing ahead. New and totally unexpected avenues are opening up. This is what he has written:

'This is exactly what I had heard during that time and it is as follows:— Please excuse me if it gives hurt to any of your family or to yourself. It is something concerning a lady related to your father. Mr. Syed Ali was living in the Manor House then but I didn't know where your father lived. Syed Ali used to go out riding and in fact I met him once on the Mission Road riding with a lady—to be exact it was at the junction of Fryer and Mission roads. I didn't really know who was that lady. I remember well about it as I wished him (Syed Ali) good morning then. I know Syed Ali well too because, I think, it was in 1925 that I was initiated in Lodge Moyde when he became Worshipful Master of that Lodge.

I suppose there was some objection by your Dad of the Lady going riding with Syed Ali and probably there was some misunderstanding between Syed Ali and your Dad. This is exactly a rumour which I cannot vouch to be true.

Sometime later I heard that your Dad was shot and killed on one of the Rides east of Maymyo. There was quite a lot of rumour floating about then, implicating Syed Ali in the case. Some thought he was thought to have been shot deliberately and some thought it might have been an accident done by a poacher. However the British Govt. seemed to have taken some serious investigation in the matter and I don't know what they found out about it. Some local hunter was heard to have been taken away for an enquiry but I did not (hear) the result.

I was working for the Bombay Burmah Trading Corporation then as Manager in a district of the Pyaungshoo Forest known as Kawng Kham some miles away, east of Maymyo. The area I worked had been on the borders of Hsipaw, Lawksawk & Mong Kung states. I used to come into Maymyo to our Head Office for specie once in three months or so.

So when I came back to my Hd: Quarter i.e. Maymyo next time I heard people talking that Syed Ali had left Maymyo for some reasons, leaving his work in the hands of his younger brother Younis and his son Rahmat. What people were supposed to have said about Syed Ali was that he had

Ian Morshead

been deported back to his own country but God knows what the cause really was.

I was living in a house called Augusta Villa, on Fryer Road, which is now known as Padauk Street, and it was at the back of or behind Manor House and the road known as Manor House Road.'

Sonny Bernard is still waiting patiently for me outside. I am invited back here to lunch tomorrow, my last day.

'I'll take you to look at Manor House first; it's quite close by . . . Here it is, biggest house in town, a prestige place that is used a a film set from time to time. See, the drive has recently been re-surfaced.'

We walk on to the Garrison Church and find the grave; the headstone is broken, deleaded and fallen, but still legible. In my imagination I hear the echoing shots of the firing party . . . a bugle detail is sounding the Last Post, its diminuendo hanging on the air, haunting the mind.

It is afternoon by the time we return (having said we would be back early), but Albert Bernard has waited lunch. He says grace and we eat together again, served like royalty by the many members of this devoted family.

Cherchez la femme! The last thing in the world that I expected to find was a *femme fatale*; and here was Henry's own sister cast in that rôle. Could Ruth have a secret? Something of which even Kenneth Mason was unaware? Was this the missing piece of the jigsaw? Suddenly I feel I have started something I cannot finish.

Had Henry named his killer in his last letter home? Nay, in the last sentence he ever wrote, an hour before his death? He says he sat next to Syed Ali at a dinner of the United Club the previous Sunday. So it was Syed Ali who lived at Manor House. . . Coming from the direction of Elephant Point the horse had to *pass* the turning to Upperfold in order to reach Manor House; it would not have passed its own home turning; it was clearly not Henry's horse. Syed Ali was the owner of the Maymyo Bank and of the Electric Supply Co. and Grand Master of the Lodge. He certainly had the money; now Fenton has supplied a motive. Henry must have fallen into the trap set at that dinner. He was a dead man from the moment he accepted the offer of a ride on Syed Ali's new Arab pony. Right . . . It's a date then . . . I'll send the *syce* round with him at 6.30 a.m. next Sunday . . . That gives him a whole week in which to hire an assassin . . . Embarrassingly for Syed Ali the pony already knew its own stable, and returned there riderless and bloodstained . . . Those marks on the suspect's ear and cheek were caused by a desperate lunge of Henry's riding-crop as the assassin manoeuvred for position with the choke barrel.

I am walking at a leisurely pace from Upperfold down the only possible

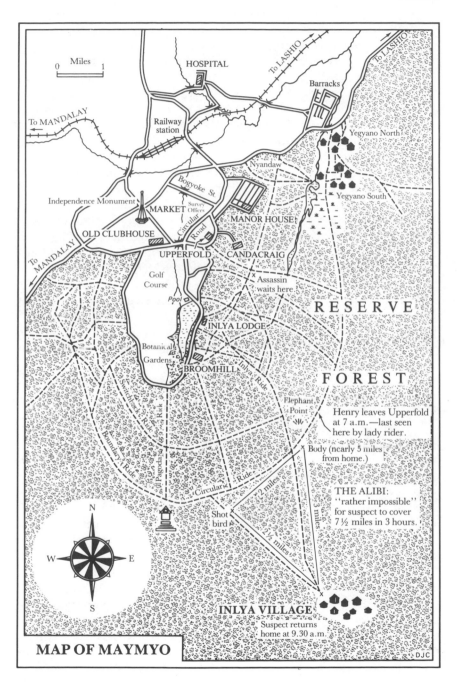

MAP OF MAYMYO

track, the one we always took, almost opposite the garden gate, out once more into what was the Reserve Forest. Here I am, at the first intersection of bullock tracks. Fifty years ago an assassin is hiding here. He has been shown the Arab pony, told where to wait, given half the money in advance and told to plant his 'shot bird' alibi on Saturday evening. A rider will appear here, on this same horse, about 7 a.m. Sunday, never mind who, and the rest of the money is yours after you've done it. Oh yes, and there's extra money the further you stalk him. I don't want it happening on my doorstep . . .

Turning right, I follow the track round to Inlya Lodge, Mason's old house, spending some more time at the old swimming pool. The round trip back to Candacraig has taken me an hour and a half at leisure. I am hunting for something to give Fenton, in token of my gratitude. The most personal present I can think of is my new Viyella dressing-gown, something quite unobtainable in Burma. He is wearing it, and it fits beautifully; but he is taking it off again. Somehow I have let slip the fact that it was my wife's Christmas present to me last month, and he declines to accept more than the token wearing of it. I stay on to tea. 'Be merciful' he adds as I am leaving. 'Of course' I reply.

I am at Dr. Game's house drinking more tea and thanking him for his help. He is dressing my four huge blisters, and I am inspecting his many golf trophies. U Mya Thein's car is back in the porch at Upperfold: he must be back from his tour. I present my bottle of 'duty-free', and go on to say farewell to the Bernards. 'The old man has gone to sleep' whisper the daughters. I book an early call for tomorrow.

Ten people, plus luggage and wicker baskets of produce, is the normal load for these World War II jeeps that still run up and down the *ghat* from Mandalay to Maymyo. I am unable to get on to the Rangoon flight, in spite of telling Burma Airways that the Surveyor General is waiting for me; but all is not lost. If I kill time until 5.15 p.m. there will be a charter flight of Japanese ex-soldiers of World War II returning from a ceremony of sorts at Myitkyina. I toy with the idea of introducing myself as a former opponent of theirs. After waiting two hours for me in Rangoon, Colonel Hla Aung has unfortunately gone home.

The pleasant young New Zealander is in the restaurant and I seat myself next to him. His week also is finished, and he never did get that game of golf. He is by now beginning to get used to our conversations being continually interrupted by my stream of contacts; he is therefore unsurprised when in walks Colonel Hla Aung. I thank the former Director General of the Burma Survey Department (1959–75) for honouring Henry by turning out a second time, late at night. Hla Aung is still President of the

Hiking and Mountaineering Association, and he hands me as a memento a photograph taken near the top of Saramati Peak, 12,533 ft., on the Indo-Burma frontier.

*   *   *

My greater pilgrimage is over, but I still have a problem. To whom can I tell my story? Can I tell it at all? Because to believe Fenton is to imply a lack of candour elsewhere. I parry one question with another as the problem chafes within me. Did I exert myself to seek the truth only to conceal what I had found? And was what I had found the truth, or just another rumour to add to the many? I had made no secret of my intentions before starting; to put the record straight was my highest ambition. Had my suspicions of a covering up been proved right for the wrong reasons?

From beginning to end I have felt propelled by a guiding force; may it not desert me now! The sense of predestination is uncanny; I cannot seem to put a foot wrong. The coincidences have been so numerous as to be scarcely explainable in any other terms. People I have met by purest chance seem to have appeared as if by appointment.

I have managed to locate Harold Oxbury, the actual Subdivisional Officer, Maymyo at the time of the murder. He has responded to my letter by return of post and kindly invited me to lunch.

My excitement mounts as I drive to meet the very man who took the first phone call from Syed Ali after the murder. This had been Oxbury's first appointment in the Indian Civil Service, and he had been intimately involved. His immediate reaction, on putting down the phone, had been to think in terms of a riding accident, but it was soon apparent that there had been too much blood for that. He started the search himself, at once, for the horse's rider. Oxbury's clear recollection of the affair is in full accord with all the contemporary press accounts that I know so well; he harbours no private suspicions, and has heard no suggestion that the horse might have been lent or borrowed. As he explains to me, there was no record of the horse's ownership ever having been disclaimed when the police made their enquiries. Given no such disavowal, the horse might logically have been assumed to be Henry's, and no one would be likely to question the assumption once made.

Equally, there was no record that the question 'whose horse?' had ever been asked; the subject is simply ignored in the Police Report.

If, as Mason wrote in his memoirs, 'the horse was identified as having been lent' to Henry; and if, as Fenton wrote, there was 'rumour implicating Syed Ali in the case', then one might expect the District Superintendent of Police to have known about it. Yet Prescott, the D.S.P., had said nothing to

Oxbury, the S.D.O., about the horse's being lent. Who then was Mason's informant? Was it Ruth herself? Apart from this one all-important clue, Mason was as much in the dark as everyone else.

Nobody in Maymyo then or since, until my visit, had ever produced a motive for the wanton killing of my father. Could Prescott himself (and he is long since dead) for whatever reason, have suppressed some information? Certain it is that he would never have found anyone to bear witness against this powerful freemason Syed Ali; and he might have been trying to shield the Colonel's own sister from scandal. No, the very idea is too outlandish and insulting to contemplate. Will I ever learn who is shielding whom? I have one throw left.

I have written to Ruth about Fenton's statement, and told her she will find me a sympathetic listener if she has any comments to make. She has accepted my invitation to tea. A log fire is blazing, and the house is empty except for ourselves. She can recall little from those far-off days, certainly nothing about Syed Ali. She never met him herself. In fact the only reason she remembers his name is because Henry did not like him.

'Your father used to refer to him as "that awful man".'

We watch the flames for a minute, interrogating the silence. No, it would be unthinkable that Ruth could have known more than she ever told. Suddenly I feel ashamed of myself. How unworthy of me to consider such a thought.

'And how are you going to tell your story?'

'I'm not sure yet. I suppose I will relate it exactly how it happened.'

John Fenton has given me a list of three names. 'All are ex-Bombay Burmah officials' he has written 'and I think their addresses are known to Wallace Brothers Bank Ltd. If they are still alive, and I hope so too, kindly remember me to them. Also to say that I always remember them in my prayer.' Wallace Brothers do know the addresses; two of them are still alive, and they very much appreciate the message.

'How beautiful!', Peter Nettleship had said to me before I left Delhi. Indeed, the whole six weeks had been beautiful; quite the most beautiful experience of my life. I have taken a small step towards Nirvana, and the silent roar of eternity. I can say my *Nunc Dimittis*: need I say more?

Bat ka khatima. . . . The end.

Notes

1 Param Vishisht Sewa Medal.
2 A former Chief Medical Officer of Burmah Oil Group.

Glossary

Ammon	wild mountain sheep
anna	one-sixteenth of a rupee
arak	liquor distilled from fermented sap
ayah	Indian nurse
bagh	garden
bandobast	arrangement, administration
barfi	sweetmeat
basam	cane foot-bridge (Tibetan)
basha	bamboo hut
bekti	edible river-fish
bharal	Himalayan sheep
box-wallah	European businessman
bund	raised embankment
chang	north
chapati	unleavened bread
chital	spotted deer
chokra	boy
chu	water, river (Tibetan)
chummery	shared household of bachelors
-chung	small (Tibetan; in place-names)
cutcherry	court-house
dacoit, dacoity	robber, robbery
dak	post
damdim	a black and yellow fly with a painful bite
dao	broad-bladed all-purpose knife
dekho	look
dhobi	washerman
dirzi	tailor
dzong	fort, headquarters of a Dzongpön (Tibetan)
Dzongpön	District Administrator (Tibetan)
ghat	range of hills
godown	outhouse, storeroom
gompa	monastery (Tibetan)

gooral	shaggy goat-like antelope
hilsa	edible river-fish
kabab	roast meat
khalasi	professional tent-pitcher, skilled handyman
khamal	stores
khansama	cook
khud	steep hillside
koel	'brain-fever' bird, a type of cuckoo
kothi	house
kukri	heavy curved knife
la	gap, pass, col (Tibetan)
lammergeyer	the Bearded Vulture, said to have a wingspan of about 9 ft.
latsa	hut or camping-ground at the foot of a pass (Tibetan)
machan	shooting platform
maidan	public land, park
mali	gardener
marwa	fermented liquor made from millet (Tibetan)
mazbut	strong (Urdu)
-me	lower (Tibetan; in place-names)
mochi	shoemaker, curer of hides, skins
munshi	interpreter, language-teacher
myo	village (Burmese)
Nyerpa	steward, headman (Tibetan)
Ovis Ammon	wild mountain sheep
Pö, Pöba	Tibet, Tibetan
razai	quilt
ri	hill (Tibetan)
rong	gorge, ravine (Tibetan)
sambar	Indian elk
serow	Asiatic antelope
shabash	well done!
shikari	hunter, ghillie
sirdar	local chieftain, title of respect
syce, sais	groom
takin	a horned ruminant
tamasha	celebration or spectacle
terai	plains country below the Himalayas
thunder box	earth closet
-to	upper (Tibetan, in place-names)
tope	grove or plantation of trees
topi	pith sun-helmet
Tsangpo	Large River (Tibetan)
tso	lake (Tibetan)

ula	free supplies, transport and accommodation provided for an official while on a journey
wallah	person, object
zenana	women's quarter

Appendix

SURVEYORS GENERAL OF BENGAL

JAMES RENNELL	1767–1777
THOMAS CALL	1777–1786
MARK WOOD	1786–1788
ALEXANDER KYD	1788–1794
ROBERT HYDE COLEBROOKE	1794–1808
JOHN GARSTIN	1808–1813
CHARLES CRAWFORD	1813–1815

SURVEYORS GENERAL OF BOMBAY

CHARLES REYNOLDS	1796–1807
MONIER WILLIAMS	1807–1815

SURVEYOR GENERAL OF MADRAS

COLIN MACKENZIE	1810–1815

SURVEYORS GENERAL OF INDIA

COLIN MACKENZIE	1815–1821
JOHN ANTHONY HODGSON	1821–1823
VALENTINE BLACKER	1823–1826
JOHN ANTHONY HODGSON	1826–1829
HENRY WALPOLE	1829–1830
GEORGE EVEREST	1830–1843
ANDREW WAUGH	1843–1861
HENRY LANDOR THUILLIER	1861–1877
JAMES THOMAS WALKER	1878–1884
GEORGE CHARLES DE PREE	1884–1887
HENRY RAVENSHAW THUILLIER	1887–1895
CHARLES STRAHAN	1895–1899
ST. GEORGE CORBET GORE	1899–1904
FRANCIS BACON LONGE	1904–1911
SIDNEY GERALD BURRARD	1911–1919
CHARLES HENRY DUDLEY RYDER	1919–1924
EDWARD ALDBOROUGH TANDY	1924–1928
ROBERT HENRY THOMAS	1928–1933

HAROLD JOHN COUCHMAN	1933–1937
CLINTON GRESHAM LEWIS	1937–1941
EDWARD OLIVER WHEELER	1941–1946
GEORGE FREDERICK HEANEY	1946–1951
IAN HENRY RICHARD WILSON	1951–1956
GAMBHIR SINGH	1956–1961
RAJINDER SINGH KALHA	1961
EUSTACE RANDOLPH WILSON	1961–1962
GAMBHIR SINGH	1962–1966
JITINDER SINGH PAINTAL	1966–1969
JAMSHED ARDESHIR FARDUNJI DALAL	1969–1971
JITINDER SINGH PAINTAL	1971–1972
HARI NARAIN	1972–1976
KISHORI LAL KHOSLA	1976–

Works Consulted

Bailey, Frederick Marshman. *China—Tibet—Assam: a journey, 1911*. Cape, 1945.

Bailey, Frederick Marshman. *Mission to Tashkent*. Cape, 1946.

Bailey, Frederick Marshman. *No passport to Tibet*. Hart-Davis, 1957.

Bailey, Frederick Marshman, *and* Morshead, Henry Treise. *Reports on an Exploration of the North-Eastern Frontier*. Dehra Dun, 1914.

Barber, Noël. *From the land of lost content: the Dalai Lama's fight for Tibet*. Collins, 1969.

Brown, Percy. *Tours in Sikhim and the Darjeeling district*. Newman, Calcutta, 1917. 2nd ed., 1922.

Bruce, *Hon.* Charles Granville. *The assault on Mount Everest, 1922*. Arnold, 1923.

Buchan, John. *The last secrets: the final mysteries of exploration*. Nelson, 1223.

Burrard, *Sir* Sidney Gerald. *Explorations on the North-East Frontier during 1911—12—13*. Calcutta, 1914.

Burrard, *Sir* Sidney Gerald. *Explorations on the Tsangpo in 1880—84 by explorer Kinthup*. Dehra Dun, 1911.

Burrard, *Sir* Sidney Gerald. 'Mount Everest and its Tibetan names'. Dehra Dun, 1931.

Burrard, *Sir* Sidney Gerald *and* Hayden, Henry Hubert. *A sketch of the geography and geology of the Himalaya Mountains and Tibet*. Calcutta, 1907—8. 2nd ed., Dehra Dun, 1932.

Collis, Maurice. *Last and first in Burma, 1941—8*. Faber & Faber, 1956.

Collis, Maurice. *Lords of the sunset: a tour in the Shan states*. Faber & Faber, 1938.

Collis, Maurice. *Trials in Burma*. Faber & Faber, 1938. 2nd ed., 1945.

Gascoigne, Bamber. *The great Moghuls*. Cape, 1971.

George III, *King. The later correspondence of George III*, ed. by A. Aspinall, 5 vols. Cambridge U.P., 1962—70. [See especially no.1597, vol.II, 1963]

Gibbs, Henry. *The hills of India*. Jarrolds, 1961.

Hillary, *Sir* Edmund Percival. *From the ocean to the sky*. Hodder & Stoughton, 1979.

Howard-Bury, Charles Kenneth. *Mount Everest: the reconnaissance, 1921*. Arnold, 1922.

Kelly, Margaret, *and* Kelly, Mary. *The Kelly Book*. Privately printed, 1954.

McRae, Alistair, *and* Prentice, Alan. *Irrawaddy flotilla*. Paton, 1968.

Mason, Kenneth. *Abode of snow: a history of Himalayan exploration and mountaineering*. Hart-Davis, 1955.

Montgomery, *Sir* Archibald Armar. *The story of the Fourth Army in the Battle* of the Hundred Days, August 8th to November 11th, 1918. Hodder & Stoughton, 1920.

Morshead, Henry Treise. Report on the expedition to Kamet, 1920. Dehra Dun, 1921.

Morshead, Henry Treise. Report on the operations of the Mount Everest survey detachment. Dehra Dun, 1921.

Morshead, Henry Treise. Report on the operations of the survey detachment with the Waziristan field force. Dehra Dun, 1920.

Murray, William Hutchinson. The story of Everest. Dent, 1953.

Newby, Eric. Slowly down the Ganges. Hodder & Stoughton, 1966.

Norton, Edward Felix. The fight for Everest, 1924. Arnold, 1925.

Robertson, David James Ian. George Mallory. Faber & Faber, 1969.

Sandes, Edward Warren Caulfeild. The military engineer in India. 2 vols. R.E. Institute, Chatham, 1933.

Scott, Sir James George. Burma: a handbook of practical information. 3rd ed. Alexander Moring, 1921.

Scott, James Maurice. Gino Watkins. Hodder & Stoughton, 1935.

Severin, Timothy. The Oriental adventure: explorers of the East. Angus & Robertson, 1976.

Smythe, Francis Sydney. Kamet conquered. Gollancz, 1932.

Somervell, Theodore Howard. After Everest: the experiences of a mountaineer and medical missionary. Hodder & Stoughton, 1936.

Survey of India. General Report for 1913—14.

Survey of India. Historical records of the Survey of India, by Reginald Henry Phillimore. 5 vols. Dehra Dun, 1945—66.

Survey of India. Notes for June 1931. Calcutta, 1931.

Swinson, Arthur. Beyond the frontiers: the biography of Colonel F.M. Bailey, explorer and special agent. Hutchinson, 1971.

Tenzing Norgay. After Everest: an autobiography. Allen & Unwin, 1977.

Theroux, Paul. The great railway bazaar. Hamish Hamilton, 1975.

Thomas, John. The West Highland Railway. David & Charles, 1966. 2nd ed., 1976.

Thubten Jigme Norbu. Tibet is my country. Hart-Davis, 1960.

Townsend, Peter. Time and chance: an autobiography. Collins, 1978.

Waddell, Lawrence Austine. Among the Himalayas. Constable, 1899; Mittal, 1980.

Woodman, Dorothy. Himalayan frontiers: a political review of British, Chinese, Indian and Russian rivalries. Cresset Press, 1969.

Younghusband, Sir Francis Edward. The epic of Mount Everest. Arnold, 1926.

Journals

Alpine Journal, November 1931; Indian Daily Post (5—6 January 1928, for H.M.'s articles Overland to India); Indian Quarterly Register; Journal of the Bombay Natural History Society; Rangoon Gazette (19 May, 20 May and 11 June 1931); Royal Engineers Journal (September, 1923)

Papers

The F.M. Bailey Collection (MSS EUR F.157) at the India Office Library and Records
Letters of Henry Morshead in the archives of the Royal Geographical Society

Photographs

Morshead Album, Royal Geographical Society Library

Index by Philip Ward

OLEANDER TRAVEL BOOKS
  I.   Come with me to Ireland
       Philip Ward
  II. Touring Cyprus
       Philip Ward
  III. Indonesia: a Traveler's Guide
       vol. 1: Java and Sumatra
       Darby Greenfield
  IV. Indonesia: a Traveler's Guide
       vol. 2: Bali & Eastern Indonesia
       Darby Greenfield
  V.   Bangkok: Portrait of a City
       Philip Ward
  VI. The Aeolian Islands
       Philip Ward

OLEANDER LANGUAGE AND LITERATURE
  I.   Translating Chinese
        Wayne A. Schlepp
  II.   Romagnol: Language and Literature
        Douglas B. Gregor
  III. Mad Nap: Pulon Matt
        Douglas B. Gregor
  IV.   Just Pick a Murricane? by
        N.E. Chantz
  V.   Indonesian Traditional Poetry
        Philip Ward
  VI.   Biographical Memoirs of Extraordinary Painters
        William Beckford
  VII. The Art and Poetry of C.-F. Ramuz
        David Bevan
  VIII. Friulan: Language and Literature
        Douglas B. Gregor
  IX.   Marvell's Allegorical Poetry
        Bruce A. King
  X.   Celtic: a Comparative Grammar
        Douglas B. Gregor

ARABIA PAST AND PRESENT

LIBYA PAST AND PRESENT

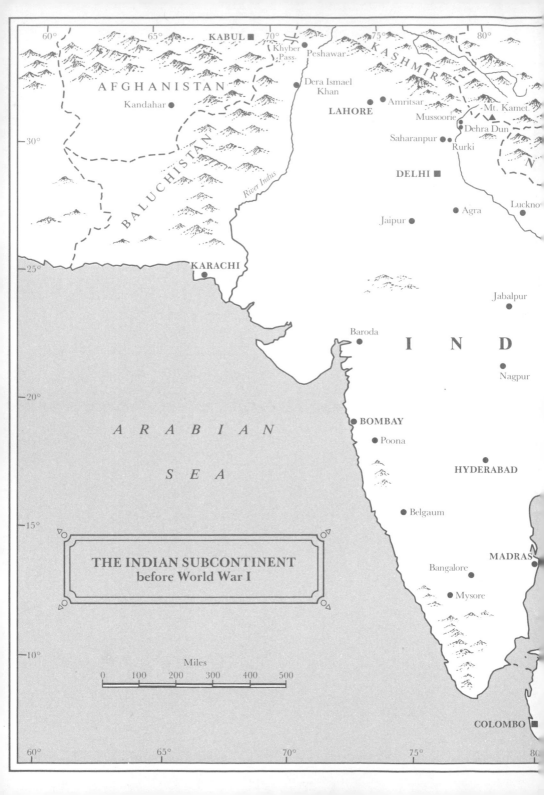

THE INDIAN SUBCONTINENT
before World War I